An Illustrated History of

THE POPES

Saint Peter to John Paul II

An Illustrated History of

THE POPES

Saint Peter to John Paul II

Michael Walsh

ST. MARTIN'S PRESS NEW YORK

'To Kate'

Editors: Felicity Smart
Elizabeth A. Holzer
Designer: Annie Tomlin
Picture Researcher: Mark Dartford

Printed in Great Britain by Redwood Burn Limited

ISBN: 0-312-40817-X

Library of Congress Catalog Card Number: 80-50818

Nihil obstat R. J. CUMING, D.D.

Censor

Imprimatur RALPH BROWN, V.G.

Westminster, 22ND DECEMBER, 1979.

The Nihil obstat *and* Imprimatur *are a declaration that a book or pamphlet is considered to be free from doctrinal or moral error. It is not implied that those who have granted the* Nihil obstat *and* Imprimatur *agree with the contents, opinions or statements expressed.*

Frontispiece: *The present interior of Santa Maria in Trastavere is mainly the result of reconstruction work in 1450 under Pope Nicholas V, but there has been a church on this site at least since the mid-fourth century.*

CONTENTS

INTRODUCTION

The Emperor Augustus divided the city of Rome into 14 regions. The last of these lay on the west bank of the River Tiber, and its most distinctive feature was a hill called the *Mons Vaticanus*. It was not one of the traditional seven hills on which Rome was built, but it is the only one which most people remember today – for it has given its name to the world's smallest independent state, the Vatican City.

When ancient writers mentioned the Vatican at all, it was to describe it as an unhealthy place: its air bad, its wine poor. Yet this tiny state now contains some of the world's most splendid buildings, housing vast collections of paintings, sculpture, books and manuscripts.

The Vatican City is wholly surrounded by the capital of Italy. Today, fewer than 1,000 people live there, fewer still are citizens carrying Vatican passports. No one is born there, very few die there, and hardly anyone is buried there. It is not a democracy, it is – at least in theory – the world's most absolute dictatorship, one which cannot sign the United Nations' Declaration of Human Rights because within its boundaries there is no freedom of religion. Its ruler has a string of titles after his name: he is Bishop of Rome, Vicar of Jesus Christ, Successor to the Prince of the Apostles, Supreme Pontiff of the Universal Church, Patriarch of the West, Primate of Italy, Archbishop and Metropolitan of the Province of Rome, Sovereign of the Vatican City, and Servant of the Servants of God. He is usually known simply as the Pope.

The Pope can be a man of any nationality. There have been Syrians, Greeks, Spaniards, Frenchmen, a great many Italians, and a single Englishman. The present Pope is from Poland. He was chosen, as were the majority of his predecessors in the last thousand years, by a small group of electors. In the course of his term of office, the Pope will select some of the men who will elect his successor. He is the spiritual leader of an estimated 710 million Roman Catholics – almost one-fifth of the world's entire population.

Many Catholics have very clear-cut views on the scope of papal authority, but there is still a wide variety of opinions. This is not surprising: what is perhaps surprising is that so many people could ever be certain about what they believe. Down the centuries, popes themselves have differed from one another in the way they understood the office and the degree of authority which goes with it. Even the meaning of the word 'Pope' has changed. Its origin is the Greek *papas*, or *pappas*, a respectfully affectionate term for 'father', and as such it was used of bishops in general during the early centuries of Christianity. Today it is still used of the Patriarch of Alexandria, and all parish priests in Greece are called *Papa*, just as Catholics and certain other Christians address their clergy as 'Father'. The first time a Bishop of Rome was called 'Pope' seems to have been in the third century, and the

Opposite: *Built over the tomb of the 'Prince of the Apostles', the great basilica of Saint Peter in Rome is looked upon by hundreds of millions of Catholics throughout the world as the central church of their religion.*

title was given to Pope Callistus, a former slave and one-time convict who appears later in this book. From his time onwards, it was so frequently used to describe the person who ruled over the Church of Rome that by the end of the fifth century 'Pope' usually meant the Bishop of Rome and no one else. It was not until the eleventh century, however, that a Pope could insist that the title applied to him alone.

Thus originally 'Pope' was not the name of an office, although we have come to think of it in that way. It was a title of respect, and the office to which that title became attached was the Bishopric of Rome. Popes have seen their task in the Church in many different ways, but no matter how little some of them may have been concerned about the spiritual well-being of the people of their diocese, or how rarely they may have actually visited it, they have always been aware that their authority comes to them as Bishop of Rome.

Jesus did not leave his disciples with a carefully worked out plan of how the Church should be organized. It seems very likely that the earliest disciples did no more than model the early Church on the way Judaism was organized. Wherever there was a group of Christians of any size there was also a local committee made up of elders and called a 'presbyterate'. These governed the early Church, but out of the presbyterate there gradually emerged one man acting as a sort of chairman or overseer. The Greek for 'overseer' is *episkopos* and it is from *episkopos* that 'bishop' is derived.

In the first letter to Timothy, written as if from Saint Paul, though it may not be by him, there is this description of an ideal bishop:

> *Here is a saying that you can rely on: to want to be a (bishop) is to want to do a noble work. That is why the (bishop) must have an impeccable character. He must not have been married more than once, and he must be temperate, discreet and courteous, hospitable and a good teacher: not a heavy drinker, nor hot-tempered, but kind and peaceable. He must not be a lover of money. He must be a man who manages his own family well and brings his children up to obey him and be well-behaved: how can any man who does not know how to manage his own family have responsibility for the Church of God? He should not be a new convert, in case pride might turn his head and then he might be condemned as the devil was condemned. It is also necessary that people outside the Church should speak well of him, so that he never gets a bad reputation and falls into the devil's trap.*

The word 'bishop' in the passage just quoted has been put in brackets as a reminder that in the first century of Christianity it probably did not mean the same as we mean by it today. 'President' or 'superintendent' might be a better translation. The two terms *episcopus* and 'presbyter' (the latter was later used to mean 'priest') were sometimes employed, even towards the end of the second century, as if they meant the same thing. But an *episcopus* was an official with duties to perform, while 'presbyter' implied status as a member of the consultative council of the local Church.

Unless some new documents from Christianity's first century are discovered, and that seems highly unlikely, we are never going to know the precise nature of the relationship between presbyter and *episcopus*. By the beginning of the second century, however, Bishop Ignatius of Antioch was describing a Church in which one bishop was in charge of administration and worship, assisted by several priests. This structure of a single bishop with his assistant clergy did not emerge from the presbyteral form of government at the same moment everywhere. But within a century and a half of Jesus' death it was the way the Church was mainly organized.

'Where the bishop is present, there let the congregation gather, just as where Jesus Christ is, there is the Catholic Church', wrote Bishop Ignatius. The word 'Catholic' means 'universal'. Although the first Christians were gathered in tiny groups within the great cities of the Roman Empire, they

Left: *The first mention of a 'Castle of Gandulf', eighteen miles south-east of Rome, occurs in the early ninth century. The villa at Castel Gandolfo, which now serves as the papal summer residence, was built by Carlo Moderna (1556-1629) on the instructions of Pope Urban VIII, and shortly afterwards re-modelled by Bernini. Since the Lateran Treaty of 1929, it has been an extra-territorial possession of the Holy See.*

were conscious that they shared the same faith. Bishops exchanged letters informing each other about new appointments or difficult points of doctrine. When a Christian moved from one town to another he carried with him, as his religious passport, a recommendation as someone sound in faith from his previous bishop. Whenever a bishop was chosen by his local Church to preside over the community, bishops from surrounding areas came to ordain him to the office, thereby giving visible expression to the unity of the Church.

But from among the many Churches there was one to which the others showed especial respect and deference. It was the Church at the heart of the Empire – the group of Christians in Rome itself. It owed its eminence not only to that city's own pre-eminence, but to the tradition which linked it with Saint Peter the Apostle.

That is why this book begins with Saint Peter, whom Catholics think of as the first Pope, and describes the lives and works of the popes in chronological order to the present day. According to the official count in the *Annuario Pontificio*, the Vatican's yearbook, there have been 262 since Saint Peter, and they are listed towards the end of this book. But not all of them are discussed here because not every pope was important in the development of the papal office, which is the theme of this book, and some were so obscure that little or nothing is known about them. *An Illustrated History of the Popes* covers the lives and works of those popes whose period of office affected the way in which later popes, and we ourselves, think of the Pope today.

For the idea of the papal office grew. As we have seen, it certainly did not spring ready-formed from the pages of the Gospels. Papal authority as it is now exercised, with its accompanying doctrine of papal infallibility, cannot be found in theories about the papal role expressed by early Popes and other Christians during the first 500 years of Christianity. But there is a line of development between early popes and modern ones, and this book sets out to trace that line in words and pictures.

SAINT PETER

Apart from Jesus himself, there is no one whose personality emerges from the pages of the Gospels as clearly as Saint Peter. We know that he was a fisherman, and one of a family of fishermen. He was married – Jesus healed his mother-in-law. He was impetuous and generous, with a propensity to great elation and deep depression. He was loyal. He could be rashly courageous, but at times was humiliatingly frightened. He was something of a visionary – one reference to him in Jewish literature suggests he was a poet – but one not always bold enough to stand by his convictions. He was an ordinary man who found himself doing an extra-ordinary job.

We know more about him than about practically anyone else in that first century of Christianity because of the way he dominates the Gospels and the Acts of the Apostles, and even turns up occasionally in the letters of Saint Paul. It is easy to see how important people thought him. He is mentioned by name 114 times in the Gospels, and another 57 times in Acts. Saint John's name comes next in the frequency-table: 38 times in the Gospels, and eight times in Acts.

There is no doubt that Peter was the leader – a born one, perhaps, or moulded into one by Jesus. He regularly spoke and acted on behalf of the group of twelve Apostles Jesus gathered round him. The Apostles are listed four times in the New Testament. The order in which the names are given, and even the names themselves, vary slightly from one list to another but the name of Peter always heads the list.

Two events narrated in the Gospels, one in the sixteenth chapter of Saint Matthew and the other at the end of Saint John, draw particular attention to Peter's pre-eminence. There are many different ways of interpreting these passages, but no one denies that in them Peter is being singled out for some special role.

The first took place near Caesarea Philippi. Jesus asked his disciples what the people thought of him. 'Who do people say the Son of Man is?' he asked. They gave him some of the opinions which were held by those he had been preaching to. 'But you,' he said, 'who do you say that I am?' Then Peter, whose name up to that point had been Simon, replied, 'You are the Christ, the Son of the Living God'.

This was a great profession of faith by Simon, and it was rewarded. 'Simon, son of Jonah', said Jesus, 'you are a happy man. Because it was not flesh and blood that revealed this to you but my father in heaven. So now I say to you: *You are Peter and on this rock I will build my Church.*'

There has been great debate over this short passage. It is important because it became, as we shall see, the crucial text by which the popes

Opposite: *Saint Peter by Giotto (1267-1337). The Saint is shown wearing the 'pallium', a stole of white lamb's wool symbolizing the fullness of episcopal authority. He is holding a book to symbolize his writings, and the key as yet another sign of his authority (see Matthew 16:19).*

attempted to justify their claim to rule over the whole Church, and not just over their local community in Rome. But whatever the interpretation of the facts, the facts themselves are these: in Aramaic, the language Jesus was using, the word 'Peter' and the word 'rock' are the same: *kepha*. Until Jesus bestowed it upon Simon *kepha* was not a personal name, and neither was its Greek equivalent, *petros*. In fact, even after Jesus had given it to Simon it was not thought of simply as a name. Names sound more or less the same, whatever language is being used. They are not translated from one language into another. But the name *Kepha* was translated into Greek as *Petros*. So those who were writing and translating the Gospels and the Acts of the Apostles clearly did not want the significance of the word *kepha* (meaning 'rock') to be lost.

The second crucial passage from the Gospels is that at the end of Saint John's Gospel. It has to be read with the story of the Last Supper in mind. During the Last Supper Jesus told Peter it was his job to encourage the other Apostles, and then went on to warn him that before the night was over he would have denied him three times. Peter, of course, vehemently asserted his loyalty, but what Jesus had prophesied came true nonetheless.

After the Resurrection, Saint John tells us, Peter and a group of the disciples were fishing in the Lake of Tiberias when Jesus appeared to them. After giving them some good advice about where to catch fish, he prepared breakfast for them on the shore. After breakfast he took Peter aside and said to him 'Simon, son of John, do you love me more than these others do?' Peter answered, 'Yes, Lord, you know I love you.' Jesus said to him, 'Feed my lambs.' A second time he said to him, 'Simon, son of John, do you love me?' Peter again replied, 'Yes, Lord, you know I love you.' Jesus said to him, 'Look after my sheep.' Then he said to him a third time, 'Simon, son of John, do you love me?' The three-fold question obviously recalls Peter's three-fold denial of Jesus, and so it is not surprising that Peter was, as the Evangelist tells us, upset when Jesus questioned him for the third time. 'Lord, you know everything', he replied this time, 'you know I love you'. 'Feed my sheep', Jesus said to him, and then went on, says Saint John to indicate the way in which Peter was to give glory to God — i.e. to die.

Although the missionary journeys of Saint Paul dominate the second part of the Acts of the Apostles, when the book opens, Saint Peter is the chief figure. He heads the list of the eleven, and it is he who takes the initiative in proposing that someone should be chosen to bring the number of Apostles back to twelve. He even lays down the qualifications the new Apostle must have. So it is not surprising that after the Holy Spirit had come down upon the Apostles at Pentecost, it was Peter who preached the first sermon, and brought about the reception into the Church of its first 3,000 converts. As in the Gospels, so in the Acts, there are two events in particular which draw attention to Peter's unique position. At first, all the believers pooled their resources, but a husband and wife called Ananias and Sapphira, though they agreed to sell all their property, kept a sum of money back instead of handing it over to the group as they had said they would. Their punishment was dramatic – first one then the other dropped dead – and it was Peter who had sat in judgement upon them.

The second occasion is not so much a single event but a whole chain of them, one which was of enormous significance for the life of the Church. The first Christians were, of course, all Jews. One day, while he was on his way to Jaffa, Peter had a vision and heard a voice telling him to eat all the animals he saw in the dream, some of which were regarded as 'unclean' by Jews, and therefore not to be eaten. So Peter was indignant. 'Certainly not, Lord', he said, 'I have never yet eaten anything profane or unclean.' But the voice answered him, 'What God has made clean, you have no right to call profane.' The vision's meaning worried Peter until he met the Roman centurion Cornelius. Cornelius himself had had a vision instructing him to send for Peter. 'The truth I have now come to realize', Peter told the

centurion, 'is that God does not have favourites, but that anybody of any nationality who fears God and does what is right is acceptable to him.'

The news that Peter had taken the initiative in receiving Gentiles into the Church did not please the other Christians in Jerusalem. He had to justify his conduct. However, he managed to persuade the Jerusalem Church of the correctness of his actions, just as later he took the lead at the council called in Jerusalem. James, who presided over the council, commented that it was Peter's testimony which carried the day and persuaded those gathered there that Christians did not have to be circumcised like the Jews.

But after the council in Jerusalem Peter practically disappears from the story. The New Testament contains a couple of letters which bear his name. He is mentioned by Paul in a letter to the Church at Corinth in a passage which seems to suggest that Peter's wife was travelling with him on his missionary journeys. But otherwise there is little or nothing more known about him after the year A.D. 48 or thereabouts.

And when there is no certain information about someone as important as Peter, then the spinners of legends step in. The 'apocrypha' are early Christian writings, similar in form to the books of the Bible, but never accepted by the Church as telling authentic stories. Peter crops up in several of them and in other writings, such as *The Preachings of Peter*, *The Gospel of Peter*, and *The Acts of Peter*. It is easy sometimes to see how the legends grew up. According to *The Acts of Peter*, the Apostle had a paralysed daughter. When the grave of a martyr called Petronella was discovered in Rome, she was immediately hailed as Peter's daughter, despite the fact that she died in the third century, too late to have been immediately related to the Apostle, and despite her name, though sounding somewhat similar, having nothing to do with the name Peter.

According to *The Acts of Peter*, the Saint spent twelve years in Jerusalem before going to Rome. There, in the capital city of the Empire, he found Simon Magus already in residence. Simon, the magician who had offered money to the Apostles for the gifts they possessed, appears only briefly in the Acts of the Apostles, but turns up regularly in the apocryphal writings. In this story he was living in the house of a certain Marcellus, a rich man who had at one time been a particularly pious and generous Christian, but who had been won over to Simon by his magic powers.

Peter decided to do battle with the magician. He went to the door of Marcellus' house and demanded that Simon come out. But the servant who answered the door refused to take the message. Not daunted, Peter unleashed a dog, which then said to him, 'What do you bid me do, you servant of the living God?' Peter sent the dog into the house with a message to Simon to come out. The talking dog was enough to convert Marcellus back to Christianity, but in all the excitement a statue of Caesar was knocked over and broken, a sacrilegious act which greatly alarmed Marcellus. At Peter's bidding, however, Marcellus sprinkled water on the marble fragments, and the statue was restored to its former shape.

It did not prove quite so easy to win Simon himself back to Christianity. A contest was arranged in the Forum. All the prefects, senators and other Roman nobility were there, *The Acts of Peter* records, and they paid a gold piece each to get in. The Prefect of the City called upon Simon to kill a young man by magic. This he did. Then Peter was called upon to restore him to life. Instead of doing it himself, however, Peter gave the young man's master – apparently he was a slave – power to bring the boy back from the dead. He himself then raised other people to life for good measure.

Not surprisingly, such events had a profound effect on the people of Rome. Many became Christians, including the concubines of the Prefect Agrippa, and Xanthippe, the particularly beautiful wife of a friend of Caesar's called Albinus. On their conversion the women gave up sleeping with their husbands and lovers (apocryphal stories have a distinct antipathy to sex). The frustrated men arranged a plot against Peter but he, warned by Xanthippe, fled from Rome. As he was leaving the city he saw Jesus entering it. 'Where are you going, Lord' (*Quo vadis?*), said Peter to Jesus. 'I am coming to Rome to be crucified', replied Jesus, and then Peter, abashed, returned to the city rejoicing. So he, too, was crucified. But feeling himself unworthy to die exactly like his master, he asked his executioners to crucify him upside down. The year of Peter's death cannot be exactly determined. It took place, in all probability, between A.D. 65 and 67, during the persecution of the Christians by the Emperor Nero.

Above: *There is an opening in the floor of the nave of Saint Peter's immediately in front of the papal altar, surrounded by balustrades. Within this opening there is a statue of Pope Pius VI kneeling facing a bronze door which leads into a small room called the 'niche of the pallia'.*

So much for the legends. The story of Jesus' appearance by the lakeside as recounted in Saint John's Gospel seems to hint at the way Peter was to die, and for his presence in Rome there is the evidence of an odd phrase in Peter's first letter. It ends in a rather mysterious fashion: 'Your sister in Babylon, who is with you among the chosen, sends you greetings; so does my son, Mark. Greet one another with a kiss of love. Peace to you all who are in Christ.' It seems quite likely that the author of this letter attributed to Peter really was the Apostle, and that he wrote it with the aid of a secretary called Silvanus while in a place he called 'Babylon'. But this Babylon was not the city in Mesopotamia. It could have been the name used scornfully for a whole variety of places, though the odds are it was Rome.

In a letter sent from the Christians in Rome to the Christians in Corinth before the end of the first century, and so written during the lifetime of people who could have known Saints Peter and Paul, the writer presumes that the two Apostles were in Rome, and died there. He does not set out to prove it, but mentions it as a matter of course. We must never forget that our questions are not necessarily those of earlier generations. The controversies which now make us look for evidence that Peter visited Rome and died there were not matters of debate in the first century. Our own generation, however, has been provided with some new evidence about Saint Peter.

Sometime during the first quarter of the fourth century Bishop Eusebius of Caesarea wrote a *History of the Church*. He was the first serious Christian historian, and a conscientious scholar. He quoted a great deal from documents, and the writings of earlier authors. We learn, for example, that Origen, who died in A.D. 254, believed that Peter had been crucified upside down in Rome, a story he clearly got from *The Acts of Peter*. An even earlier writer quoted by Eusebius recounted the martyrdom of Peter's wife: 'We are told that when the blessed Peter saw his wife led away to death he was glad that her call had come and that she was returning home, and he spoke to her in the most encouraging and comforting tones: "My dear, remember the Lord".'

But for our purposes, the most interesting remark occurs when Eusebius is writing about Nero's persecution of the Christians: 'It is recorded that in his reign Paul was beheaded in Rome itself, and that Peter likewise was crucified, and the record is confirmed . . . by a churchman named Gaius, who was living while Zephyrinus was Bishop of Rome [that is, about A.D. 200]. In his published *Dialogue* with Proclus, the leader of the Phrygian heretics, Gaius has this to say about the places where the mortal remains of the two Apostles have been reverently laid: "I can point out the monuments of the victorious Apostles. If you will go as far as the Vatican [for Peter] or the Ostian Way [for Paul], you will find the monuments of those who founded this Church".'

Gaius was clearly wrong if he thought that Peter and Paul had founded the Church at Rome in any strict sense. Peter arrived in Rome after Paul, and when Paul was writing his letter to the Romans he was writing to an already well-established Christian community. But Gaius was making no mistake when he said that he could point to the 'monument', literally the *tropaion* or 'triumphal tomb', of the Apostle on the Vatican hillside. It has been found. It lies deep beneath the papal altar of the present basilica of Saint Peter's.

Although the unscrupulous in the Middle Ages were not above stealing a saint's body or two as relics, the medieval world generally had a superstitious fear of disturbing the bones of the dead – witness the attempts to move the body of Saint Swithin at Winchester, attempts which the Saint himself thwarted, in true English fashion, by miraculous showers of rain. So the search for the tomb of Saint Peter did not begin in earnest until 1940.

The present papal altar was erected in 1594. It was built over the smaller altar of Pope Callistus II (1119-24), and during the construction workmen saw an even earlier altar, taken to be that put up under Pope Sylvester (314-35). But no investigations were made at the end of the sixteenth century, and the cracks through which Pope Sylvester's altar was visible were sealed up.

When the archaeologists began their work on the papal altar in 1940 they found remnants of much earlier structures. There was a marble column, and pieces of a second one, supporting a marble slab. The slab was projecting out of, and partly supported by, a red wall. In this red wall there was a semicircular niche both above and below the slab, the upper one going deeper into the red wall than the lower one.

It was clear that the columns and slab, with the adjoining wall, had been erected in a graveyard, which could be dated about A.D. 69 from makers' marks stamped on tiles. The columns and slab, however, had been put in place no earlier than the middle of the second century as a sort of monument. The archaeologists had found the *tropaion* mentioned by Gaius.

At the foot of the *tropaion* there was another slab, set at an odd angle to it, which suggested that the slab, or what it covered, was there first and the monument had been erected later. The slab was movable. It covered a simple grave scooped out of the soil. Like other graves of the poor, this one had probably once been covered with three pairs of tiles leaning against each other in the manner of a pitched roof. Scattered around the grave was a great quantity of coins dating from the late Roman Empire to the high Middle Ages. They had come tumbling down a channel or 'cataract', cutting through the various layers built up over the centuries, to fall on the tomb of the Apostle; these coins were the offerings of the faithful.

In a cavity hollowed out beneath the red wall, rather than in the grave itself, a jumble of bones was found. They had been put there, perhaps hidden there, deliberately. They were not laid out like a skeleton. They were the bones of one man, an old, powerful man of average height. The archaeologists were cautious, but in private were confident that they had found the body of Saint Peter. It was lying directly beneath the dome of the great church erected in honour of the Apostle. Around the dome of the church is written '*Thou art Peter, and upon this rock will I build my church.*'

There is no way of proving that these are indeed the bones of the leader of the Apostles. The area around the grave had frequently been disturbed. There is good evidence to suggest that during the persecution under the

Left: *This portrait of Saint Peter comes from the remains of a thirteenth-century 'retable', or altar piece, in London's Westminster Abbey. The abbey church is dedicated to Saint Peter who, according to legend, appeared to a boatman on the Thames and pointed out to him the spot where the Saint wanted the church erected.*

RGO DEVM COPLEXA SINV·
RVANDO PVDOREM
RGINEVM·MATRIS FVNDANS
ER SECVLA NOMEN

Emperor Valerian (257-9) Saint Peter's body was moved from the pagan cemetery on the Vatican Hill, where it had first been buried in a pauper's grave, to the comparative safety of a predominantly Christian cemetery now lying beneath the church of Saint Sebastian. In all probability, the bones were returned to the original grave at some more peaceful time. But there is one curious feature about the bones bundled together under the red wall: the skull is missing, and that is just what one might have expected.

From at least the end of the eleventh century it has been claimed that the skulls of both Saint Peter and Saint Paul were first kept in the papal palace of the Lateran, and later (from 15 April 1370) in the Lateran basilica, the cathedral church of Rome. We shall never know if these skulls were really those of the two greatest Apostles, and little remains of them now. At the end of the eighteenth century, the reliquary which contained them was

Above: *A mosaic from the Roman church of Santa Maria in Trastevere, showing the Madonna and Child between Saint Peter (with a sword) and Saint Paul. The small figure upon whom Saint Paul's hand is resting is the donor.*

stolen, but the relics themselves were left behind – a jawbone, a few loose teeth. But the seals of Urban V, the Pope at the time the relics were transferred from the palace to the church, were still in place on the reliquary.

There is a curious story about the reliquary. In 1438 a rich and powerful Venetian lay dying. He prayed to the Apostles promising that if he recovered he would give them a valuable pearl out of his collection of jewels. He did recover, and the pearl was sent off to Rome. Much to the consternation of those who should have been guarding the relics, however, the pearl turned out to be one which ought to have already been decorating the reliquary. In all, so it was discovered, twelve pearls, two rubies, three diamonds and a sapphire had been stolen. The thieves were soon discovered. They were taken to the church of Santa Maria in Aracoeli, stripped of their clerical status, exposed in iron cages in one of the city's squares, dragged at horses' tails through the streets of the city to the Lateran, had their right hands chopped off, and were then burnt to death. The man who had done no more than receive the stolen property was treated more leniently. He was brought to the Lateran riding on a donkey and wearing a paper hat. There he was tortured with red-hot tongs and hanged. The Romans took great care of the relics of those who had brought such new fame to their city.

Peter's presence in Rome, however, does not prove that he was the first 'Bishop of Rome', still less the first Pope. It would be a mistake to think in those terms. As the Introduction pointed out, 'bishop' and 'Pope' were offices which developed over the years, and it would be anachronistic to suggest that Peter had held them. But 'bishop' means little more than 'leader of the Church', and it would be very strange indeed if Peter, who played such a leading role in the Gospels and such a dominant one in the first half of the Acts of the Apostles, was not given a leading position in the Church when he came to Rome.

The earliest list we have of the Bishops of Rome dates from between the years 170 and 180. It was drawn up by Saint Irenaeus. Irenaeus was at this time Bishop of Lyons, but he had been brought up, he tells us, not in Lyons but in Smyrna under the great Bishop Polycarp who had known Saint John at Ephesus. The context in which Irenaeus mentions his list tells us something about the way Christians thought of their faith. He is attacking a group of heretics, and he compares their faith to the tradition which had been handed on from the Apostles. He is talking about all local Churches, but uses the Church of Rome as an example:

> . . . *pointing out the tradition which that very great, oldest, and well-known Church, founded and established at Rome by those two most glorious Apostles Peter and Paul . . . When the blessed Apostles had founded and built up the Church, they handed over the ministry of the episcopate to Linus. Paul mentions this Linus in his epistle to Timothy. Cletus succeeded him. After him Clement received the lot of the episcopate in the third place from the Apostles.*

Irenaeus continues his list until he reaches the Bishop of Rome of his own day:

> *Eleutherus now in the twelfth place from the Apostles holds the lot of the episcopate. In this very order and succession the apostolic tradition in the Church and the preaching of the truth has come down to us. This is a full demonstration that it is one and the same life-giving faith which has been preserved in the Church from the Apostles to the present, and is handed on in truth.*

It is clear that continuity was all-important to early Christians, and one must remember that Irenaeus was writing in the lifetimes of people who would have known the Apostles' first disciples.

There are other similar lists. Tertullian (about 160-225) provides one which has Clement as Bishop of Rome immediately after Saint Peter. These early writers had no doubt that Peter had visited Rome. But they did not think of him as a bishop. The succession of bishops begins with the one to whom he handed on the faith. Who that was is not quite so clear as the quotation from Irenaeus would seem to suggest. One interpretation of what Irenaeus wrote seems to indicate that as much of the authority of the Apostles as could be communicated to anyone who had not seen the risen Lord was handed not to Linus, but directly to Clement – in other words, in line with the list compiled by Tertullian.

The truth of the matter is now lost in time. One thing, however, is clear: Rome had a special place in the minds of Christians in the early centuries of the Church, and not just because it was the capital city of the Empire. In the words of Irenaeus, it was 'the very great, oldest and well-known Church, founded and established at Rome by those two most glorious Apostles, Peter and Paul'.

We must look further into this pre-eminence of the Church of Rome, and the best place to start the next chapter of this book is with the letter which the Christians in Rome sent to the Christians in Corinth. It was written by someone called Clement, the same Clement, one may suppose, as the person who perhaps succeeded Peter as leader of the Church in Rome.

THE CHURCH GOES UNDERGROUND

Clement is an enigma. In the last chapter he was described as leader of the Church in Rome, and someone called Clement is mentioned in the lists of Bishops of Rome which later writers have left us. But these authors were writing their books a century or so after Peter's death. By that time, the system of a single bishop in a town, with several priests assisting him, had become commonplace throughout the Empire wherever there was a substantial Christian community. Irenaeus or Tertullian would have taken it to be the normal thing.

So the question is, did they assume that the situation of their own day was similar to the situation of the Church at Rome in the first century of Christianity? It seems that they may have done so. We have a passage from a letter written by Dionysius, Bishop of Corinth, to the Christians in Rome in about the year 170, and preserved for us by Bishop Eusebius of Caesarea in his *History of the Church*: 'Today being the Lord's Day, we kept it as a holy day and read your letter, which we shall read frequently for its valuable advice, like the earlier letter which Clement wrote on your behalf.'

It sounds as if the letter was read out at church services very much as the letters of Paul, Peter, John, James and Jude are still read out today, which shows how highly the letter was regarded. And it also sounds as though Clement was writing the letter as a secretary, rather than as the author. The letter was written 'on behalf' of the community in Rome. No bishop is mentioned. It is the Church of Rome which is important, not the Bishop of Rome.

Perhaps in the years immediately following Peter's death there was no single bishop in Rome. It may be that there was a form of government by a group of priests, all of more or less equal status – Linus, Cletus and Clement. If so, it would explain the confusion over the succession lists.

Whether or not Rome was late in developing the structure of one bishop assisted by several priests, there is no doubt that Clement, whatever his rank may have been, became a person of some eminence in the Church at large, and not just in Rome. A whole series of legends grew up around him.

According to the legends, his father was called Faustus and was closely related to the Emperor. Faustus was married to Mattidia, also a relative of the Emperor. She was a very chaste woman, and when her brother-in-law made impure advances to her, she was too frightened to tell her husband. The only way she could escape was by fleeing from Rome. She left her youngest son, Clement, with her husband but took the older twin boys with her. She fled by ship towards the East, but there was a storm at sea and her ship was wrecked on the shores of Palestine. Mattidia became separated from the twins who were captured by pirates and sold into slavery.

By one of those strange quirks of fate in which legends delight, the twins

Opposite: Giovanni Battista Tiepolo (1696-1770) painted 'The adoration of the Trinity by Pope Clement' about the year 1735. The papal tiara lying on a cushion beneath the altar is meant to signify Clement's papal office, but whether later generations are right to regard him as a Bishop of Rome is open to question.

were purchased by a lady called Justa who turned out to be the Syro-Phoenician woman whose daughter Jesus had healed, according to Saint Mark's Gospel. The two boys then fell under the influence of the ubiquitous Simon Magus, but were later converted to true Christianity by none other than Zacchaeus – the same man who, so Saint Luke tells us, was so small that he could not see over the heads of the crowd, and had had to climb a sycamore tree to catch a glimpse of Jesus. Zacchaeus then introduced them to Saint Peter, and they travelled with him on his missionary journeys.

Meanwhile, Faustus had become distraught at the disappearance of his wife, so he set off in search of her. Clement was left behind in Rome, but when Faustus, too, failed to return from his travels, Clement also set off. To cut an enormously long story short, Clement met up with Saint Peter and the twins. As they all wandered about together they came across an old lady with withered hands. Using a false name, she told them a story about a noble Roman lady who many years before had lost her twin sons in a storm at sea after having had to flee from home. The old lady was, of course, Mattidia herself. Clement, the twins and Mattidia were thus reunited, and Peter healed her withered hands.

Overwhelmed by all that had happened to her so suddenly after her many years of searching, Mattidia asked for baptism. The whole group fell into prayer, observed by an old man who then told them the tale of a noble friend of his, a Roman, who many years ago had had his horoscope cast. According to the stars' predictions, this nobleman's wife would be unfaithful and would die by drowning. The old man turned out to be Mattidia's husband, Faustus. The fact that Mattidia was still alive was proof that the horoscope could not be trusted, so Faustus, too, became a Christian.

The legends which surround Clement's death are just as dramatic. So successful a preacher was he, that the Emperor Trajan became seriously alarmed. Clement was therefore banished to a remote region of the Crimea, where some 2000 Christians had already been exiled and made to work in the marble quarries. It was an arid part of the world, but wherever Clement went springs of sweet water rose to the surface and made the desert fertile. Vast numbers of the local population were converted by this miracle, so many that 75 churches were built, and the temples in the area razed to the ground. The authorities were understandably furious at Clement's repetition of his success in Rome, and decided to put him to death. They hung a heavy anchor around his neck and flung him into the sea. The spot where he drowned was two miles from the seashore, yet every year, on the anniversary of his death, the sea receded and pilgrims could walk dry-shod to the place where his body rested under a mysterious cairn of stones.

This much is legendary. Almost 700 years after Clement's reputed martyrdom, however, two saints did go to the Crimea to search for his body. They were called Methodius and Constantine, but Constantine changed his name to Cyril, and so gave his name to the Slavic alphabet – the Cyrillic alphabet – which he invented to use for the Church's liturgy and the translation of the Bible. These two missionaries found what they believed to be Clement's body, together with the anchor used to drown him, and brought it back to Rome about the year 868. It was buried in the church which even then bore his name – San Clemente. But it could never be proved that this really was Clement's body, and so the story remains part fact and part legend.

Among all this extraordinary conglomeration of miracle stories, a sort of early Christian romantic novel, there are glimmerings of what may have been the truth, though practically nothing is known for certain about Clement beyond the fact that he wrote a letter of reproach from the Christian community in Rome to the Christian community in Corinth. That was an odd enough thing to do and it was a sign that even then the Roman

Church thought of itself as having a role to play which extended beyond its geographical boundaries.

A little can be gleaned from the letter. It reads as if the person who composed it was a convert from Judaism. But then most of the earliest converts to Christianity fell into this category.

Something may be guessed from his name. Clement was not an unusual name. Paul knew someone who was called Clement, and mentioned him in a letter to the Church at Philippi. It was not long before one Christian author identified the Clement mentioned in the letter to the Philippians with the one in Rome. It may, however, have indicated membership of a particular Roman family, either by ties of blood or through employment. In A.D. 95 a certain Titus Flavius Clemens was consul. As soon as his term of office was over he was put to death by the Emperor Domitian, and his wife Domatilla was sent into exile. Both husband and wife were related to the Emperor. It seems that the charge against them was 'impiety' which, in context, can only have meant conversion to Christianity. There is still in existence a catacomb (an underground burial place) which bears the name of Domatilla, and is sited on an estate which once belonged to her. There are obvious points of contact between Titus Flavius Clemens and his wife and the legends surrounding Clement of Rome.

The church of San Clemente is not far from the Colosseum. As it stands now, it dates from the early twelfth century, but in the mid-nineteenth century it was discovered that directly beneath it lay the substantial remains of a fourth-century church, and beneath that again a first-century building.

Below: *The pagan temple of Mithras found beneath the present church of San Clemente in Rome. The carving on the altar shows the god Mithras slaying a bull.*

Above: *San Clemente typifies the 'basilican' form of church: it has a high central nave with windows along the top, and lower aisles on either side. At one end there was often a curved wall, or apse.*

This very early structure had been erected on the foundations of houses destroyed in the fire started by Nero in A.D. 64.

The first-century buildings of the third layer down are of especial interest. One side of them is a tenement block (which the Romans called *insulae* or 'islands'), in the courtyard of which was – and still is – a small temple to the god Mithras. On the other side there was an imposing mansion which probably once belonged to a man named Clement, possibly to Titus Flavius Clemens, the martyred consul. It also seems quite likely that there was a room set aside in this mansion for Christian worship, at least from the beginning of the second century or so. In Rome, as elsewhere, the names of owners of houses were often inscribed on plaques attached to the facades of the buildings. These plaques were the *tituli* or 'titles' of ownership. Some

private houses which were regularly in use as places of worship eventually became churches, but still appear to have been known by the 'title' of their previous owner – whom later tradition often turned into a saint. Thus the house *titulus Clementis* (belonging to Clement) became the church of Saint Clement, and the church subsequently built on the site, and which exists today, became San Clemente. There is no absolute proof that the mansion beneath San Clemente actually did belong to Titus Flavius Clemens or, indeed, to anyone called Clement at all, but the archaeological evidence strongly points that way.

And so this is all we know of Clement: he was possibly a slave or a freedman of Jewish descent, working in the household of the aristocratic Christian couple, Titus Flavius Clemens and his wife Domatilla, perhaps in a house on the site of the present church of San Clemente. He became one of the leaders of the Christians in Rome, maybe even a bishop, certainly a man of eminence whose reputation spread far beyond the confines of his Church.

This is not a great deal of information, but it is more than we have about some of his successors in Rome. There is a *Book of the Popes*, the first draft of which seems to have been put together about the middle of the third century. As we now have it, the *Book of the Popes* chronicles the lives of the Bishops of Rome from Saint Peter to Pope Pius II, who died almost 1400 years after the death of Peter. There are an increasing number of records as the *Book* progresses.

For the first two centuries, however, this series of lives of the Bishops of Rome, arranged in chronological order, is about as much information as we have. The *Book of the Popes* gives the name of each Pope, his father's name, his country or place of origin, and the length of time he governed the Church in Rome. The *Book* also records any legal or liturgical decisions made by the popes, any donations given to churches, how many priests and bishops each ordained, and how many churches were founded. Unfortunately, not all this information is supplied for each pope. Although the list appears to have been based on fairly accurate, if incomplete, records, some details cannot be trusted, for the compilers have sometimes read back into history the situation as it existed at their own time, and quite arbitrarily assigned to one Pope or another the various different pieces of legislation which governed the organization of the Church in their own day.

What we know of the popes from Clement to the middle of the third century is therefore little more than a list of names, together with some dates which must have a question mark after them. The first Bishop of Rome whose death can be accurately dated is Zephyrinus, Pope Victor's successor. He died in 217. In the traditional list of popes he comes fourteenth, not including Peter. He was a Roman, as four of his predecessors had been, another three had come from elsewhere in Italy, four had been Greeks, and there was one Syrian and one African.

The bishop was, for the most part, chosen from among the clergy, who met in synod to do this, and the clergy was chosen from among the people. If there were Africans, Syrians and Greeks as well as Italians among the popes, this reflected the make-up of the Christian community in a city which saw constant immigration from all the provinces of the Empire. We know little about the early Christians – there is just the occasional inscription on a tomb, or some other brief written record. They seem, however, to have come from every class in society and by A.D. 200 numbered about 10,000 or so in a city whose population would have been about a million.

However, we know a great deal more about Callistus, the Pope who succeeded Zephyrinus in 217. The portrait we have of him is all the more vivid because it was drawn by his arch-enemy Hippolytus, a priest with whom he had serious theological disagreements. Callistus was born in Rome and came from the region across the Tiber called Trastevere, then inhabited by poor people and those of doubtful character. His father, Domitian, was probably a slave, because Callistus himself was certainly one, working in the

house of Carpophorus, a nobleman who was a friend of the Emperor. Both Callistus and his master were Christians.

Callistus was clearly a man of some ability. Carpophorus entrusted money to him with which to set up a bank. Possibly because of their faith, other Christians deposited considerable sums of money in the new bank. But for some reason it failed, and Callistus tried to flee the country. He was caught by Carpophorus and thrown into prison, though not before he had tried to commit suicide by jumping into the sea. If rogue he was, Callistus must have been a likeable one. He had friends who managed to persuade Carpophorus to release his former slave.

According to the hostile account provided by Hippolytus, Callistus once again tried to commit suicide, this time by the unlikely expedient of picking a fight with some Jews. But they simply hauled him off to a magistrate, and had him condemned to the mines in Sardinia. He stayed there for a time, but then managed to get his name put on a list of prisoners to be amnestied – much to the irritation of Pope Victor who had drawn up the list. Victor therefore gave him a pension and told him to stay out of the city, but Victor's successor, Zephyrinus, brought him back to Rome, ordained him priest, and put him in charge of a Christian burial ground on the Appian Way which still bears his name: the Catacomb of Callistus. The tombs of nine popes are to be found there.

There are many catacombs in and around Rome. There is no special significance about the fact that they are underground. The soil of Rome is particularly suited to tunnelling, and it was simply more convenient to

expand downwards for cemeteries than to take up more land on the surface. Tunnels were dug into the earth, and bodies were laid in niches in the sides of the tunnels. When a gallery was full it was expanded downwards by excavating the floor, so producing corridors of great height, with the oldest interments nearest the surface.

Christians probably held some sort of service in the catacombs from time to time, but they were not places of regular worship or of refuge in time of persecution. As refuges they would have been useless. The location of burial grounds had to be registered with the imperial authorities. There was no point in hiding from Roman soldiers in the one place the magistrates knew all about.

From custodian of one of these cemeteries, Callistus rose to become Bishop of Rome on Zephyrinus' death. From Zephyrinus he inherited the problem of Sabellianism. Sabellianism was so called after Sabellius, its ablest exponent, who was possibly a Roman presbyter. It was a version of Christianity which held that God the Son and God the Holy Spirit were not distinct from God the Father, but were ways in which God the Father existed. The complaint had been made against Callistus that before his election to the office of Bishop he had been too closely identified with people who held these heretical views. There was even talk of bribes being passed to allow Sabellianism to be taught to Christians in Rome. But once he was Bishop, Callistus took steps to see that those who held these heretical opinions were not allowed to spread them.

Hippolytus accused Callistus of promising to forgive people's sins provided

Above: This marble slab from the Catacomb of Callistus is the inscription from the tomb of Pope Pontianus (230-5). Although Pontianus was exiled to Sardinia in the Persecution of the Roman Emperor Maximin and died there, his body was brought back to Rome. The inscription, which records his name and the fact that he was the bishop, was reconstructed from fragments found scattered about the catacomb in the early years of this century.

TRVS   CO ORNELI YSPP IVLIVS PPC

Above: *A twelfth-century mosaic depicting from the left Saint Peter, shown in Roman dress, Popes Cornelius (251-3) and Julius (337-52) wearing the 'pallium' or woollen stole as a sign of their office, and the martyr Saint Calepodius.*

they accepted his doctrinal views. There was a division in the Church as a whole about the forgiveness of sins. Some people believed that sins could only be forgiven once after baptism, if at all. But the Pope's view seems to have been that sins could be forgiven provided the person involved was truly repentant.

The Church was thus divided into two groups: one which saw the Church as a handful of saints in constant conflict with the world, and another which saw it as a means to help sinful mankind work out its salvation – people needed encouragement precisely because they were

30

not yet saints. Callistus put it picturesquely when he said that there were both clean and unclean animals in Noah's Ark. It was natural that bishops, with their pastoral responsibilities, should take Callistus' view, and that visionaries and prophets should see the Church as an embattled but unbowed group of saints.

The 'Church of the pure' group was scandalized that Callistus tolerated what they saw as low standards of behaviour from his clergy. He allowed bishops, priests and deacons who had been married two or even three times to remain in office, and permitted those who were already priests to marry. He was also accused of allowing Roman women to live with the slave or freedman of their choice because to marry beneath them would contravene Roman law. It was said that he would even tolerate abortions if they were necessary to disguise the existence of such liaisons.

Hippolytus' supporters elected him Bishop of Rome in opposition to Callistus, and so he became the first of many anti-popes. But Callistus was not Bishop of Rome for long. In 222 he was attacked by a pagan mob and died violently when they threw him into a well. This happened in Trastevere, the part of Rome where he had been born. The mob had been inflamed because Callistus had apparently been taking over property to turn into churches, and the crisis had come when he tried to turn a pagan tavern into a church. The pagans could not turn for support to the Emperor Alexander Severus because he was sympathetic to Christianity. Callistus was regarded as a martyr.

Curiously, Hippolytus also came to be numbered among the martyrs. In 235 Alexander Severus was murdered and his successor Maximin revived the persecution of Christians. Hippolytus fled into exile, together with Pontianus, who was the legitimate Pope at this date, and there both of them died.

Pontianus was succeeded by a Greek, Pope Anterus, who survived his election by only a month. At the time of the election for another new Bishop of Rome a farmer called Fabian decided to visit Rome with a few friends. He was in the gathering where names were being put forward. According to Bishop Eusebius, the historian, a blue dove came down from heaven and settled on his head. The crowd took this as a sign from God, seized him, and set him on the Bishop's chair.

It proved to be an excellent choice. The Church was at peace for the 14 years of Fabian's reign, and he used the time well. For civil purposes, Rome had been divided into 14 regions. For ecclesiastical purposes, Fabian divided it into seven, with a deacon in charge of each. In a famous letter, quoted at length by Eusebius, Fabian's successor described the sort of organization which the Church at Rome had developed: 'there are 46 presbyters, seven deacons, seven sub-deacons, 42 acolytes, 52 exorcists, readers and door-keepers, and more than 1500 widows and distressed persons'. The size of the Church as described suggests that the total Christian population of Rome in the mid-third century was 30- to 40,000.

They were accommodated for public worship in 25 churches, or *tituli*, which were grouped together in a few areas of the city where the Christian population was expanding. They were so close to each other that they probably housed congregations of differing traditions – perhaps even congregations which were at odds with one another.

The *tituli* of Fabian's time appear to have had two priests each, while the administrative work in the seven ecclesiastical regions was carried out by a deacon who had a sub-deacon as his personal assistant, and six acolytes to do the more menial tasks.

Fabian is also credited with erecting buildings at the cemeteries. It was a pagan custom to hold memorial feasts at the graves of relatives or close friends on the anniversaries of their deaths. Christians apparently extended this practice to holding feasts in honour of the most distinguished among the martyrs. The accommodation provided by Fabian seems to have been

31

intended for the greater numbers who were coming to these feasts.

Pope Fabian was a formidable man. A contemporary bishop in Africa is reputed to have said that the Emperor Decius would sooner have had to cope with a pretender to the imperial throne than with the Bishop of Rome. So when the Decian persecution began in 250, Fabian was among the first to die. This persecution was one of the fiercest Christianity has ever had to face. Hitherto, persecutions had, for the most part, been sporadic, and were often the result of private local enmities rather than public policy. Christians in prison could be visited by deacons, without the deacons finding themselves in prison too. A good many Christians were sent to the mines or marble quarries, rather fewer were executed by beheading, and only a handful were thrown to the lions. As far as is known, the Colosseum in Rome never witnessed a single martyrdom.

Decius, however, managed to make the Christians condemn themselves. He ordered everyone in the Empire to offer sacrifice. They had to line up, throw a few grains of incense on a brazier in front of a statue, pour a drop or two of wine on the floor (a libation), and then take a mouthful of the flesh of a sacrificial victim. Having done all this, those who had sacrificed were provided with a document, a *libellus*, duly signed and witnessed, to say that they had done so.

It was possible to escape by fleeing to the countryside, by bribing the officials handing out the *libelli*, or by apostatizing, and many Christians took this last course. They scattered the incense, poured the wine, ate the victim, collected the certificate, and then presented themselves as penitents in front of a bishop – if a bishop could be found, that is. It was fourteen months from the death of Fabian before a new Bishop of Rome could be elected. And when he was, he found himself faced with an enormous pastoral problem. What was to be done with all those who had apostatized, the *lapsi* as they were called? When they presented themselves for forgiveness, they were often clutching letters of recommendation from the 'confessors', those who had gone to prison rather than betray their faith. In Carthage, the great Bishop Cyprian came to the conclusion that though the *lapsi* might be reconciled, they would first have to undergo severe penance unless they were in danger of death. As was the custom in any Church when a major decision was reached, Cyprian communicated his policy to Rome.

But when his letter arrived, no successor to Fabian had yet been elected. A priest called Novatian replied on behalf of the Church. He expressed his approval of what Cyprian was doing, but insisted that Rome had to wait for a new Bishop and the calling of a synod. Novatian may himself have expected to be Bishop, but the choice was a Roman priest called Cornelius.

Cornelius' father, Castinus, may have belonged to one of Rome's noble families. He was a Christian, for his son had worked his way up from the very bottom of the ecclesiastical hierarchy – the first Bishop of Rome known to have done this, and Cyprian very much approved of it. He had been chosen, wrote the Bishop of Carthage, for his prudence, goodness and humility, though given his background he might have been expected to be ambitious.

Novatian had himself ordained Bishop in opposition to Cornelius, and split the Church at Rome over the question of the *lapsi*. He now wanted a much tougher line, while Cornelius adhered to the policy propounded by Cyprian. The Pope immediately had that policy endorsed by a Roman synod, attended by 60 bishops and numerous other clergy. Cyprian showed his support for Cornelius by writing a book entitled *On the Unity of the Church*. He saw this unity expressed in the person of each bishop, and by bishops through their union with each other. The Bishop of Rome had a special part to play in this union because the Church began with Saint Peter, and therefore Peter and his successors had primacy in the Church. Though Rome and Carthage were united, other Churches did not accept the synod's decision or Cyprian's views. Antioch, for example, supported Novatian, and this kept the schism alive.

Cornelius died in exile at Centumcellae (later to be called Civitavecchia) and was hailed as a martyr by Cyprian. After the short pontificate of Lucius I, which lasted only a few months, Pope Stephen became Bishop of Rome in 254. The problem of the *lapsi* continued. Cyprian discovered that the Bishop of Arles was allowing them to die unreconciled, so he wrote to Stephen demanding that he take action about it, thus demonstrating that he thought Rome had special authority extending beyond the local Church. But he quarrelled with Stephen over the question of the validity of baptism carried out by heretics. Stephen had informed him that the practice at Rome was to recognize baptism by heretics, and simply to receive people so baptized into the Church by a laying-on of hands. Cyprian thought that such people should be rebaptized. So angry was he at Stephen's attitude that he rewrote a chapter in his *On the Unity of the Church*, playing down the part Rome had to play in that unity. It is clear from the acrimonious correspondence between them that Stephen was bolstering his position by quoting from the sixteenth chapter of Saint Matthew's Gospel, verses 18-19: 'You are Peter and on this rock I will build my Church and the powers of death shall not prevail against it. I will give you the keys of the Kingdom of Heaven, and whatever you shall bind on earth shall be bound in Heaven, and whatever you loose on earth shall be loosed in Heaven.' As far as we know, Stephen was the first Pope to do this.

The dispute was not immediately resolved, but on this occasion it did not continue for long. Pope Stephen died in 257 and Cyprian, who had fled from the persecution of Decius, died a heroic death in 258 under the persecution of Valerian. But two years later the Emperor Gallienus issued an edict which not only brought peace to the Church for 40 years, but restored to it all the property which had been seized in earlier persecutions.

Left: *A bust of Alexander Severus, who was born in what is now the Lebanon in 208. He became Roman Emperor in 222, and was murdered by his troops in 235. A devout man, he not only tolerated Christians, but is also reputed to have placed a statue of Christ in his 'private chapel', alongside his gods.*

THE RISE OF
THE POPES

In the year 298 Diocletian and his assistant Emperor Galerius were following the Roman custom of consulting the augurs – those religious officials who interpreted omens and foretold the future. They were surrounded by high officers of state from the army and civil service. Sacrificial animals were slain as offerings to the gods, and their livers removed because they were supposed to show the signs which the augurs could read. There were no signs. Again animals were slaughtered and the livers cut out, but still there were no signs. The chief augur blamed this ill-omen on the presence at the ceremony of Christians who had crossed themselves to ward off evil spirits. Diocletian was furious. He ordered every member of the palace staff to offer sacrifice, or be beaten. Military commanders were to see that soldiers offered sacrifice or were dismissed the service.

So began the longest, and probably the bloodiest, persecution that Christianity had known. It was all the more fierce because Diocletian was such a competent Emperor. He had thoroughly overhauled the machinery of state, especially the army, police and secret service. He could ensure that edicts were obeyed.

The first edict was issued in 303. It was imposed more harshly in the Eastern part of the Empire than in the West, where Constantius, father of the future Emperor Constantine, was in charge. There was a series of edicts against Christians, each one more severe than the last. All Christian writings were to be burnt, all churches to be pulled down. For twenty years a cathedral had faced the imperial palace in Nicomedia. It was demolished. Priests were imprisoned, Christians deprived of their rank in the army and civil service. In 304 all Christians were ordered to offer sacrifice to the gods.

It is not clear how harsh the persecution was in Rome itself, but the confused records of the Roman Church in the early fourth century suggest that it was very severe. The Pope at that time was called Marcellinus. 'He fell victim to the persecution', a contemporary historian remarked laconically. Since it is known that he died a natural death, it seems that 'falling victim to the persecution' may be a euphemistic way of saying that he gave in and offered sacrifice or perhaps even handed over the Scriptures to be burnt. It was nearly four years before he was replaced as Bishop of Rome, and not until 311, when Miltiades became Pope, is there a sure account of succession to the Bishopric.

It may be that the confusion in the records reflects bitter division in the Church. The problems which Cornelius and Cyprian had had to cope with in the previous century now recurred. Some Christians wanted to be lenient and to receive back into the Church all those who had cast incense into the braziers or who had handed over the Scriptures to be burnt. Others demanded that such people, called 'traditors', do penance for the rest of their lives.

Opposite: *In the thirteenth century the curiously named church of the Quattro Santi Incoronati was regularly in use as a governmental palace. Hence the frescoes in the chapel of Pope Sylvester, painted about the year 1246, which narrate the legend of that Pope, leading up to the 'donation of Constantine'. The story is told in pictures which run most of the way around the chapel walls.*

Some rigorists, especially in Africa, insisted that sacraments administered by traditors were ineffective, the view held by Cyprian but rejected by Pope Stephen. Those who supported the African rigorist party were known as Donatists, after Donatus, Bishop of Carthage, one of its founders. Like the followers of Novatian, the Donatists believed that the Church was the Church of the perfect, not of sinners. For more than a century they were a source of disquiet both to the Pope and the Emperor. The Emperor became involved because, in A.D. 312, there occurred an entirely unexpected event – one which was to change the whole history of the Church.

Constantius died at York in 306. The Roman armies in Britain declared his son Constantine Emperor. He established his authority over Britain and Gaul (Gaul covered what is now modern France and part of Germany), and on 28 October 312 he arrived at the Milvian Bridge which led over the Tiber into Rome. At the battle of the Milvian Bridge he decisively defeated Maxentius who had been elected Emperor by the Praetorian Guard and the city of Rome. He achieved this victory despite the fact that Maxentius could call upon a far greater number of troops.

What makes this battle one of the turning-points in history was Constantine's claim that he was fighting under the protection of the Christian God. The Christian 'Chi Rho' symbol, from the first two letters of the Greek word for Christ, was painted on his soldiers' shields. The reason for this was that Constantine had seen a vision of a cross with these words beneath it: 'In this sign you will conquer.'

Constantine the Great may not have been the first Christian Emperor, but he was the first one whose Christianity made a difference to the future of the Church. But he accepted baptism only a few days before his death at the age of 57 or thereabouts, in the city of Nicomedia. He was baptized by the Bishop of that city, Eusebius, and he died on Pentecost 337. For almost the whole of the time between Constantine's conquest of Rome and his death, the Bishop of Rome was Pope Sylvester I.

During his lifetime Constantine dominated the Church to such an extent that little is known of Sylvester beyond the name of his father (Rufinus), the date of his election (January 314), and the date of his death (December 335). But since it seemed strange that so little was known about someone who ruled the Church of Rome at so important a time, legends provided what history did not record.

According to the legends, Sylvester was a Roman by birth, and his mother was called Justa. He was brought up in Christian ways by a priest named Cyrinus and, being a very pious youth, he was particularly welcoming to all who came to Rome on pilgrimage. One such, a holy man from Antioch named Timothy, arrived in the middle of Diocletian's persecution. Timothy went about preaching Christianity until he was arrested and executed. Sylvester bravely collected Timothy's body and buried it in the garden of a pious lady, near the tomb of Saint Paul. This courageous act almost brought about his own capture, but he miraculously escaped and fled from Rome. He had been ordained deacon and priest by Miltiades, Pope from 311 to 314, and was still living as a fugitive on Monte Soratte when he was elected Bishop. (Timothy was an historical figure, martyred in the year 303.)

After capturing Rome, the story goes on in cheerful disregard of historical fact, the Emperor Constantine launched a bitter persecution against the Church, but was punished for doing so by contracting leprosy. Pagan priests recommended a bath in the blood of small children. The children were gathered together for slaughter, but Constantine, moved by the tears of their mothers, repented. The blood-bath was cancelled. That night the Emperor had a dream in which two figures told him to seek out Sylvester. He did so, and Sylvester revealed that the two figures had been none other than Saints Peter and Paul. What Constantine really needed, Sylvester went on, was the baptism of regeneration which would heal not only his body but his soul as well. The Emperor underwent baptism, and was healed.

The Emperor's mother, Helena, had meanwhile become a Jewess, so a trial of strength was arranged between Jewish magicians and Christian priests in which the magicians demonstrated their power by slaying a bull simply by whispering a spell into its ear. Sylvester promptly restored it to life and in so doing converted Helena to Christianity. But the Pope's troubles were not yet over. Living in the middle of Rome was a dragon, a pet of the Vestal Virgins, which had to be kept quiet by being fed on human flesh. With the disappearance of the Vestals, along with the other pagan priesthoods, the dragon began to terrorize the inhabitants of the city. Sylvester used his powers to immure it in the Tarpeian Rock near the Forum.

As a reward for all these endeavours, the legends go on, Constantine heaped honours and gifts on the Pope. He endowed Sylvester and his successors with buildings and palaces in the city and, because he was about to depart for his new city of Constantinople (now Istanbul), the Emperor made the Pope responsible for the well-being of the whole of Western Europe. As a sign of the Pope's new authority over the Western Empire, Constantine wanted him to wear a crown, but Sylvester refused to do so, putting on his head instead a humble cap or mitre. In addition to this secular authority for the Western world, Constantine gave the Pope spiritual authority over the whole Church, including authority over the patriarchs ('patriarch' derives from the Greek word for bishop) of Alexandria, Constantinople, Antioch and Jerusalem.

Above: *This thirteenth-century fresco illustrates a scene from the legends surrounding Saint Sylvester, who was Pope from 314 to 335. Two figures appear in a dream to the Emperor Constantine the Great who was, according to the story, suffering from leprosy – hence the spots on his body. They tell Constantine to find out their identity from Sylvester, who tells the Emperor that they were the Apostles Peter and Paul. Thereupon Constantine was both converted and cured.*

Latin inscription text visible in upper left portion of the drawing, and the labels "Pinea aenea", "Palatium Innocentij viij.", and "Dominicus Castellinus de lugo" within the image.

Above: *This drawing, taken from a book now in the Vatican library, shows the forecourt and facade of the original basilica of Saint Peter. In the foreground stands an unusual fountain in the shape of a pine cone.*

None of this makes sense. It was concocted to explain, and provide justification for, papal intervention in the politics of Europe, the Church's possession of such magnificent buildings in Rome, the Pope's special head-dress, and so on. The list of privileges and gifts contained in these legends became known as the 'Donation of Constantine', a theme which provided material for Raphael and his pupils in the Vatican, as it had for many a medieval artist before them.

The legends were exotic. The reality was a good deal more prosaic. The Emperor's reasons for embracing Christianity can only be guessed at, but his commitment was real enough, even if his faith was shared by only one in ten of his subjects. The Lateran palace, hitherto an imperial residence, was made over to the Church to provide Rome's Bishop with his first permanent home. The barracks of a cavalry regiment which had opposed Constantine was razed to the ground to accommodate the Lateran basilica.

The Lateran was not the first purpose-built church in Rome, but it set a new style for Christian places of worship. Though 'basilica' now means church, in the late Roman Empire the word was used to describe a special type of building: this was a large hall containing at one end a free-standing dais, or perhaps an apse, where a magistrate or teacher could sit. It was a public building, used for meetings or for the transaction of imperial business. Pagan temples, on the other hand, were simply shrines for the statues of gods, accessible to only a small number of worshippers, and usually entered

only by priests. Christian churches rejected the pagan temple as a model. With the bishop's chair in place of the magistrate's, they were places where congregations gathered, and where a large number of believers could worship God.

Thus the church Constantine built on the ruins of the barracks, the basilica now known as Saint John Lateran was a 'hall' church. It would have held a congregation of several thousand. There was room in the sanctuary for about 200 priests and deacons – in other words, for the entire Roman clergy. There were seven gold altars, sixty gold or silver candlesticks, and the apse where the bishop sat was covered with gold leaf and mosaics. The columns down the aisle were coloured yellow, red and green, the nave was lit by 45 chandeliers, and the sanctuary by five more. Over the main altar there was a canopy of solid silver, similar to the one under which the Emperor sat when holding court.

Other churches were built round the tombs of the martyrs. The church of Santa Croce was constructed within the Sessorian Palace, perhaps by the

Above: *The interior of the old basilica of Saint Peter, showing the papal altar over the Apostle's tomb. This building was demolished in the sixteenth century to make way for the present basilica.*

Above: *The Council of Nicaea was convened by the Emperor Constantine the Great in 325. This fanciful reconstruction by the sixteenth-century painter Giovanni Speranza shows Pope Sylvester presiding, seated between two cardinals. But there was no such thing as the office of cardinal in 325, and Pope Sylvester did not attend the Council. Constantine, shown in the foreground, attended occasionally. The Bible, in the centre of the picture, lay open throughout the proceedings. The Council condemned the Arian heresy, and devised a new formula for unity within the Church.*

Emperor's mother, Helena, to house a relic of the True Cross. In A.D. 333 the building of the great church of Saint Peter began; situated across the Tiber from the pagan centre of Rome, it was carved out of the Vatican hillside and was constructed over the tomb of the Apostle. It was a magnificent building. There was a beautiful fountain shaped like a pine-cone in the courtyard, and inside there were marvellous decorations.

The Emperor's decision to tolerate Christianity – a decision known to history as the Edict of Milan, though no such edict was ever issued – meant more than the restoration of property to Christians and the construction of churches. Privileges granted to them distinguished them from those of other beliefs. Some new legislation was of a generally humanitarian nature: slaves were granted their freedom; Sunday was henceforth to be a public holiday, except for farm labourers; the clergy were freed from public duties which certain classes of Roman citizens were obliged to carry out – in particular, from having to organize and pay for the public entertainments which went with some civil offices. So many of the overtaxed Romans flocked into the Christian priesthood to take advantages of these privileges that the Emperor was eventually forced to curtail some of the exemptions he had made.

An unexpected bonus for the higher ranks of the clergy was authority to use the imperial post and transport system. The result was larger and more frequent gatherings of bishops to resolve the problems which were arising in the Church. One such was the complaint by Donatists that they had been left out when property was restored to the Church. Instead of deciding the

matter himself, Constantine referred it to Pope Miltiades and chose a group
of bishops from Gaul to assist him. Miltiades, perhaps to indicate that a
Bishop of Rome was not to be dictated to by an Emperor, added 14 bishops
from Italy to the ones chosen by Constantine. This little gathering found
against the Donatists, who once again appealed to the Emperor, and he,
once again, referred the question to the Bishop of Rome, who by this time
was Pope Sylvester.

A Council was called at Arles in 314, just ten months after the gathering
in Rome. Though Sylvester did not travel to Arles – the Bishops of Rome
usually sent representatives to councils rather than attending themselves –
the meeting was important. It was attended by bishops from widely scattered
cities of the Western Empire, including Britain, and decided many matters of
a disciplinary and ethical kind, as well as yet again condemning Donatism.

'What has the Emperor got to do with the Church?' a Donatist leader
was finally driven to ask. But the Donatists had appealed to the Emperor
against the Church when they had turned to Constantine after failing to get
satisfaction from Bishop Miltiades. The consequences of involving the
Emperor were far-reaching. Constantine believed that the Church could
contribute much to the strength of the Empire both by its prayers and its
solidarity. Hence his hostility to the Donatists once Pope Miltiades and his
council had decided the issue, and hence his desire for a quick solution to the
problem posed by Arius – a problem which became known as the Arian
heresy.

41

Arius was one of the senior clergy at Alexandria. About the year 319 he began to teach that Jesus was not eternal. Arius argued that he had been created by the Father and only afterwards elevated to the rank of Son of God. Arius was condemned at a local council in 320, but this did not put an end to his heresy which, in all its ramifications, divided the East and affected the West for the rest of the century.

Anxious as always about the unity of his Empire, Constantine summoned a great council to meet at Nicaea in 325. It was the first in a long series of councils which were called 'ecumenical' because they were, in principle at least, councils of the world wide Church, and not just of local bishops. There were some 250 bishops present at Nicaea, almost all of them from the Eastern part of the Church although there were a handful from the West including Hosius, Bishop of Cordova, who acted as the Emperor's personal representative. Two priests attended in place of Pope Sylvester.

Below: *Raphael's pupil, Giulio Romano, was engaged to complete his master's series of frescoes in the Vatican on the life of Constantine. In this scene, which may perhaps be set in what Romano remembered of old Saint Peter's, the Emperor hands over to Pope Sylvester a statuette, a symbol of his 'donation'.*

IAM TANDEM
CHRISTVM
LIBERE PRO
FITERI LICET

ECCLESIAE DOS
A CONSTANTI
NO TRIBVTA

Proceedings were conducted like a meeting of the Roman senate. The Emperor sometimes presided, though he did not speak. Hosius spoke first, as 'leader of the house', followed by the priests representing Sylvester even though they were of a lower rank than the bishops present. The remaining council fathers gave their opinions in order of seniority. The Book of the Gospels lay where, in the senate, the altar of victory would have stood.

Jesus Christ, the Council declared, was 'God from God, light from light, true God from true God, begotten not made, of one substance with the Father'. The formula, still repeated in the Nicene Creed, was intended to restore unity but instead only gave rise to new problems, as the debate about the exact meaning of 'one substance with the Father' went on. By the time Constantine died, however, only one bishop was still excluded from his diocese for rejecting the formula.

But if Constantine helped to solve one problem, he sowed the seeds of another. In May 330 the new city of Constantinople which he had founded was dedicated with pagan rites – Constantine was sensitive to the fact that he was operating in a largely pagan society, though he himself was sympathetic to Christianity. Constantinople was to be a new Rome and its site, its palaces, its baths, its churches, its offices of state and its senate closely mirrored the Empire's old capital city. It was in a good strategic position, and was to be the seat of the Eastern Emperors. The seaport upon which Constantinople was built had been called Byzantium, and this ancient name survived to describe the Eastern half of the Roman Empire.

The establishment of Constantinople was destructive of the unity of both Church and State. The richest provinces, and the best recruiting areas for troops, were made over to the Eastern Emperor. The prestige of the Emperor in the West was gradually eroded, and the ecclesiastical standing of Rome was also challenged. This challenge took formal shape at the Council of Constantinople in 381. Damasus was Pope at this time, and as his pontificate was crucial in the development of the papal role, his life merits some examination.

He became Pope in 366, and died in 384. He was about 80 years of age when he died, so he must have been born during Diocletian's persecution. The *Book of the Popes* says he was of Spanish descent but he was certainly brought up, and probably born, in Rome where his father served the Church first as a lawyer and later as lector, deacon and then priest at the church of San Lorenzo. Surviving fragments of inscriptions tell us a little about Damasus' family. His mother died at the age of 90, after having been vowed to chastity for 60 years. Before her vow, she had given birth to Damasus, his sister – who was also vowed to chastity – and to at least one other child.

By 355 Damasus was already a deacon. In that year the Emperor Constantius, the pro-Arian son of Constantine the Great, exiled Pope Liberius for supporting the Bishop of Alexandria in his refusal to compromise with the Arians. Damasus accompanied Liberius into exile, but changed his mind on the way and returned to Rome to support Felix, a pope forced on the Roman Church by the Emperor. Liberius returned three years later on the death of the Emperor and reasserted his authority. Damasus made his peace with him, but the bitterness of his betrayal lingered on.

After the death of Liberius, the party which had most strongly opposed the anti-pope Felix immediately held an election in the Julian basilica. This was organized by three deacons and seven priests. The deacon Ursinus was elected and consecrated. The vast majority of Christians in Rome, however, acclaimed Damasus in the basilica of San Lorenzo and he was consecrated, in accordance with the rules which Ursinus had flouted, by the Bishop of Ostia after an interval of seven days.

Battles broke out between supporters of the rival popes. They continued for three days before the civil authorities exiled Ursinus and the two deacons. For a time, however, the seven priests remained and set up a separate Church, much to Damasus' irritation. He again turned to the civil authorities to have them driven from the city, but once again the priests evaded the police and this time took over the basilica built by Pope Liberius on the spot where, he had been told in a vision, he would find snow on 15 August. Damasus hired gangs of thugs to drive them out. There was a great battle around the basilica in October 366 which left 150 people dead and Ursinus' party still in possession.

Even when Ursinus was finally exiled he continued to harass Damasus. The Pope was even accused of adultery, an unlikely charge against a man who was some 75 years of age, and not one that was treated very seriously. In any case, by that time the Church was faced with a new problem.

There was a group which resented the way penitent Arians were being received back into the Church. They even had their own bishop, and their own very popular holy man called Macarius. They lacked churches, of course, but held services in private houses. They were a threat to Damasus because he himself had been obliged to repent of his association with Felix, but he could not drive them out of the city on his own. He appealed to the imperial authorities for help as well as using his own gang of thugs. In the ensuing brawl Macarius was so badly beaten up that he died of his wounds.

So Damasus destroyed his enemies by using violence in an age of violence. He also had to win the total support of the people of Rome. He was relentless in his opposition to Arianism, thereby redeeming his lapse at the time of Liberius' exile. His firmness did much to restore the fortunes of the Bishopric of Rome at a time when Milan was not only the seat of the Emperor in the West, but the See of Bishop Ambrose, one of Christianity's most powerful thinkers and astute politicians.

Damasus was determined to do still more to restore some of Rome's eminence. Because he had been born at the time of the last great persecution he would have been too young to recall the deaths of the martyrs, but old enough to have talked to people with vivid memories. One such may even have been his own father, who was in charge of the archives of the Roman Church housed in the basilica of San Lorenzo. While he was Pope, Damasus excavated, enlarged and generally restored the cemeteries. He opened up the catacombs to visitors. In the course of his investigations he discovered several martyrs' tombs. He placed inscriptions over them telling something of the story of whoever was buried beneath. The inscriptions were in verse, and he seems to have been fairly conscientious about excluding anything he did not know to be true. For the most part, therefore, the verses say very little. The same is true of the inscriptions he put over the graves of his predecessors as Bishops of Rome. He was clearly interested in the history of his diocese, and it has been suggested that he had a hand in drawing up the first chronological list of the popes from Peter to Liberius.

Like his father, Damasus was something of an historian, but his interest in his illustrious predecessors and the Roman saints was motivated by more than just curiosity. By the time the persecutions came to an end, no diocese had so many martyrs' tombs as Rome and yet so few accounts of their martyrdoms. Yet their stories would have been part of local Christian folklore. So Damasus wrote them down, reporting hearsay for what it was, but showing himself interested in, and concerned about, the local heroes of the Christian city of Rome. It helped him to purge his temporary disloyalty to his predecessor.

The Christian Church owes much to him. His irascible secretary Jerome was commissioned to produce a better edition of the Latin Bible, and Jerome's translation, known as the Vulgate, was the standard version for many centuries. It was also during Damasus' time as Pope that the official list, or canon, of which books should be included in the Bible and which left out was finally decided. But important as these decisions were for biblical scholarship, Damasus earns his place in any history of the papacy chiefly for the effect which his period of office as Bishop of Rome had upon the development of papal claims.

Other Churches were ready enough to give Rome some sort of special place in the life of world-wide Christianity, but the degree to which they were prepared to do so depended very much upon the character and abilities of the Bishop of Rome. Damasus' predecessor-but-one, Pope Julius, had been a strong-minded, astute ecclesiastical politician. He had claimed, and had the claim endorsed by a Council of the Church held in Sardica, that his See (or bishopric) was the final court of appeal when bishops disagreed with one another. Rome's prestige was high. It tumbled under the vacillations of Liberius.

So far did it fall that it was the Eastern Emperor Theodosius rather than Pope Damasus who put an end to the fourth-century conflicts over Arianism, and to disputes over the succession to the bishoprics of Antioch and Constantinople. But, as mentioned earlier, the real challenge to papal authority came at the Council of Constantinople, convened by the Emperor in 381. The Council was famous because it insisted upon the divinity of the Holy Spirit – but no bishop from the Western part of the Empire attended and so, without consulting Damasus, the Council also made the fateful decision that the Bishop of Constantinople should rank immediately after the Bishop of Rome simply because his See was the New Rome.

Damasus could not, and did not, accept such a state of affairs. He refused to recognize the decision about Constantinople, and the Council became accepted as a proper council of the Church only when, 70 years later, the account of what had happened during it was written into the records of the Council of Chalcedon.

To add to the Pope's distress, the Emperor Theodosius endorsed the decisions of the Council of Constantinople even though, just the year before, he had decreed that the faith of Damasus and the faith of the Bishop of Alexandria were to be taken as the standard test of orthodoxy because their faith had come to them from Peter.

Damasus tried to regain the initiative by calling his own council at Rome a year after the one at Constantinople. For the most part, this was something of a fiasco, but in the course of the gathering it was for the first time stated unequivocally that the Church at Rome had precedence over all other Churches because it had been founded by the Apostle to whom Jesus had said, 'You are Peter, and on this rock I will build my Church.' Because the See of Alexandria had, according to tradition, been founded by Saint Mark, Peter's disciple, and because Peter was supposed to have presided over the See of Antioch for a time before moving on to Rome, these Churches were to rank second and third. And as extra proof of Rome's pre-eminence, if more proof were needed, the Council pointed out that a second Apostle, Saint Paul, had been associated with Peter in founding the Church in the Empire's capital city. Constantinople came nowhere. Ecclesiastical status was not to depend upon civil status as far as the authority of the local Churches was concerned.

This 'primacy of the Roman See' as it was defined by the Council in Rome reflected Damasus' ambitions for his Church. He was the first Pope to speak regularly of the 'Apostolic See'. The full import of his claims for Rome became evident during the 15–year reign of his successor, Pope Siricius, who was elected in December 384.

Siricius was a Roman, and clearly well versed in Roman law. He called himself the 'heir' of Saint Peter, knowing perfectly well that in law an heir took over the legal status of his predecessor. He also adapted the Emperor's law-making technique to the needs of the Church. The Emperor would reply to a question from one of his subordinates by a letter saying '*decretum est*': 'it has been decided'. Siricius used this method of replying by 'decrees', or 'decretals' as they were called, to questions put to him by bishops of the Western Church. This became the papacy's standard method of resolving the problems that came to Rome. The decretals eventually built up into a body of 'case law' through which every aspect of the Church's life could be regulated.

ROME OF THE POPES

The Bishops of Rome, rather than Emperors living in **Milan, Ravenna,** or far off Constantinople, were by the beginning of **the fifth century** the true guardians and protectors of the city. If anything **served to** drive this point home to the inhabitants of Rome with **sharp emphasis, it** was the invasion of the barbarians.

'Barbarian' comes from the Latin word *barbarus*, itself of Greek origin and meaning something rather like our English 'babble', or 'gibberish'. It was a term of contempt used to describe the uncouth warrior tribes from beyond the Rhine and Danube frontiers of the Empire, who spoke an unintelligible language. From the mid fourth century onwards they were entering Europe in successive waves from the heartlands of Asia. Such was their impact that 'Hun' or 'Vandal' (the names of two of the tribes) are terms which are still used to describe someone who is hated or feared. The adjective 'Gothic' is derived from the name of another tribe. It is applied to a style of medieval architecture which is now much admired. But tastes have changed. When the term was first used it meant crude and unpolished, an expression of scorn.

The Romans despised the barbarians, but needed them to fight their battles. Barbarian soldiers served as allied troops and their kings, with names which sounded harsh in Roman ears, became Roman generals. Many of the tribesmen were pagans, so for a time at least the pagan senators in Rome looked upon them as their natural allies. Even those who had become Christians were, for the most part, not Catholics but heretical Arians.

In 394 the last Olympic Games until modern times were held in Greece. Shortly afterwards the Gothic hordes swarmed into the peninsula, right up to the gates of Constantinople. To buy off King Alaric, their leader, the Emperor made him a Roman general. This was not enough to appease him. Though he withdrew from Greece, he led his troops into Italy in the spring of 403, only to be defeated by the army of the Emperor Honorius.

Rome had been in a panic at the approach of the barbarians, so now the Romans celebrated. In December they put on a triumph, the last to be observed in the city for a victorious Emperor. News of it reached the town of Hippo on the coast of North Africa. But it was not the jubilation which attracted the attention of the bishop there, the great Saint Augustine. He pointed another moral. When Honorius entered the city, he said in a sermon, he did not go first to the Templum Urbis, the City Temple. Instead, he first went to give thanks at the shrine of the fisherman.

Presiding over that shrine in December 403 was Pope Innocent I, who had been unanimously elected Bishop just two years before. Little or nothing is known of Innocent's early life. The *Book of the Popes* says that he was born at Albano, and that his father was also called Innocent. But Jerome, the irascible former secretary of Pope Damasus who had retired to a hermitage

Opposite: *This enormous relief – it is nearly 25 feet high – is in Saint Peter's in Rome. It was executed by Alessandro Algardi (1595-1654) towards the end of the sculptor's life, and depicts the meeting in 452 between Leo I and Attila. The Pope is pointing to the Apostles Peter and Paul who are coming to the defence of Rome, and the King of the Huns is turning away in fear. It is clear from the way the other figures in the group are standing that no one except the Pope and King can see the vision.*

Above: *Saint Augustine, Bishop of Hippo in North Africa (354-430). He was one of the most influential thinkers that Christianity has ever produced. A great deal of later theology has been either a commentary upon, or a reaction against, the teaching contained in his voluminous writings.*

in the Holy Land, claimed that he was not only the successor to, but also the son of Pope Anastasius. Possibly the words were meant figuratively, but there is just a chance that Jerome was speaking literally. A man who had been, or still was, married could enter the higher ranks of the clergy provided certain conditions were fulfilled, and provided he no longer lived with his wife. Just over a century later Hormisdas was succeeded by his son Silverius as Bishop of Rome, although only after a gap of a dozen years.

Having celebrated his triumph, Honorius retired behind the fortified walls which guarded the approaches to Ravenna. When Alaric once more advanced on Rome, he refused to come out to meet him in battle. The pagans blamed all the city's misfortunes on the abandonment of the city's gods, and wanted to offer them sacrifices once more. But to do so they had to break an explicit law of the Emperor Theodosius banning such sacrifices as offensive to the Christian religion. The pagans turned for authorization to do so to the most unlikely person, the Bishop of Rome, and, even more strangely, Pope Innocent granted them what they asked. This odd story is recorded by a fifth-century writer hostile to the Christians. True or false, the fact that it was written down is a sign of how much authority the Bishop now exercised in the city of Rome.

The sacrifices were not effective. Alaric laid siege to Rome. But Gothic troops were unused to this form of warfare, and their king was content to be bought off with gold and silver stripped from statues of the gods. The respite was short. Alaric was soon back, and this time Innocent went out to try to arrange a truce. Terms were agreed, and the Pope went off to Ravenna to negotiate with the Emperor. But Honorius was not interested in the fate of Rome. While the Pope was still in Ravenna, the Salarian Gate was opened to the Goths on 24 August 410, perhaps by a conspiracy of pagans, Arians and barbarian slaves, and for three days Rome was pillaged.

Alaric had ordered that the churches, especially the basilicas of the Apostles, were to be sacrosanct, and could therefore be used as places of refuge by frightened Roman citizens. In the event, the basilicas of Saints Peter and Paul were for the most part untouched, but others lost much of their wealth. One contemporary historian tells the story of a Goth going into a house and finding the treasury of Saint Peter's vigorously guarded by a single courageous woman. He was so startled he took the woman and the treasure along to Alaric, who ordered both to be returned to the basilica of the Apostle.

Rome was to be sacked on many occasions, but the first time the capital of the Empire fell shock waves reached out to the farthest parts of the civilized world. Senatorial families fled to their country estates, some seeking refuge in North Africa. They came to Carthage, and some fled on to Hippo. To console them, and to explain how everything was part of God's purpose, Augustine of Hippo composed one of Christianity's greatest books, *The City of God*.

Innocent returned to Rome in 412, and once again began to piece together his administration. Although his confrontation with Alaric may have been the most dramatic incident in his life, it is as an administrator that he has become most famous. In reply to queries from bishops all over the Western Empire, he wrote letters which came to be regarded in later centuries as the earliest formulations of the Church's Law – Canon Law as it is called. In February 404, for example, he was writing to Bishop Victricius of Rouen, laying down rules about admission to the higher ranks of the clergy. No one could be ordained, insisted Pope Innocent, who had married a woman who was not a virgin, or who had married twice, or who had married a widow. Such signs of sexual degeneracy clearly marked a man as unsuitable for ecclesiastical office in the Pope's eyes, even if marriage itself did not. No one who had performed a public penance could be ordained, went on the Pope, nor anyone who had served in the army since baptism,

taken part in trials involving capital offences, paid for public games in the amphitheatres, or held a pagan priesthood. This, said Pope Innocent, was the discipline in force at Rome, and therefore it ought to be followed everywhere.

His argument that all should follow Rome was based on the claim that the Churches of the West began as a result of missionary work by Rome. Therefore all of them should have the same laws and the same liturgy as the See of Peter, and although lesser squabbles might be settled locally, more important disagreements were to be referred to the Bishop of Rome. He based his claim to decide major matters on the Book of Exodus, where Moses set up judges over Israel but reserved matters of greater moment to himself. Alongside Pope Damasus' use of the Petrine text from Saint Matthew, this story in Exodus provided the popes with scriptural justification for their claims.

The popes' claims to regulate the liturgy and law of the Churches were for the most part restricted to the Western Empire. The great exception was Illyricum, that Greek-speaking buffer zone between the two halves of the Empire which we now call the Balkans. Pope Siricius (Bishop of Rome from 384 to 399) had made the Bishop of Thessalonika his representative in the area, and tried to establish Rome as ultimately responsible for the Churches there. In a letter sent in June 412 to Rufinus, the new Bishop of Thessalonika, Pope Innocent described the way he (Rufinus) was to look after Illyricum on Rome's behalf. Innocent was trying to assert over Illyricum the same sort of authority he exercised over Italy. Such action was bound to bring the Bishop of Rome into conflict with the Patriarch of Constantinople.

Relations with Constantinople were strained enough as it was. The problem was John Chrysostom. John was the son of a general and had abandoned a promising career in the imperial civil service to become a monk in the Syrian desert. Harsh fasting damaged his stomach, so he came back to Antioch and was ordained priest. His reputation for holiness of life and his outstanding gifts as a preacher ('Chrysostom' means 'golden-mouthed') were so great that when a new Patriarch was needed at Constantinople he was kidnapped from Antioch and brought to the New Rome. But John was too outspoken, too much of an ascetic and a reformer, to remain popular long. Although at first a favourite of the German-born Empress Eudoxia, he soon upset her by a sermon on the frailties of women. He equally upset the male population of Constantinople by preaching that

women had as much right to fidelity from their husbands as husbands had from their wives. He had to go. Before he did so, however, he preached a violent sermon comparing Eudoxia to Jezebel and Herodias, and his excited supporters set fire to the great church of Sancta Sophia. Eventually packed off into exile, John kept up a voluminous correspondence with his sympathizers.

He appealed for support to Pope Innocent. He had, he claimed, been wrongly deposed. The Pope was at first wary of becoming involved, but finally came down firmly on John's side, to no avail. John Chrysostom died, still in exile, in 407, and the Patriarch of Constantinople and the Bishop of Rome remained at odds until after Innocent's own death in March 417.

The next three popes after Innocent – Zosimus, Boniface I and Celestine – were renowned for their piety, but their pontificates were uneventful as regards the development of the papal role. But fifteen years after the death of the saintly and determined Innocent, a man of very different character was elected Bishop of Rome. We know a little about Pope Sixtus III before his election from chance remarks in letters written by his contemporaries. We know, for instance, that when he was a priest he did not meet with the approval of the great Augustine, Bishop of Hippo. His orthodoxy was in doubt in 418, but he defended himself vigorously, and in the end was believed.

His consecration as Bishop on the last day of July 432 was unusual for the

Above: *These ivory carvings date from the late fifth century and represent, allegorically, the capital cities of the divided Roman Empire: Rome and Constantinople. By the time they were made there was no longer an Emperor in the West.*

presence of two Eastern bishops, spokesmen for Cyril, Patriarch of Alexandria, who had come to win Rome's support for the Patriarch in his quarrel with Bishop John of Antioch. Sixtus replied that he wanted to see the long drawn out conflict between the two Sees come to an end, and revealed that he had been the author of earlier letters about the dispute sent out by his immediate predecessor as Bishop of Rome. Unity was achieved in 433, and John of Antioch, in an enthusiastic letter to Pope Sixtus, said he hoped the successors of Saint Peter would be as much a beacon to the Churches in the East as they already were to the Churches in the West. It was music to Sixtus' ears, even if in practice the concord between the patriarchal Sees of Rome, Constantinople, Alexandria and Antioch was destined not long to survive.

But it was not as a theologian or diplomat, like his distinguished successor, Leo I, that Sixtus was to become famous, nor as an administrator or canon lawyer like his predecessors. His particular glory was to preside over the restoration of the city of Rome to something like the splendour it had enjoyed before the pillaging by Alaric's warriors. His greatest monument can still be seen today: it is the magnificent basilica of Santa Maria Maggiore.

Sixtus' gifts to the Roman churches, and those he inveigled from the Emperor, are gloatingly enumerated by the *Book of the Popes*: over 50 pounds' weight of gold, and a thousand pounds and more of silver. But the importance of Sixtus' work was not so much in its extravagance as its style. Now that the Pope had replaced the Emperor as Rome's leading personage, that point was to be driven home by the construction and decoration of Christian churches. The palaces and administrative buildings used by the Emperors, their families and their highest officials had a style of their own. Because the Emperor was a divine figure, buildings closely associated with the imperial family had a pagan religious stamp about them. Christians therefore avoided imitating the imperial style in their own buildings, although they adapted imperial symbols to Christian usage in their decoration.

The gold and silver with which Sixtus endowed his churches have long since disappeared. The buildings he erected have been hidden under centuries of reconstruction – although just occasionally, as in the baptistery at the Lateran, the main lines can still be made out. But, much faded now, the mosaics decorating the triumphal arch of Santa Maria Maggiore remain in place. They depict the life of Christ, but are in a different order to the accounts given in the Gospels. It may be that the order was derived from the sequence of scenes depicted on the pedestal of the monument to the Emperor Arcadius, with the figure of Christ replacing that of the Emperor. The scenes chosen, the dress of the people in them and the poses they strike, all recall traditional images from imperial monuments.

At the top left-hand of the arch, for example, there is a picture of the Annunciation. Mary is dressed as an imperial princess, and is guarded by angels as if she were a sovereign. The angel bringing news of Christ's birth is depicted as the ancient Roman symbol of Victory. Across the arch, the Presentation shows not the Temple in Jerusalem but the Templum Urbis, the City Temple, symbol of peace and concord in the minds of Roman citizens. Mary and Joseph stand, Simeon goes down on his knees in a pose recalling the figure on coins issued to commemorate the thousandth anniversary of the city of Rome. The message seems to be that a new era, a new millenium, begins with the birth of Christ, when there will be peace and concord between the Old Testament (Simeon) and the New (Christ), and between the Church (Christ) and the Empire (the Templum Urbis).

Examples of the use of imperial symbols to exalt Christ and his Church are many, but perhaps the most explicit is in the centre of the arch, between the Annunciation and Presentation. The Empire's symbol of unity was the goddess Roma, and she was usually shown seated on a throne decorated with lions' heads. This ornate throne is shown at the centre of the arch, but the book of the Gospels replaces the figure of Roma. Above the throne are the symbols of the Evangelists, and Peter and Paul appear on either side. Beneath are the words XYSTVS EPISCOPVS PLEBI DEI ('Sixtus the Bishop, for the People of God').

Sixtus died in August 440. It is typical of his Archdeacon and successor that, at the time of his election, he should be in Provence trying to mediate in a squabble between rival generals. A delegation was dispatched to bring him back, and Leo I was consecrated Bishop of Rome on 29 September.

The new Pope was a Roman by upbringing and possibly by birth, though his father came from Tuscany, and so Leo may have been born at Volterra, south-east of Pisa. As with Sixtus, we hear only incidentally of his early life. It may have been Leo who, as an acolyte, went over to Africa in 418 to assure the bishops of Sixtus' orthodoxy. A couple of years later, when he had probably become a deacon, he is described in John Cassian's *On the Incarnation of Christ* as an 'ornament of the Roman Church and the sacred ministry' and an 'honoured friend' of the author. Ten years afterwards Cyril of Alexandria refers to him as Archdeacon of the Roman Church. As such he was Sixtus' chief adviser, and we know that he dissuaded the Pope from an act of doubtful orthodoxy on at least one occasion.

Orthodoxy was one of Pope Leo's main preoccupations. Like most of the fourth and fifth-century popes, however, he understood the word very simply: he merely wanted to preserve the faith handed down to him. Much of the debate in the Eastern Church, if he understood it at all (there were translation problems), seemed over-subtle.

The question of the day was this: fourth-century councils declared that Jesus Christ was truly God. But was He truly man, and if so, how? The Council of Ephesus of 431, at which the Roman delegation arrived late, decided that because Mary was mother of Jesus she was Mother of God: Jesus, in other words, was God from the moment of his conception as man. (It was to celebrate this that Sixtus dedicated his great church to Santa

Below: *This fresco by Raphael in the Stanza d'Eliodoro in the Vatican shows a very sixteenth-century Pope Leo I turning Attila back from the gates of Rome. The scene was perhaps painted to recall the deliverance of Rome from the French after the disastrous defeat of the papal forces at Ravenna in 1512, and thereby to glorify the political role of the popes in general and Pope Julius II in particular.*

Maria.) But disagreement about how Jesus was both God and man continued, and the Emperor Theodosius II determined that another council was needed. He solicited the support of the influential Bishop of Rome, but Leo was against the idea. Eventually, however, he had no choice but to send delegates to Chalcedon in 451. Their brief was a letter, Leo's 'Tome', which the Pope had written to the Patriarch of Constantinople two years earlier. It explained very simply that Jesus Christ is one person, but in Him there are two natures, the nature of God and the nature of man, both present in their fullness and neither absorbing the other. 'Peter has spoken through Leo' acclaimed the assembled bishops when the Tome was read out, and although it singularly failed to close the controversy which had occasioned it, the Tome became from that moment the accepted expression of the faith of the Catholic Church.

But the Council he had tried to avoid was not an unmitigated triumph for Leo. The seventeenth canon (or regulation) laid down by Chalcedon said that the ecclesiastical status of a city was to reflect its civil status, and the twenty-eighth elevated Constantinople to be on a par with Rome. Leo believed on the contrary that Rome enjoyed a *plenitudo potestatis*, a 'fullness of power' over the whole Church. Peter, he believed, was the *princeps* of the Apostles. *Princeps* does not mean, as it is usually translated, 'prince' but 'first citizen', rather as the American President is first citizen of the United States. So Peter had an authority over the other Apostles, and not just an honorary position – and the popes were his heirs. Again, Leo developed a Roman legal idea for his own purposes: in Roman Law an heir simply took over the legal status of the deceased. The logic of Leo's argument was inescapable: he had authority over the whole Church. 'Let nothing be done against or without the authority of the Roman Church', decreed the Emperor Valentinian in 445, thereby making Leo's understanding of his office part of the constitutional law of the Roman Empire. Leo appropriated the once pagan title of *Pontifex Maximus*, still used by the popes today, and borne, until towards the end of the fourth century, by Roman Emperors to indicate that as civil rulers they had a right to intervene in religious affairs.

With Leo, however, the position was reversed. He was a religious ruler who intervened in civil affairs. Just as refugees had fled to Africa when Alaric threatened Rome, now they came flooding back as Carthage fell to the Vandal King Genseric. Rome was full of them, and almost half Leo's surviving sermons are about giving alms. All offerings for the refugees, he suggested in his simple, direct, and very Roman style, should be distributed from churches in the various regions of the city. Such exhortations to charity, along with others asking clemency for serfs, slaves and those in illegal private prisons, indicate how much the Bishops of Rome were now part of the social life of the city.

There was one group of refugees, however, for whom Leo had no time at all: the Manichees. These people believed in two equally powerful gods, one of all that was good, the other of evil, and the two were locked in perpetual combat. Men could identify with the good god by eating certain things and thereby releasing the particles of light locked up in them, by fasting, and by refraining from sexual intercourse. It seems a very debased form, then, which came back to Rome from Africa. Leo had been shocked to hear of ritual sexual intercourse between a youth and a girl of ten. Since the time of Diocletian it had been the State's duty to search out and punish Manichees, but in 444 Leo took this upon himself, presiding over a court composed both of clergy and Roman senators. Though the culprits were found guilty the sentences were light, provided they renounced Manichaeism. Leo then asked Christians to inform upon other Manichees in the city, and forbade dealings with them. Eighteen months later the Emperor, quoting Leo's action, forbade Manichees to live in cities, to inherit property, to work in the civil service, or to bring cases to court. If Leo's leadership had been doubted in social and political, as well as in religious affairs at Rome it could scarcely have had better confirmation than this by the Emperor.

Attila, King of the Huns, provided the most dramatic illustration of the position Leo had attained in Rome. The Huns had marched across the Empire for many years before Attila determined, in 452, to turn his attention to Rome. Why he did so we shall perhaps never be sure. It may be, however, that he had become dissatisfied with his rank of general in the Roman army and the annual tribute paid him, and wanted to advance himself and his tribe by marrying into the imperial family. He was unexpectedly presented with an opportunity. The Roman Emperor Valentinian was incompetent, but he had a highly competent sister, Honoria, who was becoming bored with her brother and her subordinate role. To divert herself she engaged in an affair with a steward of her palace. When this was discovered it was decided to marry her off to a senator of unimpeachable character. Honoria was having none of it. In desperation, she sent her ring to Attila and asked him to come to her rescue. Attila interpreted this as a proposal of marriage, no matter how unlikely it seemed that she really intended 'to deliver her person into the arms of a barbarian, of whose language she was ignorant, whose figure was scarcely human, and whose religion and manners she abhorred', as Edward Gibbon wrote in his *Decline and Fall of the Roman Empire*. But whatever her real intentions, Attila responded by marching into Italy.

The Roman senate panicked. Pope Leo and two senators were dispatched to open negotiations with the barbarian King. They found Attila encamped with his army near Mantua, close to the southern shores of Lake Garda. Leo talked to him, and begged him to turn back. To everyone's amazement Attila agreed.

It may not have been Leo's words which persuaded him. The barbarian King had problems. The previous year Italy had experienced a famine, and food was short for the Hunnish warriors. It may be that Attila had received word of the approach of Roman troops sent from Constantinople to defend Rome by the Eastern Emperor Marcian. There is a story that the Huns, perhaps weakened by hunger, had been attacked by plague, and there is another story that they went in superstitious dread of Rome, remembering that, within a year of the sack of 410, Alaric was dead. Attila withdrew his troops from Italy and a year later he, too, the 'scourge of God' as the Christian chroniclers called him, had died. But whatever the background to Attila's decision, the meeting at Lake Garda, by the banks of the River Mincio, was a triumph for Pope Leo.

In a similar situation three years later, however, Leo had less success. In June 455 the Vandal King Genseric, having conquered Africa, set sail for Rome. The city was defenceless, and when Leo met Genseric at the city gate he could only beg the barbarian leader not to burn the city down or pillage its churches, and to spare the lives of its citizens. Genseric agreed, and in the looting which followed, the riches – or at least some of them – of the larger churches were spared. But private houses and smaller churches were ransacked, and even the seven-branch candlestick which the Emperor Titus had brought back to Rome from the sack of Jerusalem nearly 400 years before disappeared in the ransacking.

Yet without Leo's intervention the destruction might have been greater, and the Pope was still the city's best protector. In a sermon on the Feast of Saints Peter and Paul following the sack by the Vandals, Leo voiced a new view of the role of the city of Rome. He argued that because of the presence there of the See of Peter, Rome's spiritual dominion over the world would be greater than any it had achieved by force of arms. As Romulus and Remus had founded the city, he said in another sermon, so Peter and Paul had refounded it, and it was upon them that its true glory was to be built. To the disheartened citizens this dazzling amalgam of Roman legal and political ideas, Scriptural quotation and Christian tradition, offering hope of a new

Left: *The Huns arrived in southeast Europe about the year 360, and survived until their defeat at a spot beside the still unidentified river Nedao, by an alliance of other barbarian tribes in 455. Their skill as fierce mounted warriors – and especially as archers – struck terror into the inhabitants of Europe. From 434 to 453 they were ruled by Attila, at first in partnership with his brother whom he murdered in 445.*

role to the battered city, must have been a heady vision. By the end of Leo's episcopate – or 'pontificate', as it was now called since he had adopted the title *Pontifex Maximus* – the Pope had replaced the Emperor as the most important figure in the city of Rome.

Leo continued Sixtus' policy of building, renovating and ornamenting the basilicas and churches of the city, and he seems to have paid special attention to those in some way linked with the name of the Emperor Constantine. It was as if he had set out to replace the work done for the Church by a secular ruler of Rome by the work of the new ecclesiastical ruler of the city. And in imitation of the *cubicularii* (gentlemen of the bedchamber) who guarded the Emperor he set up clerical *cubicularii* to guard the tombs of the Apostles.

Leo was probably about 70 years of age when he died on 10 November 461, his Archdeacon Hilarius being elected to succeed him. He was buried in the entrance of Saint Peter's, the first Pope to be interred in the basilica of the 'Prince of the Apostles' built by Constantine. Later, his body was exhumed and moved to a more honoured place within the church and, still later, he was reburied in the new Saint Peter's. Like Pope Innocent and Pope Sixtus, he is looked upon as a saint. But more than that, he was the first Pope to be endowed with the title 'the Great'. In the middle of the eighteenth century Pope Benedict XIV added Saint Leo the Great to the small group of 'doctors of the Church' whose teaching on the things of God have special authority within the Catholic Church.

POPES AND THE WIDER WORLD

In 476 a barbarian king named Odoacer, who had once been in the service of Attila, deposed the last Roman Emperor of the West. The Empire itself survived, but its ruler was in Constantinople rather than in Milan, Ravenna or Rome. Secure in their control of the Empire's former capital, the Bishops of Rome remained loyal to the ideal of a united Empire for two and a half centuries until circumstances forced them to look West, rather than East, for support.

The memorials of Rome's past grandeur helped to keep the loyalty alive. A Greek historian who toured Italy in the entourage of an Eastern general during the first half of the sixth century complimented the Romans on their eagerness to preserve the city's monuments, despite the depredations of barbarians. But had a guidebook of the day been written it might have described a stroll through Rome as easily in pagan as in Christian terms. In front of the Lateran Palace, for example, there was an equestrian statue of the pagan Emperor Marcus Aurelius: it was for a time thought to be a representation of the Christian Emperor Constantine. The Lateran itself, once an imperial residence, was now the centre of papal administration. From there to the Vatican the route passed the church of the 'Four Crowned Martyrs', a titular church from Christianity's earliest days in Rome, and continued on to San Clemente. Near San Clemente a pilgrim would see the Colosseum, associated, however inaccurately, with the sufferings of the martyrs, and beyond that the Arch of Constantine, a monument erected when the senate was still largely pagan. Its inscription spoke, somewhat ambiguously, of Constantine achieving his victory 'by divine guidance'. Further on there was the church of San Lorenzo, on which Pope Damasus had lavished such care, and beyond that again the pilgrim would pass the vast tomb of Hadrian, now called Castel Sant' Angelo, which Pope Leo had unfavourably compared with the tomb of Saint Peter.

Rome, as well as the Romans, had been baptized. Saint Peter had called the city 'Babylon', but in A.D. 500 a bishop visiting it for the first time compared it to the heavenly Jerusalem: 'How beautiful the heavenly Jerusalem must be', he wrote, 'if the earthly Rome is so splendid'. When Zeno, the Eastern Emperor, wrote to Pope Gelasius to complain that he had not been informed of his election in 492, Gelasius replied, 'Glorious Prince, as a Roman-born, I love, respect and honour the Roman Emperor. As a Christian, I desire that he who has zeal for God shall have with it an accompanying knowledge of the truth'.

Gelasius' problem was that the Emperor was interfering in ecclesiastical affairs in a way which the Pope could not approve. To unite the warring factions after the Council of Chalcedon – for the Council's solution to the problem of the nature of Christ had not proved acceptable to all – the

Opposite: *Fresco of Saint Gregory the Great (590-604) portraying a legend from his life, according to which he dictated his books from behind a curtain. On one occasion, says the legend, his secretary pulled back the curtain and saw the Holy Spirit in the form of a dove whispering in his ear, telling him what to say.*

Emperor had produced a formula of unity. The Patriarch of Constantinople at the time was called Acacius, and as far as the Roman Church was concerned it was Acacius who was held responsible for the formula which Rome found objectionable. Hence the schism (or division) which arose when the Emperor tried to impose his creed forcibly came to be known as the Acacian schism.

There is no doubt that Gelasius had well-learned the doctrine of papal authority. He had served as secretary to two popes, and came to the chair of Saint Peter with his ideas clearly worked out. The letter to the Emperor went on:

> *There are mainly two things, august Emperor, by which this world is governed: the sacred authority of the pontiffs and the royal power. Of these priests carry the greater weight, for they must render an account to the Lord even for kings before the divine judgement. You know, most merciful son, that though you surpass the human race in dignity, yet you must bend a submissive head to the ministers of divine things, and that it is from them that you must receive the conditions of your salvation.*

Precisely what Gelasius meant by this is much debated. Quite possibly he was simply telling the Emperor not to meddle with doctrinal matters, and there was nothing new in that. But later generations took him to mean rather more, and sometimes what someone is thought to have said can prove more important than what he actually did say. Gelasius was taken to mean that there was a hierarchy (the word 'hierarchy', describing an ordered system of command, was invented at this time) of priest over layman. The laity were important in their own sphere, but because the clergy were ultimately concerned about eternal things, the clergy had authority over the laity. Gelasius contrasts the *authority* of the pontiffs with the royal *power*, but events increasingly obliged the Bishops of Rome to use not only their authority, but also such power as they could muster.

The problem, once again, was the barbarians. This chapter opened with Odoacer, the barbarian King, deposing the last of the Western Emperors. Theoretically, he now ruled under the lordship of the Byzantine Emperor, but in practice he was an independent monarch. It was a situation which the Emperor Zeno tolerated for a while, but Odoacer's expeditions into Dalmatia brought him too close to Constantinople for comfort, and so Theodoric, King of the Ostrogoths, was commissioned to overthrow him. Theodoric murdered Odoacer at a banquet, and thereby emerged as undisputed ruler of Italy. He was a great believer in settled government, and an equally great respecter of learning, because he had grown up as a hostage at the imperial court in Constantinople. He was an Arian, but still welcome to Gelasius as bringing stable government to the devastated countryside.

The Pope then undertook the first survey of the Church estates – at least, it is the first to have survived. These estates consisted of lands scattered throughout Italy and elsewhere too, which had been given to the Bishop of Rome from time to time to help him finance the running of the Church in Rome and, more especially, its charitable activities. In this first ecclesiastical 'Domesday Book' the location and size of the estates were described, and what income the Church might expect. Such financial foresight was becoming increasingly necessary. The Emperor was virtually cut off from Rome, so the popes took over responsibility for the well-being of its citizens. To do so, the popes needed a regular income.

Throughout his brief reign, Gelasius' organizational skills were much in evidence: during a famine the Church was able to feed the people of the city. But he was no heartless bureaucrat. He may have been scholarly and personally very austere, yet he was as generous with his own wealth as with the Church's. He was fiercely protective of the Church's doctrines, pledging himself to oppose innovation. He discovered a sect of Manichees in the city, drove them from Rome and had their books burned outside Santa Maria Maggiore. He himself wrote four books condemning heresies. He also condemned the Lupercalia, a pagan fertility festival which had managed to survive with the backing of members of the senate. He thus made himself unpopular with some of the Roman aristocracy who revenged themselves by accusing him of neglecting his obligation to see that the Christian clergy behaved properly.

The accusation was unfair. If anything, Gelasius was a bit too zealous. It is true that with the Church in chaos after the Gothic invasions, Gelasius had thought it necessary to relax some of the regulations surrounding ordination, but only in order to speed up the process. Procedures for selection were still very strict: no illiterate person was to be ordained, no proven criminal, no physically deformed person and definitely no woman was to become a priest.

His fierce opposition to the formula worked out by the Emperor, endorsed by Patriarch Acacius and intended to achieve unity in the Church was not shared by his successor, Pope Anastasius, who was elected within a few days of Gelasius' death at the end of November 496. The new Pope was not prepared to rehabilitate Acacius (now dead in any case), but he was ready to receive into communion a deacon who had been very much in favour of the formula. But Anastasius' action caused a split in the Roman Church which erupted into open warfare on his death two years later.

Elections took place in Rome on 22 November 498. One party of clergy and laity met in the Lateran basilica and chose the deacon Symmachus. Another faction, gathered in Santa Maria Maggiore, elected the Archpriest Laurentius.

Symmachus was a convert from paganism. He had come to Rome from Sardinia, and pursued his new-found faith with all the zeal of a crusader. He was not at all willing to come to terms with the Emperor over the Acacian schism, and in this he seems to have had the support of the younger element among the clergy. Symmachus was probably a fairly young man himself. The *Book of the Popes* tells us that he was Pope for over 15 years, an extraordinarily long time for a Pope at that period. To win support, he offered a rise in clerical salaries, and tripled the level of poor relief dispensed by the papacy. He built hostels for the destitute and even provided a public lavatory in Saint Peter's Square. But the older, more senior clergy, who were already wealthy enough not to be bought, and the aristocracy who wanted a settlement with the Emperor, backed Laurentius.

The Emperor in Constantinople was a sufficiently distant figure for Symmachus to treat coldly. Not so King Theodoric. Those who took a hard line against imperial meddling in ecclesiastical affairs approached Theodoric and asked him to settle the issue of who was the 'real' Pope. He first set up a synod of bishops, but they evaded their responsibility: 'the simplicity of priests is not equal to the cunning of the laity', they wrote to the barbarian king. The decision therefore went in favour of Symmachus, since he fulfilled the requirements laid down by Theodoric: he had been elected first, and had the greater support. Laurentius accused Symmachus of winning Theodoric's favour by bribes, but seemed ready enough to accept the ruling. He was among those who signed the statute, introduced before a Roman synod just four months after the disputed election, which was to regulate procedure in elections for the future.

It laid down that there was to be no electioneering during the lifetime of a pope. Any cleric found doing so, or discovered promising anyone his vote, was to be removed from office and excommunicated. If a pope died suddenly, whoever was the unanimous choice was to be accepted. If there had to be an election, the winner was to be the man who won most of the votes, freely given. The implication of the statute is that one pope seems to have been expected to nominate the next, or at least to make it clear who

Above: *This mausoleum at Ravenna was built by the Ostrogoth King Theodoric who ruled Italy from 493 until his assassination in 526. Though he was buried in his still uncompleted tomb, his bones were eventually removed and the mausoleum converted into a church. The dome, a single slab of Istrian limestone, is cracked from the centre to the rim. Though later legends attribute this to lightning, it is more likely that the crack occurred when the slab was being lifted into place.*

should be elected. Symmachus' predecessor, Pope Anastasius, had reigned for only a short time, and so possibly he did not have time to make his preference obvious. But it also seems likely that part of the trouble sprang from a senator called Festus who was sympathetic to the Emperor.

His first attempt to get a pope elected who would have accepted the imperial formula for unity misfired. Two years later he tried again. With some of the leading Roman clergy, he accused Symmachus of celebrating Easter on the wrong day, of being unchaste, and of misusing Church funds. Symmachus might have been prepared to argue about the date of Easter. He had followed the Roman calendar, whereas Festus and his associates wanted to follow the Greek one. But the Pope took fright at the other accusations and locked himself up in Saint Peter's. Festus and Laurentius took this as evidence of guilt. They assembled the bishops in synod to sit in judgement on the Pope. Symmachus was then summoned to appear. As he set out to cross Rome he was attacked by a mob, and several of his supporters were killed, including two priests. Not surprisingly, he retreated to Saint Peter's and refused to come out. A new synod had to be arranged, but this time the bishops decided that the wisest course was to concede that the Pope was above the bishops, and could not be put on trial. Symmachus had won, even though the troubles dragged on for four more years, with much of Rome, including all the larger churches, being in the hands of the supporters of Laurentius. The Lateran was among these, and so Symmachus made Saint Peter's his headquarters: he was the first Pope to do so, and he considerably expanded it.

Both sides engaged in literary propaganda. Laurentius was supported by a monk named Dionysius Exiguus (or Denis the Little) who put together on Laurentius' behalf the first collection of the laws of the Church to be widely used. He had been called to Rome in the first place to prepare a new table showing the dates of Easter, because the one then in use was about to run out. He calculated the dates starting from the year which he took to be that of Jesus' birth. He may have got the year wrong, but it is his system which is still followed, and which divides the years B.C. from those which are A.D.

Laurentius' propaganda was in vain, even though the Emperor accused Symmachus of being invalidly ordained, of being a Manichee, and of conspiring with the senate to excommunicate him. The Pope made it quite clear that he was not going to accept lay interference in ecclesiastical affairs. Symmachus' concern for the papal estates made him popular with the people of Rome who were relying increasingly upon papal generosity. The profits from the estates paid the clergy, aided travellers to Rome, and ransomed the many prisoners who had been taken by the Goths in the course of the wars. His opposition to the Emperor made him popular with Theodoric, who was playing an ever more independent role as King of Italy, and he ordered Laurentius to give up his Roman churches and retire to Festus' estates. This he did in 506. In his retreat he fasted so vigorously that he died, and from then until his own death in July 514 Symmachus' reign was relatively undisturbed. This fiery, stubborn but shrewd man was outlived by a dozen years by his protector, Theodoric.

In the year following Theodoric's death, Justinian became Emperor in Constantinople. He was determined that the Western provinces of the Empire should not slip from his grasp, and so for twenty years war between the Eastern Empire's troops and the Gothic soldiers of Theodoric's successors devastated Italy, while tax-gatherers from both sides bled what they could from the people. Though Justinian claimed victory, it was at a tremendous price. Italy had become a frontier province, no longer the centre of the Empire. Its civil service, like its garrisons, was staffed by people who spoke Greek. In Ravenna an Exarch, or governor-general, was installed, and the bishopric there was built up to rival Rome, Ravenna being the most easily defended of the Byzantine strongholds on the Italian mainland.

Justinian appointed Maximian of Pola as Archbishop of Ravenna and had him consecrated by Pope Vigilius. It was still unusual for the Emperor to interfere directly in episcopal elections, and thus when Maximian arrived in Ravenna the people would not accept him, and he had to take refuge in the palace of the former Arian bishops outside the town. But gradually he won over the town's leading citizens, and was permitted to take up residence. Visitors to Ravenna can still see many of the buildings he completed and much of the decoration with which he adorned them. The Gothic mosaics in San Apollinare Nuovo were removed, though the hands of some figures, probably representing personages at the court of Theodoric, can still be seen unattached to bodies. The new mosaics celebrate the triumph of Catholicism (the Emperor) over Arianism (the Goths). The close links which the Emperor wanted between Rome and Ravenna account for the constant repetition of the Petrine theme. But most of all, the mosaics served to enhance the glory of the Emperor himself who had provided money, materials and land. On either side of the apse in the church of San Vitale there is a picture of the heavenly court, and below a picture of the earthly court. On one side the Emperor Justinian advances with Archbishop Maximian beside him, holding out a golden plate on which the host would be placed during Mass.

Right: *This famous sixth-century mosaic is still to be seen in the church of San Vitale in Ravenna. It depicts the Emperor Justinian (483-565) advancing towards the altar, carrying the bread for use at Mass. On his right are his entourage, and on his left the Bishop of Ravenna, Maximian, carrying a cross, and two of the Bishop's acolytes. Across the apse from this mosaic is a similar one of Justinian's wife, the Empress Theodora, bringing the wine for the Mass.*

Directly opposite is Justinian's Empress, Theodora. She is accompanied by ladies of her court and two attendants, and carries the chalice to be used during Mass. The figures are not just majestic. They have an ethereal quality which almost indicates divinity. Most striking of all are the huge, compelling eyes of the Emperor.

Imperial control of Rome was not quite so direct, but it was tight. No new bishop was to be consecrated until the Emperor had given his consent, and the terms in which the Roman Church begged imperial approval were humiliating, even allowing for the extravagantly obsequious language of the day. But the language reflected the reality. The Emperors had come back to Italy, and Rome needed them.

As the imperial and Gothic armies fought their way up and down Italy, Rome was taken by force five times. Its population fell to some forty thousand by the middle of the sixth century, but when Totila captured and sacked it in 546, after four treacherous imperial soldiers had opened its gates, there were only five hundred people within its walls. Totila threatened to pull the whole place down, and set some of it on fire. He drove the remaining population out of the city, and left it entirely empty for forty days. Rome's vulnerability was evident to all.

It would have been particularly evident to Gregory, the son of Gordianus and Silvia, who first appears in the records in 573 as Prefect of the city. By that time the Gothic threat had been replaced by another.

The Lombards, who have left their name on one whole region of Italy, were living somewhere in the Baltic in the first century of the Christian era, but like other barbarian tribes they gradually drifted south, entering Italy in 568 and swiftly taking control of much of the peninsula north of Rome except, of course, for the area around Ravenna. Pavia became their capital. They were wild-looking, shaggy-bearded men. Their hair was close-shaven at the back, but long and parted on their foreheads, hanging down over their cheeks. For a century and a half the Bishops of Rome had to maintain a delicate balance between the Emperors and the Lombard Kings.

Gregory was well aware of the dreadful effects of the Lombard wars. 'Our cities are destroyed; our fortresses are overthrown; our fields laid waste; the

land is become a desert. No inhabitants remain in the countryside, scarcely any in the towns . . . some we have seen led into captivity, others mutilated, others killed', he wrote, shortly after his election to the papacy in 590. He lists the disasters: two monks were hanged, an abbot was killed, a deacon beheaded, forty peasants were put to death in one massacre and four hundred captives in another. The world was slipping into chaos.

Gregory had been born about the year 540 into an ancient senatorial family famous both for its nobility and its piety. Two sisters died renowned for their sanctity, one of them, it was said, with skin on her knees like that of a camel from so much kneeling in prayer. The third sister, when freed from the influence of the others, eloped with the steward of her estates.

Not long after becoming a civil servant, Gregory decided to enter a monastery. In the past, men of his standing were expected to make a career either in the senate or the Church. But such was the chaos of the world, and so appealing were the ideals of Christianity that Gregory, like many others, determined to retire into a monastery founded in the tradition of Saint Benedict who, about the year 500, had left Rome to live in a cave at Subiaco, east of Rome. There a community grew up around him which moved to Monte Cassino, south of Rome, in the year 530. In 581 it fell to the Lombards, and the monks fled to the Lateran, where they took up residence, and there Gregory met them. On joining the community, he gave them his family house on the Coelian Hill, which became the Benedictine Monastery of Saint Andrew. As a monk, Gregory would have followed the rule of life devised by Saint Benedict, though since the monastery was in the middle of the city there would have been much less emphasis on manual labour in the fields, and much more on study. He spent three years as a monk, the happiest ones of his life, he later recalled, before being ordained deacon and sent to

Above: *Some believe this painting, in one of the vaults of the church of Saint Francis at Assisi, is by Giotto (c. 1270-1337), but the attribution is much disputed. It is a picture of Pope Saint Gregory the Great, who is instantly recognizable because of the dove, symbolizing the Holy Spirit, whispering in his ear. Medieval artists, in order to indicate which saint they were depicting, regularly used the same symbols with the same saint. So Saint Peter, for example, is frequently shown as holding a key or keys, as on page 10.*

Constantinople, as papal ambassador, an assignment which he hated.

He lived in the Byzantine capital for six years, but never learned to speak Greek. His closest friend there was a Spaniard, and it was to him that he dedicated his commentary on the Book of Job, a work which enjoyed great success in the Middle Ages. Full of allegory and curious symbolism, it was meant to move hearts rather than minds, as indeed was the monastic movement as a whole. Job had seven sons. That is the perfect number, said Gregory, because seven is made up of three plus four, and three times four equals twelve, which is the number of the Apostles! But while writing such things, he was also engaged in rather more learned debate with the Patriarch of Constantinople over the nature of the risen body. The dispute reached such levels of acrimony that both protagonists fell ill, and when the Emperor decided in favour of Gregory, the Patriarch finally died.

In 586, Gregory returned to his monastery in Rome, bringing religious relics with him: the head of Saint Luke and the arm of Saint Andrew. He was elected abbot. It was while he was abbot that he first caught sight of a group of tall, fair-haired boys being sold in the Forum as slaves. He asked who they were, and on being told they were 'Angli' made the famous reply: '*Non Angli sed angeli*' – 'Not Angles but angels', and determined there and then to undertake their conversion. He asked Pope Pelagius II for permission to set off on his missionary journey to England. This was granted, but when he was only three days' journey from Rome, a locust settled on the page of the Bible he was reading. '*Locus sta*', said Gregory, which means 'Stay in this place' – it was one of those puns which made his writings so popular in the Middle Ages. However, he took this as an omen that he was not meant to go any further, and went back to Rome.

But the conversion of the English remained very much in his mind. His first plan was to acquire English youths as slaves, who might then be trained for the priesthood and sent back home, but he was presented with the possibility of much quicker results when King Ethelbert of Kent married the

Christian daughter of the King of Paris. The princess travelled to England accompanied by a Frankish bishop, with the promise that she would be allowed to practice her faith.

So, in 596 Augustine, a close friend of Gregory's and a member of the community of the Monastery of Saint Andrew, set off somewhat timidly for England. His efforts were met with almost instant success. Ethelbert was baptized on Whitsun's Eve, 597, and on Christmas Eve of the same year, Augustine, now the 'Archbishop of the English', baptized over ten thousand people. It had been the intention to move from Canterbury to London, once the initial work of evangelization had been done. London was to share with York the responsibility for the English Church, and seniority was to be determined by the date of appointment of the two archbishops. It was a confused arrangement, and one not satisfactorily worked out to this day. The Archbishop of York is titled 'the primate of England', while the Archbishop of Canterbury is called 'the primate of all England'.

Gregory was less successful in Gaul than he had been in England. The Franks had been Christians in name since the baptism of their King Clovis in 496, but they were still half pagan. The Pope managed to establish regular communication with the Frankish bishops, and made firm friends in the royal household. But Gregory's policy was not conversion at any price. Jews were subjected to stringent restrictions. Although the Pope insisted that the law be carried out to the letter, he made it clear that only persuasion could bring about a true conversion, compulsion would not. The degree of toleration he showed was quite remarkable for the age in which he lived, though he was not above taking advantage of the fear induced by the plague which ravaged Italy in the last decade of the sixth century (possibly the first signs of the Black Death) to frighten Arian Christians into becoming Catholics.

Popes belonging to religious orders were destined to play a large part in the history of the papacy. Gregory was the first of them. He brought in monks to run the central administration, to look after the *tituli*, or parish churches, and to oversee the papal estates outside Rome. It did not make him popular with the ordinary Roman clergy, with their jealously-guarded privileges, distinctive dress and tight-knit colleges and jurisdictions. It is not by chance that in the *Book of the Popes* the account of Gregory's life is remarkably short, or that his first biographer was a monk in far-away Whitby, in England, or that very few monks became pope in the following three centuries. The Roman clergy wanted to forget him.

Not so the Roman poor. Though he founded two singing schools, he cut down the time deacons spent in singing so that they could look after the charitable works of the Church. Gregory was generous not just to the inhabitants of the city but also to the many refugees who poured in from the Lombard wars. He so emptied the papal treasury that his successor was forced to sell, rather than give away, the corn supply, and so had a riot on his hands. There is a legend that he died as a result of a kick in the head from Gregory's ghost.

Money and supplies for Gregory's corn dole came from the papal estates. These were leased out to tenants who paid a rent to the manager of the regional patrimony, who had the title of rector. There were 15 such regions when Gregory became Pope, and their rectors – usually deacons but sometimes priests – were sent out from Rome after swearing on Saint Peter's tomb to protect the poor and defend the interests of the Church. As well as their concern for the management of the estates, the rectors also had the task of overseeing episcopal elections, and rectifying abuses in monasteries and other ecclesiastical institutions.

The income from the estates was not only used for charitable purposes. When Gregory became Pope he found Rome threatened by Lombards from without and by mutinous imperial troops within. The troops had not been paid by the imperial authorities. Gregory gave them their wages, and seems even to have contemplated making a separate peace with the Lombards.

So he was acting not only as Bishop in Rome but also as its civil governor.

Gregory I died in March 604, and was buried at the entrance to Saint Peter's. History has accorded him the title of 'Saint Gregory the Great'. When a second Gregory, also a monk, was elected Bishop of Rome in May 715 the diplomacy and statecraft which had been thrust upon a reluctant Gregory I by force of circumstances were now being taken for granted as part of the role of the Pope. Both Gregories reigned for the same number of years, both came from monastic backgrounds, both turned their family houses into monasteries. Both of them came from noble families, and had served at the imperial court, but the differences in their style were much greater than the similarities, and draw attention to the way the papal office had developed.

Gregory the Great strove for apostolic simplicity in his life and in his administration. He appointed monks to the main positions of authority in the Lateran palace. Laymen and non-monastic clergy were out of favour, but by the time of Gregory II they were back in favour, and the complex bureaucracy, staffed with laity and clergy rather than monks, served a glittering court. Simplicity had been the keynote of the first Gregory's revision of the liturgy. By Gregory II's time, singing flourished, and a good voice was a passport to high office. The simple, pastoral spirituality of Gregory I had been replaced by convoluted theological reasoning in the Greek tradition.

But though there were more Greeks in Rome, and a great deal of Byzantine influence on art and liturgy in the seventh century, with the dedication of Roman churches to Greek soldier-saints, this did not mean that Rome and Constantinople were on any better terms.

When Gregory I was elected Bishop, the Patriarch of Constantinople was the saintly John the Faster, whose devotion to the rigours of asceticism was equalled only by his devotion to the privileges of his See. He took the title 'Universal' (or Ecumenical) Patriarch, which the Patriarchs of Constantinople use to this day. But it was resented by Gregory because it challenged the primacy of the See of Rome. By the end of the seventh century Constantinople was claiming not just to be Rome's equal as a bishopric, but its superior.

In the negotiations over this claim, Gregory II had been to Constantinople as part of the entourage of his predecessor, Pope Constantine. Gregory was born a Roman, the son of Marcellus and Honesta, and had a meteoric rise through the ranks of the papal civil service, eventually becoming, as a sub-deacon, responsible for the papal treasury. Because the Roman banking system had collapsed, this meant he had to look after a whole range of civil as well as ecclesiastical funds. He was promoted to the rank of deacon, and given charge of the papal library – he was the first librarian to be named individually – which meant that he was one of the Pope's chief advisers.

As soon as he became Pope, he embarked upon major restoration of the defences of Rome, though the Tiber floods of 716 put an end to his plans. He also restored the monastery of Monte Cassino, and sent monks back from the Lateran monastery to restart the community. Much of the papal treasure was spent in bribing the Lombards, now largely converted from Arianism to Catholicism, but still not trusted by the Pope, and buying back captured cities. And if bribes allied to threats of divine vengeance did not prove enough to deter them, Gregory was ready to take more active measures. When the Lombards cut communications between Rome and Naples, Gregory sent one of his sub-deacons to advise the Duke of Naples about military strategy.

Gregory's loyalty to the Empire remained real, but it was severely tried. For reasons which still remain obscure the Emperor Leo decided that the devotion shown by Christians to images (icons) was displeasing to God. He was not supported in this by the Patriarch of Constantinople who retired to his estate to keep out of trouble, and there was at first only one major incident of image-smashing, or iconoclasm. The whole affair might have blown over had not news of these events in Constantinople reached Rome at the same time as an immense tax demand, which Gregory refused to pay. Leo then had an army dispatched from Ravenna to collect the money and murder the Pope, but this only succeeded in uniting the Romans and Lombards against the imperial troops. Next, the Duke of Naples together with his son – who had been excommunicated for marrying a nun – marched upon Rome, but they, too, were defeated and put to death by the Romans. The imperial governor, the Exarch, in Ravenna then tried an alliance with the Lombards. This time, the imperial and Lombard armies descended upon the Pope, but Gregory won over the Lombard King, who laid down his spear on Saint Peter's tomb. Despite these attempts against his life by the imperial authorities, Gregory remained remarkably loyal, even supporting the Exarch when a rebellion broke out in Tuscany.

Yet Gregory could do nothing to persuade the Emperor of this loyalty. The taxes he had refused to pay were replaced by a drastic confiscation of papal estates in southern Italy and Sicily, some of the most profitable areas of the patrimony of Saint Peter. Territories held by the papacy outside Italy had also disappeared by this time, but they were replaced by lands nearer Rome, and the Roman See does not seem to have been impoverished.

Despite his fundamental loyalty to the Emperor, Gregory shows in his letters a quite surprising degree of independence. Other alliances were becoming popular, such as with the Lombard King himself, or with individual Lombard dukes. Increasingly, the papacy was looking for support from the barbarian tribes. During the seventh century, Saxon kings left England to spend their last days in Rome, and guidebooks were being written for them about the city and its monuments. So persistent were the Anglo-Saxons in their visits to Rome that hostels were built in an area near Saint Peter's which they called 'the borough', and which is still known as the Borgo. After the manner of the English, they lived in wooden houses, which constituted a constant fire hazard. This separate community was called the *schola* of the Saxons, and there were other *scholae*, those of Greeks, Lombards and, eventually, Frisians.

A monk from Crediton in Devon came to Rome in 718, when he was 40 years of age. He was called Wynfrith, but changed his name to Boniface before setting off from Rome, with Gregory's blessing, to evangelize the tribes living in what is now Germany. When rumours of his unorthodoxy reached Rome he was recalled by the Pope for questioning. He claimed that he could not understand the Pope's language, so he put his profession of faith in writing and laid it on the tomb of Saint Peter. It was enough to win the Pope's confidence once more, and Boniface was made a bishop and sent back to Germany. His story belongs for the most part to the next chapter, but the example of his complete, if not uncritical, devotion to the Roman See is evidence of the growing influence of the papacy in the West.

A Roman synod held by Gregory II declared that Rome was 'the head of the Church of God and of the priests throughout the world'. The Lombard King incorporated the claim into his own code of law. When Gregory died in February 731, the iconoclast controversy had separated him from the official Greek Church, which was dominated by the Emperor Leo, but had won him the support of many individuals in the East who were out of sympathy with the imperial religious policy. In Italy, bishops had come to rely increasingly on the Pope not only as a spiritual but also as a secular leader. Outside Italy, there were few areas which had not experienced the reforming or missionary activity of monks and priests sent out from Rome.

As the influence of the Pope – who now, like the Patriarch of Constantinople, called himself 'the Universal Bishop' – declined in the East, it grew in the West. The pattern had been set by the beginning of the reign of Gregory II: it was to take dramatic form at the very end of the eighth century.

SCS
PETRVS

SCISSIMVS

DNLEODPP

DN CARVLO REG

BEATE PETRE DONAS
VITA LEONI PP BICTO
RIA CARVLO REGI DONAS

POPES AND EMPERORS

In the church of Santa Maria Antica in Rome there is what may well be the earliest surviving portrait of a pope. It shows a slightly built young man with receding dark hair and an alert expression. He looks exactly as the *Book of the Popes* describes him: a 'suave' figure. He is Zachary, son of Polychronius, born in Calabria, a part of Italy still dependent on Constantinople. He was elected Bishop of Rome in December 741, after serving the Roman church as a deacon for at least nine years.

He was soon to need all the suavity he could muster. Two years earlier, King Liutprand of the Lombards had appeared before the walls of Rome, and Zachary's predecessor, Gregory III, had appealed for help to Charles Martel, the Frankish ruler. Nothing came of the appeal, but it was a significant step: the Pope had looked for help to the West rather than to the East. Zachary, however, was more realistic. He knew that help would come from neither side, and so to prevent further aggression he determined to treat with the Lombard King himself. Soon after his election he set off for Liutprand's court on a mission that proved more successful than he could have hoped. On the Saturday, the King and the Pope had a political discussion, the following day they met socially over dinner. So charmed by Zachary's conversation was Liutprand that he said afterwards he had never enjoyed a meal so much.

Liutprand agreed that all papal lands lost to the Lombards should be returned to the Pope, but what Zachary promised in return has not been recorded, possibly he agreed that the See of Rome would not ally itself with any of the Lombard Dukes against the Lombard King: Roman forces allied to the Duke of Spoleto's army had inflicted a defeat on Liutprand's troops.

The Lombards had thus been dissuaded from attacking Rome. They made no promises about Ravenna, still the seat of the Exarch. When Liutprand turned his attention to Ravenna in 743 the Archbishop appealed to Zachary for help, and the Pope set off again, protected on his journey to Ravenna, the legends recount, by a cloud which sheltered him from the sun. He found Liutprand in his capital of Pavia. The King agreed to return to the Emperor much of the territory around Ravenna which he had already seized. Not unnaturally, the Emperor was delighted, and rewarded Zachary's work with the grant of estates, making some reparation for the lands in southern Italy he had confiscated from the Pope just ten years before.

Zachary was soon to need this new-found wealth. Liutprand's successor was a peaceable man by nature, but was forced by the other Lombard dukes to engage in some sabre-rattling. He marched against papal and imperial territories, and was bought off with papal treasure, whereupon he decided to give up the bellicose life for good and, along with his wife and daughter, entered religious life. The new Lombard King was much more warlike, and

Opposite: *This mosaic originally decorated the hall built by Pope Leo III (795-816). It shows Saint Peter on a throne giving a pallium to Pope Leo and a banner to Charlemagne. It was probably erected about 798 before Charlemagne had been made Emperor. Across the arch from this group another mosaic depicted Christ handing keys to Pope Sylvester and the labarum to Constantine. In 1625 the mosaics were thoroughly restored and in 1743 they were moved. During the move, however, they were badly damaged and most of what remains is based upon conjecture, relying on drawings of Pope Leo's hall.*

71

determined to establish his rule over the whole of Italy. Ravenna was the first town to fall to him, and the Emperor's inability to win it back was final proof, if further proof were needed, that the popes had to look other than to Constantinople for their secular protectors. Then Zachary was presented with a problem which was to shift the balance of power for good: he was appealed to by Pepin.

For two and a half centuries the area which is now France had been ruled by the Merovingians. But long before Zachary's election this royal line had become so weak that effective power lay in the hands of an official called 'the mayor of the palace', or major-domo. Charles Martel had been just such an official – Zachary's predecessor had addressed him as 'sub-king' – and the task was now being performed by Pepin. The nominal ruler was Childeric III.

Was it right, an emissary from Pepin asked the Pope, that the person who wielded the authority of a king (meaning himself) should not be king, but only 'mayor of the palace'? Zachary's answer favoured Pepin, and Childeric was made into a cleric and packed off to a monastery. At Soisson, Pepin was anointed King of the Franks by, in all probability, Saint Boniface. Thus the first of the new royal house of the Franks came to power with the consent of the Pope, and with an anointing by a papal legate.

Boniface himself, meanwhile, had been so successful as a missionary in Germany that he was able to hold a national German synod to reform abuses in the Church. Pepin's brother, Carlomann, who ruled the German part of the Frankish Kingdom, gave the decrees the force of law. Two years later, and again with Boniface presiding, a similar gathering was held in Pepin's part of Francia, and Boniface presided once more over a combined meeting in 745 when it was decided that he would fix his See at Cologne, on the borders of what was still pagan territory. Zachary determined otherwise, however, and appointed him to Mainz, with Tongres, Cologne, Worms, Spire and Utrecht all subject to him, together with the entire German people.

In the year of the combined synod, Carlomann, to atone for his violent life, united both parts of the Frankish Kingdom under Pepin and gave Boniface some land at Fulda to build a monastery. Boniface, who is now called 'the apostle of Germany', told Zachary that he wished to be buried at the monastery, and so Zachary granted to Fulda, as he had granted to Monte Cassino, exemption from all jurisdiction except that of Rome. Carlomann himself journeyed to Rome, became a monk, and founded a monastery at Monte Soratte, not far from Rome. The proximity to Rome was a mistake. Lombard and Frankish noblemen travelling to and from Rome would call to see him, and so he had to go and live at Monte Cassino to find the peace he desired.

Pope Zachary was as busy reforming his own diocese as he was encouraging Church reform elsewhere. In 743 he held a synod at Rome that was attended by some 40 bishops and about half that number of priests. Various disciplinary measures concerning priests and nuns were laid down, marriages within certain degrees of kindred were restricted, and Christians were forbidden to celebrate January 1 and December 25 according to the pagan fashion. The synod also condemned all those who sold Christian slaves to Jewish owners.

The synod decreed that bishops subject to the Pope's jurisdiction must come to Rome each year to report on the state of their dioceses, unless distance made this impracticable. If they lived too far away for an annual visit, then the frequency was to be determined between bishop and Pope. The bishops were to come, said the synod, *ad limina Apostolorum* (to the threshold of the Apostles), and visits of Roman Catholic bishops to the Pope are called *ad limina* visits to this day.

Papal authority was reaching out to the newly-converted lands. Four years after the Roman synod, a similar meeting was held at Cloveshoe in England. Among its many declarations on Church reform was the decision that in all things concerning the saying of Mass and the singing of the chant the practice of the Roman Church was to be followed.

Reforms were also brought to the running of the papal estates. The Campagna is a great stretch of low-lying plain to the south of Rome. Its climate is unhealthy. In Zachary's time it had scarcely recovered from devastation by Huns, imperial troops and Lombards. Yet in this region the Pope set up five small settlements with churches and houses to bring it under cultivation. The extra funds which such colonies brought in, and the income from the lands given him by the Emperor, enabled Zachary to be generous not just to the poor but also to the clergy. It was the Bishop of Rome's practice to make an annual gift of money to his priests and deacons. Zachary doubled the sum.

He died, much loved, in 752 and was buried in Saint Peter's. His successor, the priest Stephen, lived only four days after his election, and is sometimes omitted from the list of the popes. It was the shortest pontificate on record. Confusion is made all the worse because the elected successor to Stephen was another Stephen, a deacon of the Roman Church.

This second Stephen's father, Constantine, had died when the boy was very young, and he had been brought up under the special protection of the popes. He had grown up very well aware of the political problems which confronted the Bishop of Rome. On his election he sent gifts to the Lombard King Aistulf, and Aistulf agreed to a forty-year peace. It lasted four months. Then Aistulf demanded a tribute of a gold coin from every Roman citizen. Pope Stephen went in procession through the city, a picture of Christ on his shoulders, and ashes on his head. The treaty Aistulf had broken was nailed to a cross and carried before them. Then in 753 he journeyed north to see Pepin, making the hazardous crossing of the Alps in midwinter, escorted by the Bishop of Metz.

Papal chroniclers record that the King met the Pope on foot and, acting as groom to his horse, led Stephen into the palace between rows of chanting clergy. Non-papal chroniclers, on the other hand, report that Stephen dressed in sackcloth, with tears in his eyes and ashes on his head, begged for Pepin's support. At the Abbey of Saint Denis the Pope anointed Pepin and his son, declared them to be 'patricians of the Romans' (that is to say, protectors of the city), and forbade anyone not of Pepin's blood to succeed to the Frankish throne. In return Pepin, at Quierzy-sur-Oise, named the territories he would guarantee to the Pope.

Some six months after the agreement at Quierzy, the Franks marched against the Lombards. Besieged in Pavia, Aistulf capitulated and promised to hand over to the Pope the cities he had captured, including Ravenna. It was a promise he did not keep. In January 756 he was outside the walls of Rome, and Stephen wrote a letter, as if from Saint Peter himself, once again pleading for Pepin's assistance, which he obtained. Aistulf surrendered and handed over the keys of all the cities he was supposed to have ceded to the papacy before, including those of Ravenna and other towns of the former Exarchate. These were then gathered together and laid on the tomb of Saint Peter.

Stephen's pontificate was a fairly short one; he died in April 757. It was, however, a momentous one, for the papacy had found a new protector. And it was more than a political alliance. When the Bishop of Metz had arrived in Rome to accompany Stephen on his visit to Pepin's court in 753, he had been enormously impressed by the chant he had heard in the Lateran basilica and had ordered the same type of singing to be introduced into the churches of his diocese. Years later, the Bishop of Rheims, Pepin's brother, had sent monks to Rome to study in the singing schools there. Thus, Roman liturgical practice, and Roman liturgical books, were given an ever wider currency.

The Christianization of what is now modern Europe was undertaken in the name of the See of Rome. Boniface died a martyr's death in 755, but conversion was not solely a religious enterprise – it became part of statecraft, especially under Pepin's son, Charlemagne. He dominated religious events at the end of the eighth century and the beginning of the ninth. After the collapse of the Lombard Kingdom in 774, the central Italian duchies had come under Frankish overlordship. But in order to preserve the clerical nature of the papacy, an election decree of 769 had laid down that no layman was to intervene in the choosing of a new pope and that only 'cardinal priests' of the Roman Church could become Bishops of Rome. The name 'cardinal' was not at first a title of honour but indicated a role in the Church. Bishops, priests and deacons usually served the churches in which they were ordained, but in Rome some of them had to be moved to other duties. The seven bishops immediately dependent on the Bishop of Rome were required to provide liturgical services in the Lateran basilica, and the 28 parish churches had to supply priests for the other three major basilicas of the city: Saint Peter's, Saint Paul's Outside the Walls, and Santa Maria Maggiore. The bishops and priests who performed these functions outside the church of their ordination were called cardinals.

The day after Christmas 795 Leo, cardinal priest of Saint Susanna, was unanimously chosen Bishop of Rome. His father, Atyuppius, and his mother, Elizabeth, were possibly of barbarian background, not members of the Roman aristocracy. Leo himself was learned in scripture, eloquent, and a good singer. He was pious, and fond of the society of pious people. At the time of his election he was head of the papal treasury.

He informed Charlemagne of his election, and sent him the keys of the tomb of Saint Peter, together with the city's standard. He begged the King to send someone to receive the city's oath of fidelity. He was trying to get Charlemagne to commit himself to protecting the city of Rome. Charlemagne agreed to do this on condition that the Pope prayed for victory for the Frankish army.

He was soon to need the King's protection. In the spring of 799, during a procession to ask God's blessing on the fruits of the earth, Leo was attacked by a gang of thugs hired by the late Pope's nephew who had hoped to become Pope himself. Half dead, Leo was bundled into a monastery from which he had to escape by rope, and he then fled to Charlemagne's court at Aachen. At the end of the year he returned to Rome at the head of a large

Left: This tower was built by Pope Leo IV (847-55) a year after his election. It was part of the fortifications surrounding the Vatican. Known as 'Saint John's Tower' it was, until 1929, the site of the Vatican Observatory, which moved out to Castel Gandolfo that year after the signing of the Lateran Treaty. Pope John XXIII turned the tower into a four-storey apartment, complete with lift, and it became one of his favourite retiring places.

œuure du noble Charlemaine ror de fr

tailles que Charlemaine eut alencon

Frankish retinue, but his troubles were not over. Accusations were made against him of impurity, accusations which Charlemagne dismissed when he visited Rome the following year. From the pulpit of Saint Peter's, and holding a book of the Gospels in his hand, Leo swore his innocence. This happened two days before Christmas. On 25 December 800, Charlemagne made his way to Saint Peter's for Mass, dressed in the long tunic and green mantle of a 'patrician' of the Romans. He wore sandals on his feet and a gold circlet round his brow. He walked through the vestibule before the high altar, which was flanked by 12 twisted columns of white marble supporting beams covered with silver plate. On the beams were silver candelabra, and the way was paved with plates of silver. There were silver gates at the end of the vestibule, which led into a choir enclosed within walls of marble and decorated by images made of silver. On four days of the year, and Christmas Day was one of them, all 1365 candles in a huge candelabrum given by Leo's predecessor were lit.

Through the choir was the tomb of Saint Peter, surrounded by golden railings, and before this Charlemagne knelt. After reading the Gospel,

Above: *This scene, from an illuminated manuscript in Paris, shows the coronation of Charlemagne as the first 'Holy Roman Emperor' on Christmas Day 800. The Pope in the picture is Leo III (795-816). The name 'Holy Roman Empire' dates only from the middle of the thirteenth century, and the last Emperor to be crowned as such was Charles V (1500-58). The title stayed in use until 1806, when it was finally abandoned by the Hapsburg family which had appropriated it.*

Pope Leo III crowned Charlemagne Emperor of the Romans. The new Emperor's praises were sung, litanies recited, and Charlemagne was then 'adored', Byzantine fashion, by Pope and nobility. The Holy Roman Empire had been established. In name at least it was to last almost exactly a thousand years.

Leo was an astute man. It was his action which made the Frankish King into a Roman Emperor: the highest secular office was to depend upon the highest spritual one. By his initiative he ensured that Charlemagne and his successors would be protectors of the city of Rome. But a price had to be paid. Leo was soon complaining of imperial interference in the papal estates but, despite the problems, Leo was proud of his achievement. He erected a huge hall, and one of the mosaics with which he decorated it shows Christ giving keys to Saint Sylvester and a military standard to Constantine, while another shows Saint Peter giving the pallium (the woollen stole worn by the pope and other bishops to show their unity with each other) to Leo and a standard to Charlemagne.

The new Emperor dominated Leo's life, even in purely religious matters. For instance, Charlemagne held a synod at Aachen which approved the addition to the Creed of the word *filioque*, meaning 'and from the Son', when talking about the 'procession' of the Holy Spirit from the Father. The expression was theologically orthodox, Leo agreed, but it ought not to be used because it did not have the sanction of ancient Church laws.

More troublesome than theological controversy was the threat from the

Saracens. The town of Centumcellae was entirely destroyed by these Islamic invaders, and the Pope handed Corsica over to the Franks because he could not guarantee its safety.

Leo III died in 816. He had made a tentative start on fortifications for Saint Peter's, but the Leonine walls running from the Tiber round Saint Peter's and back to the Tiber take their name from Leo IV, who was elected in 847, a year after the Saracens had sacked Rome.

Leo IV was well aware of the responsibilities that would come to him as Bishop of Rome. He was of Lombard origin, or so it seems from the name of his father, Radwald. He became a monk in the monastery of Saint Martin, close to Saint Peter's, then sub-deacon in the Lateran before being transferred as priest to the church of Quattro Incoronati. He had to be carried forcibly from there back to the Lateran for his consecration. He knew the hazards of the papal office and probably did not welcome them. Building walls was therefore a prudent move. His walls took four years to complete. They were of great height and thickness, and were fortified by 44 towers. There were only three gates in them. When they were finished, solemn processions of clergy, some of them barefoot, dedicated them with sacred litanies.

Leo's building was not only for defensive purposes. He refounded Centumcellae on a site not far from the old town. The new town, Leopolis, was not a success, and its inhabitants eventually moved back to the 'old town', or

Left: *As part of his campaign to exalt the Empire at the expense of the Papacy, Frederick Barbarossa had the Emperor Charlemagne, whose private life was anything but holy, declared a saint by the anti-pope Pascal III. Some churches in France, Germany and even Spain accepted the canonization and had feasts in honour of Charlemagne. In 1215 his relics were put into this magnificent sarcophagus, which can still be seen in Aachen where the feast continued to be celebrated down to recent times.*

civitas vetus – hence it was renamed Civitavecchia. A fire in the Anglo-Saxon quarter of Rome itself, which he was reputed to have extinguished by making the sign of the cross, gave him the opportunity to redevelop part of the city, and his contemporaries remembered him for the splendour of his embellishments to Saint Peter's, and to his old church of Quattro Incoronati. This latter church was the centre of devotion to Saint Sylvester, the Pope whose legendary life helped to justify the secular aspirations of the papacy.

But with the Saracens at the gates, the popes hardly needed any such justification to bolster their temporal authority. Leo blessed the combined fleets of the maritime cities of Italy and the Byzantine Empire when they assembled at the mouth of the Tiber to face a large Saracen fleet in 849. With a little help from the weather, the Christians defeated the infidels, and prisoners were sent back to Rome to work on the fortifications of the city. Raphael was later to depict this victory – and also Leo stopping the fire with the sign of the cross – in his decoration of the *Stanze* (salons) in the Vatican.

The pressure of events made the Pope into a warrior, but he never forgot that he was also a religious leader. A synod reformed the liturgical life of his diocese and laid down, among many other things, the rule that the sacred vessels used at Mass must be made of precious metal, and cleaned only by the clergy themselves. Outside Rome, he required bishops to reside in their dioceses, to visit their parishes, and to establish schools.

Leo was particularly conscious of the need to foster learning, but in Rome this had its problems. A revival of interest in learning meant a revival of interest in antiquity, and the study of the city's secular origins. A group began to promote the ideal of a unified Italy with Rome as its capital city. One of its leaders was the brilliant Cardinal Anastasius, whose ambition led him into excommunication several times over, and into exile. On Leo's death in 855 he was a contender for the papacy, and had Frankish support. He failed to win the election and retired to the monastery of Santa Maria in Trastavere, from where he could influence the policy of successive popes, including one of the most outstanding, Pope Nicholas I, whom he served as secretary.

Like many of his predecessors, Nicholas had been destined from his earliest years for high office in the Church but, unlike most of them, had entered papal service late, remaining in the house of his father, Theodore, during his education. Theodore had responsibility for one of the regions into which Rome was divided, and so his son grew up well versed in the problems of the papacy. When elected Pope he fled and, like Leo IV, had to be brought back by force to be consecrated in Saint Peter's on 24 April 858. He may have been the first Pope to be crowned. In San Clemente there is a figure, possibly of Nicholas, in a picture of the burial of Saint Cyril. Around this figure's head is a diadem adorned with gems.

The Frankish Emperor, Louis, had been present at the consecration. Six years later he marched to Rome to force Nicholas to permit his brother, Lothar of Lorraine, to marry his (Lothar's) mistress, Waldrada. The problem was complicated because Lothar had originally married Waldrada according to ancient Germanic law, and had had children by her, but he had then been persuaded into a dynastic marriage with Theutberga, the daughter of the Count of Burgundy. Dynastically, however, the marriage had proved a disaster: no children were born. Lothar wanted to return to his first love 'because since infancy', he said, 'or at least since boyhood, I have been used to having women' and could not, therefore, live chastely outside marriage.

The Archbishops of Trier and Cologne approved his marrying Waldrada. Nicholas did not, and deposed the two Archbishops. The Frankish bishops retaliated by excommunicating the Pope, and when Louis arrived in Rome at the head of his troops the charges against Nicholas were thrown down on to the tomb of Saint Peter. In the battle of wills between Pope and Emperor the Emperor lost. He was ill with fever, and too weak politically to risk alienating Nicholas for ever. Eventually, even Theutberga petitioned the

Pope to grant Lothar's wish to marry Waldrada, so tired was she of the whole affair. But Nicholas was adamant. Both women ended their days in convents despite all the efforts they had made to escape such a fate.

What was at issue was primarily the question of Christian marriage and papal authority over it, but in standing firm on that issue Nicholas had also deposed two of the most powerful ecclesiastics of northern Europe, packed them off to monasteries, and instructed that their posts be left vacant. It was an exercise of papal power such as the West had not seen for a long time. It showed a degree of ecclesiastical independence unknown in the East.

Nicholas's problems at Constantinople also began with an illicit love affair. The Emperor's uncle abandoned his wife and went to live with his nineteen-year-old daughter-in-law. When the Patriarch Ignatius dared to criticize he was exiled, and a young monk, the charming, learned, unscrupu-

Above: *Raphael (1483-1520) was employed by Pope Leo X to glorify the name of Leo by depicting a series of incidents from the lives of earlier popes of the same name. This picture shows a legend from the life of Leo IV (847-55). A fire broke out in the 'borgo' – the area where the Anglo-Saxon community lived – near the basilica of Saint Peter, and the Pope was reputed to have put it out by making the sign of the cross.*

lous Photius was put in his place. Photius sought recognition from Rome, and even won over the legates Nicholas sent to investigate the matter. But no Bishop of Rome worthy of the name could fail to be swayed, as indeed Nicholas was, by the deposed Ignatius addressing him as 'our most holy and blessed president of all the Sees, the successor of the Apostles, the ecumenical Pope'. By the time of Nicholas's death in 867, Photius had been exiled, Ignatius reinstated, and the Emperor Michael III assassinated on the instructions of Basil – his assistant Emperor and former groom – but not before the Bulgars had become involved in the conflict between the two Sees.

King Boris of the Bulgars had been baptized after the conversion of his people by Cyril and Methodius. These two saintly missionaries had been sent, at Boris's request, by the Emperor in Constantinople, and the Emperor had stood as godfather to the King at his baptism. But now the Bulgar King turned towards Rome, perhaps to avoid too much involvement with the Eastern Empire. Nicholas sent Bishop Formosus of Porto to preach the Gospel to Boris and his subjects. He carried with him a letter which laid down the standard to be observed: no forced conversions of pagans; no torture; marriage was to be by mutual consent; there was to be no polygamy, and no superstitious practices among Christians; there were to be fast-days, though fewer in number than at Rome; no one was to work on holy days; the Bulgar battle-flag should be a cross, not a horse's tail. The King then requested the appointment of a patriarch. This could not be, said Nicholas, because patriarchal Sees had to have been founded by the Apostles and so even Constantinople had the title of patriarchate only by courtesy, not by right. He would grant them an archbishop, he declared, but it could not be Bishop Formosus – to whom Boris had taken a great liking – because Formosus was needed elsewhere. He was firm, and so the Bulgars turned back to Constantinople.

Nicholas was a strange and powerful blend of idealism and political realism, as is shown by the following events. A king of Wessex, returning from a pilgrimage to Rome, married Judith, daughter of Charles the Bald of France. But when the King died soon afterwards she married her stepson, to the great scandal of all. That marriage, too, soon ended with the death of her husband and Judith came back to France to be locked up under episcopal supervision at Senlis. But from Senlis she eloped with Baldwin, Count of Flanders, and Baldwin came to Rome to ask the Pope's approval. He gave it, and wrote to Judith's father, pointing out that if Charles the Bald did not also grant permission then Baldwin might very well ally himself with the Norsemen who were just beginning to attack the coast of France. Charles gave in, and the wife of William the Conqueror was one of the descendants of the marriage.

As the Norsemen threatened Europe from the north, so the Saracens, encamped at Bari, were a threat in the south. Within Europe, the Emperor was weak, the kings at war with one another. The papacy was a fixed point. The renaissance of learning born in France had reached Rome, and its ablest exponent was Cardinal Anastasius, papal librarian and secretary, once pretender to the Bishopric of Rome but now Nicholas's closest adviser. Europe now had something of a cultural, as well as a religious unity, and papal jurisdiction welded it into rather more than a geographical entity. So it is no accident that it was about this time that the 'False Decretals' appeared, not, at first, in Rome but possibly in France. They were a collection of documents, some genuine but many spurious which, it was claimed, had been compiled by Saint Isidore of Seville. The compilation defended the rights of bishops against archbishops but, more important, it emphasized the rights, privileges and authority of the Roman See. So much importance was given to the False Decretals that Nicholas could use them in support of the Bishop of Soissons against the Bishop's superior, the powerful Archbishop Hincmar of Rheims. In the struggle, Hincmar was forced to give in but he remained ready to support the Pope and set his monks hard at work writing against Photius.

Nicholas died in November 867. His moral authority had been enormous, but to a great degree much had depended upon his own strong personality. Soon after his death, dissenting factions within Rome reasserted themselves, and brought the status of the Bishop of that city to the lowest point it was ever to reach.

Below: Charles the Bald, grandson of Charlemagne, was King of the West Franks and, later, Emperor. This picture shows Charles's coronation with Hincmar, Archbishop of Rheims on one side and the Bishop of Trier on the other.

CONCILIVM
CONSTANTINOP·IV

THE PAPACY IN DECLINE

The century which separated the deaths of Pope Nicholas I and Pope John XII, murdered on the way to see his mistress, was one of the worst in the history of the papacy. Though the office of Pope may still have sometimes commanded respect, the persons who came to fill it very often did not command the same respect.

And there were many of them. Between Nicholas and John there were 24 popes, all of them Italians, most of them Romans. Though one reigned for 14 years, the pontificates of others can be measured in days. They passed so fleetingly that little is known of them, and it is in this period that the story of Pope Joan is set.

The first mention of Pope Joan occurs in chronicles written in the thirteenth century, four centuries after the date she was supposed to have reigned. But by about the year 1400 enough people believed in the legend for a statue of her to be erected in Siena cathedral.

There are variations of the story. According to one version, Pope Joan was English, though born in Mainz. As a girl she had fallen in love with an English monk and, disguised as a man, had followed him to Athens. There she studied, and when later she came to Rome she became a scribe, a papal notary, a cardinal, and eventually Pope. One legend has her ruling for two and a half years, and her sex being discovered only after her death. A more dramatic account records that she was pregnant at her election, and gave birth during her coronation procession. The Roman crowd, the story goes on, furious at being made to seem foolish, dragged her off her horse, out of the city gates, and there stoned her to death.

It is a gruesome, highly improbable story. There is no legitimate place in the history of the popes for her supposed two-and-a-half-year pontificate, shadowy and unsettled though much of the period was. Those who concocted the legends could not at first even agree on a name. Joan was decided upon only in the fourteenth century, and up to that time Agnes and Ghiberta had been possible alternatives. What gave some credibility to the story, however, was not so much the degradation of the late ninth- and early tenth-century papacy as the fact that one particular family, named Theophylact, and especially the women of that family, came to play a large part in the lives and the decision-making of the Bishops of Rome. The rest of this chapter pieces together the main events, as far as they are known, in the decline of the papacy during this dark and chaotic age.

Pope Nicholas's successor, Hadrian II, was aged about 75 when he was elected, and proved not to be a strong character. But, unlike many of his successors, he was a virtuous man. He came from a Roman family who lived in the city's third region – an area which had already produced two Popes, Stephen V and Sergius II. Hadrian's father, Talarus, was himself a

Opposite: The Fourth Council of Constantinople met between October 869 and February 870 in an attempt to heal the breach between the two great Sees brought about the Photian schism. The Byzantine Emperor seen in the background is Basil I (867-886) who gave the decisions of the bishops the force of law throughout his territory. The Council made one of the clearest affirmations of papal primacy over the whole Church hitherto made by a gathering of bishops from both parts of Christendom, but the papacy's triumph was short-lived.

Above: *The Archbishops of Metz and Salzburg complained to the Pope of the 'novelties' introduced among the Slavs by the two missionaries Cyril and Methodius. Nicholas I (858-67) summoned them to Rome, but it was Pope Hadrian II who listened to their arguments and approved their plan of action – including the use of the Slavonic language in the liturgy. This scene, depicted by the Italian artist Nobili, shows the two saints presenting their case to the Pope.*

bishop, and Hadrian, too, was married, with at least one child. He had been made a sub-deacon by Gregory IV, and was ordained cardinal-priest of Saint Mark's in 842. He was consecrated Pope in 867. His wife and daughter moved into the Lateran palace with him, but this did not meet with universal approval, even though he and his wife probably lived in strict celibacy.

At first, it seemed that he was not going to continue his predecessor's policies, and clearly thought that compromise was the only way to reconcile the city's opposing factions. But the party which had formed round the formidable Bishop Formosus of Porto would not let him compromise. He was persuaded to ratify Nicholas's decisions, especially that forbidding the divorce of Lothar of Lorraine. Those who opposed this policy reacted fiercely; one of them, who was called Eleutherius, and who was related to the ambitious Cardinal Anastasius, broke into the Lateran palace and kidnapped the Pope's wife and daughter. He forced the daughter to marry him, but then felt that he needed imperial support for his actions. His father went to the Imperial court to plead for him, but he died on the way there. Eleutherius panicked and killed both his captives.

Events such as these undermined Hadrian's authority at the very beginning of his pontificate. For a time, Anastasius was in disgrace, but his family was too powerful for him to stay out of favour for long. In any case, Hadrian already had enough enemies. Duke Lambert of Spoleto had dared to loot Rome during the celebrations that marked Hadrian's consecration, and now treated Rome as if it were part of his dukedom.

The Frankish Emperor, Louis, had remained in Italy following the

HADRIANVS II· PONTIFEX CVIII·
ANNO DOMINI DCCCLXVII·

dispute with Pope Nicholas, but he was incapable of intervening, both because he was a weak character and because his forces were totally committed to defeating the Saracens. Also, in trying to build a Christian alliance against these Moslem marauders, he had been obliged to give almost complete independence to the individual dukes in return for their support. It was a mistaken policy and the Western Empire forfeited all respect. It was therefore not the Western Emperor who was to play the decisive role in driving the Moslems from Italy, but Basil, the Byzantine Emperor.

Basil wanted to restore peace to the Empire, and tried to win support for his policies from the Bishop of Rome. He reversed his predecessor's support for Photius and brought back Patriarch Ignatius. Envoys were sent to the Pope. They carried a statement from Ignatius supporting the pre-eminence of the Bishopric of Rome within the Christian Church; it was the most explicit statement on this subject ever to have been made by a Patriarch of Constantinople.

At Rome, the synod called by Photius in 867 was condemned, even though the minutes of the meeting had been signed by the joint Eastern Emperors, Michael and Basil. The first signature had been obtained when Michael was drunk, said the envoys, and the second was simply a forgery. The minutes were then burnt. The resultant fire was reported to have given out a vile smell, and to have flared up suddenly, so that not even a shower of rain could dampen down the flames.

A council was then held in the East. The Council of Constantinople of 869-70 was the last joint meeting to be held in the East which the Western Church has accepted as being ecumenical – that is to say, binding on the whole Church. Photius was condemned, iconoclasm repudiated, speaking or writing against the Bishop of Rome forbidden, and it was agreed that not even a universal council could pass decrees in opposition to him. It seemed to be a triumph for the papacy. The triumph, however, was short-lived.

Annoyed that the Bishop of Rome had not permitted Bishop Formosus of Porto to remain with him as an Archbishop, the King of the Bulgars sent representatives to the closing stages of the Council. The Patriarch of the East and the Pope of the Western Church then had to decide under whose jurisdiction the newly-converted people should come. Hadrian's representatives met with those of the Patriarch Ignatius. Cardinal Anastasius, now the

…AVATICANO FER TVR PP NICOLAO IMNISDIVINIS QDAROMATIB, SEPELI

…O MARIAMACELLARIA PTIMORE DEI E TREMEDIO ANIME MEE HEC P

Pope's most capable adviser, was in Constantinople on business for the Western Emperor, but was not allowed to take part in the gathering, and the Latins were permitted only one interpreter. Jurisdiction in Bulgaria was duly granted to the Byzantines, who moved into the country, driving out the Roman missionaries. The papal envoys in Constantinople were sent home with an inadequate escort, they were captured by pirates and imprisoned. The Council, which had seemed to augur so well for the Roman See, ended in confusion.

However, what was lost by Rome in Bulgaria was regained elsewhere. The work of Cyril and Methodius in Moravia, Bohemia and Silesia had been extremely successful. The two missionaries had been summoned back to Rome by Pope Nicholas, but he had died before they had arrived bearing the body of Saint Clement. A fresco in the church of San Clemente shows the burial of the saint and depicts a pope, probably intended to be Nicholas rather than Hadrian, in the procession. Cyril died soon after his arrival in Rome, but Hadrian consecrated Methodius as Archbishop of the Slavs and sent him back to them with permission for the Mass to be said in their own language. There was a theory current at the time which held that the Mass could be celebrated only in the three languages used on the crucifix: Latin, Greek and Hebrew. As a concession to those who adhered to this belief, Hadrian insisted that the readings at Mass should be in Latin as well as in Slavonic.

Hadrian died some time in December 872. The uncertainty about the exact date is perhaps a further indication of how ineffective he was and how little impression he made on contemporary chroniclers. A pope of a much more dominant personality was needed if the prestige of the papacy was to be restored. The electors found such a person in Archdeacon John. He proved to be a forceful pontiff, but was also a ruthless opportunist, as were many of those around him. He was a Roman by birth, and records tell us that he was among the signatories at the Roman synod of 853, and that he read out Hadrian's attack on Photius at the Council of Constantinople in 869.

He was elected in the same month that Hadrian died, despite strong opposition from Bishop Formosus, who tried to become pope himself. Formosus was a strong-minded but temperamental man, much put out at not having been made Archbishop to the Bulgars. However, on this occasion he was prepared to concede the papal title to John VIII, and prepared to act as papal envoy when the Emperor Louis died and the Imperial crown was accepted by Charles the Bald of France.

John was in dire need of Imperial support. The Saracens were still threatening southern Italy, and even Rome itself. The inhabitants of the city were too afraid even to venture outside the walls to gather in the harvest. John was determined to break up the alliances which had developed between some of the southern city-states and the Saracens, and from which both sides were profiting through trade. He was prepared to threaten excommunication if he were not obeyed, which no other pope had done before. But his first efforts to force the Italians into an alliance with the Emperor were a complete failure.

There were also problems in Rome itself. He returned from a journey to southern Italy to discover that the city had been almost taken over by Bishop Formosus and his followers. Whatever the Bishop of Porto's qualities, and he had a reputation for piety, he was supported by a remarkably unsavoury group of people. One of the leaders was Gregory, an official at the Vatican in charge of foreign affairs. His family was particularly nasty. His son-in-law, George of the Aventine, a general in the Roman army, had led an extremely bloodstained life. As a single man, he had poisoned his brother to please his own mistress; to improve his fortunes he had then married Pope Benedict III's niece; he was unfaithful to her, and then murdered her in order to marry one of Gregory's daughters. Pope John claimed that the

Opposite: *This fresco from the basilica of San Clemente shows the relics of Clement being carried to their burial place in the church. The inscription attributes the event to the reign of Pope Nicholas I, and he is seen twice in this picture, identified by the halo round his head. On the left he is taking part in the procession, and on the right he is shown saying Mass after the relics had arrived at the basilica.*

murder had taken place 'almost in public'. Gregory's other daughter was no example of virtue either. She had married, left her husband for another man, and then eloped with a third.

Another leader was Sergius, also a Roman general. He had married a niece of Pope Nicholas, but abandoned her to live with his mistress. He was reputed to have robbed the papal treasury as Pope Nicholas lay dying. But apart from the unsavoury reputation of the group, John suspected them of trying to bring the Saracens into Rome. He tried to break their power by ousting Gregory from his post and replacing him with his own nephew. It may have been this which finally caused them to revolt. However, they were not successful and fled from the city, taking many of the Church's valuables with them, and leaving the city gates open so that any passing band of Saracens could enter Rome. All were excommunicated. Formosus was stripped of his offices and accused of conspiring against the Pope.

Formosus' party gained the support of Bishop John of Ravenna, who was hostile to the Bishopric of Rome, and also of the Duke of Spoleto. They tried to build up a pro-German party to counteract the influence of Charles the Bald of France. Retribution was eventually to catch up with some of them. Gregory was murdered in the entrance to Saint Peter's and his widow was whipped naked through the streets. George of the Aventine had his eyes put out. But Formosus escaped such a fate and was later to regain his former power when the Dukes of Spoleto became protectors of the papacy. He was even to become Pope.

But at the time the group fled from Rome, Pope John was short of allies. Charles the Bald was of little help. He gave John certain lands and promised him a freer hand in Rome itself, but as Emperor he was ineffective, and in any case died within a year of taking office. This was Duke Lambert of Spoleto's chance. He came to Rome and tried to force a German king on the Pope as Emperor. Now it was the Pope's turn to flee as the Formosan party returned in force. He sailed for France in a vain attempt to find a new candidate for the Imperial crown, and had to return to Rome humiliated. Eventually, Charles the Fat, who ruled Alsace, accepted the title of Roman Emperor, but he was too weak a man to be of much help. In his struggles with Duke Lambert, Bishop Formosus and the Saracens, Pope John had to look for allies outside the Western Empire.

Under Basil, the Byzantine Empire was recovering its confidence and building up its military strength, especially at sea. Both Basil and Photius, once again Patriarch after the death of Ignatius, were loud in their praise of Pope John. John recognized Photius' claim to the See of Constantinople, but good relations foundered after John failed to persuade the Byzantines to withdraw from Bulgaria. The temporary reconciliation between Rome and Constantinople, however, was not without its long-term effects.

The Eastern Emperor re-established Christian control over the southern Italian city of Bari, and it was ruled by Byzantium, much to its advantage and adornment, for the next two centuries. This display of military success inspired Pope John to build up his own navy.

In April 876 a naval squadron, under John's personal command, captured almost a score of Saracen ships and freed some six hundred captives. The Pope also bred horses for his cavalry – he asked advice on this from the King of Galicia – and fortified Saint Paul's Outside the Walls, building a castle which commanded the Tiber. He was very much a warrior, which was what the times demanded of a man who ruled a city in central Italy.

But in all his battling with emperors, dukes and Saracens he did not forget his ecclesiastical duties. He was particularly concerned about the reform of the Roman clergy, and ordered the cardinals to meet twice a month to inquire into the behaviour of the lower ranks of the priesthood, and to settle cases within the jurisdiction of the papal court.

Confronted with so formidable a character in the office of Bishop of Rome,

25

with his readiness to change sides as occasion suited, it is little wonder that the possible candidates for the title of Emperor were so unwilling to take up the office, with its obligation to defend the papacy.

John seems to have died as violently as he had lived. There was an attempt to poison him. When that failed, he was beaten to death with a hammer. History does not tell us who did this but, as we have seen, he did not lack enemies. His struggle to maintain the independence of the popes from the dukedoms which surrounded the city of Rome was at an end. Stephen VI, who became Pope in 885, accepted the protection of the Dukes of Spoleto. Duke Guy and his ambitious wife, Ageltrude, were crowned Emperor and Empress in 891.

In that same year, Pope Stephen died and Bishop Formosus was elected Pope. It seems to have been a popular choice, although a controversial one. For half a millenium it had been a rule that bishops were 'married' to their dioceses, and therefore could not change them. This rule had technically been broken after the death of John VIII when Marinus, already Bishop of Cere, had been chosen as Bishop of Rome in 882, but Marinus could claim

Above: *In the Middle Ages the Lateran was for the whole of Christendom what the Vatican is for Roman Catholics today – the centre of the Church's administration. This drawing of Saint John Lateran, the cathedral church of Rome and therefore the episcopal seat of the popes, and of the papal palace alongside it, was made by Maerten van Heemskerck, a Dutch painter, during his stay in Rome from 1532 to 1535. Both buildings were reconstructed towards the end of the sixteenth century, and this picture shows what they would have been like just before that.*

with some justice that consecration to the See of Cere had been forced upon him, so he was not really a bishop at all. The same could not be said for Formosus, already Bishop of Porto, but legal niceties do not seem to have worried the electors.

A much more pressing concern was to rid Rome of the influence of Formosus' former allies, the Spoletans, who were becoming dangerously powerful. The Emperor Guy was dead, but his redoubtable widow, on discovering that the Pope had appealed for help to a German king, threw Formosus into prison and herself supervised the defence of the city walls against German attack. Though the Germans won the day, and their King, Arnulf, entered the city across the Milvian Bridge to be crowned Emperor by Formosus on the steps of Saint Peter's, Spoletan influence was not broken.

Formosus did not long survive the coronation. He died in 896, to be followed first by Pope Boniface VI, who lived only a fortnight after his election, and then by Stephen VII. Like Formosus, Stephen was already a bishop at his election, and he was under the influence of Ageltrude. In her

presence, and that of her son, Duke Lambert of Spoleto, a synod was held to arraign Pope Formosus. His body, nine months buried, was exhumed in February or March 897, and dressed in papal vestments. A grisly trial then began. The dead Formosus was charged with usurping the papal throne although already Bishop of Porto, with opposing Pope John VIII, with re-entering Rome when under a ban, and with being guilty of ambition.

Pope Stephen was on dangerous ground, having himself been a bishop before his elevation to the papacy, so when inevitably Formosus was found guilty, all his actions, including the promotion of Stephen, were annulled. His corpse was stripped of its papal vestments, the fingers he had used for blessing were cut off, and what was left of him was thrown into the Tiber. These events, the most macabre in the chequered history of the See of Saint Peter, horrified the Romans. They rose in revolt and threw Pope Stephen into prison, where he was strangled.

He was followed by Pope Romanus, who lasted four months, and Romanus by Theodore, who survived only 20 days. But in the latter's short pontificate, Formosus' body, which had been washed up on the Tiber bank, was once more dressed in papal vestments, and honourably buried.

After the death of the next Pope, Theodore II, in 897, the Dowager Empress Ageltrude tried to force a deacon called Sergius, who had taken part in what came to be known as the 'synod of the corpse', upon the people of Rome, but the papacy went in the end to yet another John, the ninth of that name. He reached an understanding with Duke Lambert, and put the city back under the protection of the Duchy of Spoleto. Sergius fled, and set about preparing an armed invasion. John's successor, Benedict IV, elected in January 900, was himself succeeded three and a half years later by Pope Leo V, who survived his election only a few short months before he was murdered by Christopher, a priest who was an anti-pope for somewhat less than a year. Early in the year 904 Christopher himself was assassinated—possibly by followers of Sergius, who then returned to Rome.

Despite the manner of his accession to the Bishopric of Rome, Sergius has left behind him a very good reputation. As Pope, he rebuilt the Lateran basilica, adding to the original dedication to the Saviour another to

Saint John, by which the church is still known. For a time, it replaced Saint Peter's as the burial place of the popes. He also adorned the Lateran palace with splendid frescoes and mosaics. He was anything but frivolous. Nonetheless, gossips got to work and associated his name with Marozia, the daughter of Theophylact. The family of Theophylact was to dominate Rome for half a century, and to remain influential well into the eleventh century. Its origins were fairly humble. Theophylact himself began as a simple papal official, but rose rapidly to take charge of the papal treasury and then the militia. He was married to a pious, charitable woman called Theodora, who remained faithful to her husband. But her example was not followed by her two daughters, Marozia and Theodora the younger.

The gossips claimed Marozia had been Sergius' mistress before he became Pope, that the relationship continued afterwards, and that her illegitimate son John, who was also to become Pope, was fathered by Sergius. But such impropriety is out of keeping with what else is known of him.

After the death of Sergius, and the brief reigns of two other popes, Anastasius III and Lando, Theophylact chose John, Bishop of Ravenna, and forced him on the See of Rome as Pope John X. The gossips were active again: John of Ravenna, it was said, had been the lover of Theodora the younger. To strengthen the house of Theophylact, Marozia married the Duke of Spoleto. He was lynched by a Roman mob for trying, it seems, to take over entire control of the city, but not before Marozia had borne him a son, Alberic. For a time the power of the family of Theophylact was shaken. The founder of the house had died, and Pope John X tried to install his brother into all the offices Theophylact himself had held. But the attempt to break the family's control failed. Marozia married the most powerful nobleman in Italy: Guy, Count of Tuscany, and with his help won back the city. John X was murdered in 928. His two successors, Leo VI and Stephen VIII, were also murdered. In 931, Marozia's illegitimate son, supposedly by Sergius, was made Pope at the age of 25. He became John XI.

Marozia had two sons, the Pope and Alberic, who was a rising star in Rome's political firmament, but her husband had died and so for her third marriage she chose his half-brother, Hugh, who arrived in Rome with a large army. The intention, it seemed, was to annex the city to Hugh's duchy. Neither Alberic, now Duke of Spoleto, nor the people of Rome would have any of it. At the splendid wedding reception, held in Castel Sant'Angelo, Alberic picked a quarrel with his new stepfather. The Romans, humiliated at being so long subjected to rule by a woman, and now threatened by an alien army, rallied to Alberic's side. Hugh and his soldiers fled the city.

From 933 to his death 21 years later, Alberic was effectively in charge of the Church as well as the city of Rome. He used his half-brother, the Pope, to advantage. He wanted better relations with Constantinople whose armies, allied to his father and Pope John X, had finally driven the Saracens from the Italian mainland in 915. The price the Byzantine Emperor demanded for better relations was high. He wanted his son consecrated as Patriarch of Constantinople. John XI was forced to agree, and to send envoys to perform the ceremony, though the new Patriarch was only 16 years old. All papal appointments were made by Alberic, and he undertook the reform of monastic houses in and around the city, by force if need be. For this purpose, he made use of a branch of the Benedictines which had only recently come into being: the Cluniacs, who played a major role in the reform of the papacy.

Under Alberic, Rome became something of an independent city-state. Now that the Saracen threat had been removed, vines and olives were planted, and the countryside began to look prosperous once more. But Rome's security was gained at a price. The city was isolated. Pilgrims and scholars ceased to journey there, and its Bishop was no longer the effective head of the Christian Church. That does not seem to have worried Alberic.

He had married the daughter of Hugh, the man his mother had taken as her third husband, and whom he had driven out of Rome in 933. Their son he called Octavius. Alberic called himself Augustus, after the divine Roman Emperor, and when Octavius was 17 he was invested with the ancient title of *Princeps*. The Roman senators were compelled to swear that when the Pope died, Octavius would be elected to that office. This occurred in 955, two years after his father's death. Octavius was not thought to be a suitable name for a pope. He changed it to John, the twelfth of that title. This was not the first time a pope had changed his name. In 533 a priest called Mercurius had been elected Pope, and thinking it improper that a god's name should be associated with the papacy, he had changed it to John II. But from the election of Octavius it became the common practice.

Alberic had thought of the pope as little more than the performer of liturgical ceremonies. His son did not consider even those of any consequence. He was ordained at 18, and looked on the papacy as a means of enjoying life to the full. He ordained to the priesthood his companions of the stable; his chief pleasures were women and hunting; his ignorance was startling even to his contemporaries in an age not noted for its learning. But he had territorial ambitions far beyond the narrow limits his father had set.

His major adversary was King Berengar of Italy, who was determined to take over Rome. John XII needed help to repel him. He turned to Otto I, King of the Saxons, and one of the most powerful forces of the day in Europe. But one of the reasons for Otto's strength was the control he exercised over the Church. Every important diocese or abbey in his territory depended directly upon him. His ideal was to create a unified Europe which he would govern, with Rome as its capital. The Church would be subject to him. He was ready to hear John's call when it came. He marched into Italy and was crowned Holy Roman Emperor at Rome on 2 February 962. Pope John had an ornamental copy made of the Donation of Constantine, and presented it to him.

Otto then realized his ideal: he liberated the states of the Church seized by the King of Italy, but he did so by reconquering them for himself and making their inhabitants his own subjects. This was clearly not what Pope John had intended, and he now turned to his former enemies, the King of Italy and the Byzantine Emperor, who had troops encamped south of Rome. Otto had returned to Germany, and so the Pope tried to persuade the imperial officials he had left behind to come over to his side.

An imperialist group among the Roman nobility now seized Saint Paul's Outside the Walls, and invited Otto to return. He arrived in time to catch a glimpse of Pope John XII in full armour on the other side of the Tiber. As the Emperor approached, the Pope fled.

John XII was deposed for his immorality, and scorned for his bad grammar. In 963 the Romans took an oath not to elect another pope without imperial consent, and future popes, before their consecration, were to take oaths of allegiance to the emperors: Otto was reducing the status of the Bishop of Rome to that of any other bishop in his dominions. The man chosen as pope by the Emperor, and elected by a Roman synod, was a blameless papal civil servant who had won the Emperor's favour during negotiations with John; he became Leo VIII in December 963. But as soon as Otto had once more left Rome, John came back. He wreaked terrible vengeance on his adversaries, and even on some of his former friends: the man who had prepared the illuminated copy of the Donation of Constantine given to Otto had his fingers cut off. Pope Leo took refuge with the Emperor. The Romans elected the deacon Benedict as Pope Benedict V in May 964. The Emperor hurried back to Rome, deposed the new Pope in June 964 and reinstated Leo, who ruled until his death in 965. But before the Emperor had arrived in Rome, Pope John had been murdered on his way to visit his mistress. It was the night of 14 May 964, and the point at which this sorry episode in the decline of the papacy was brought to a close.

THE REFORM
OF THE PAPACY

The reform of the papacy began under the German Emperor, Otto I. It took another decisive step forward under his grandson, Otto III, who was only 16 years old when Pope John XV appealed to him for help against the family of Crescentius Nomentanus, distant relatives of Alberic, 'the prince and senator of the Romans'. Crescentius himself, rather than the Pope, controlled most of the city of Rome, including the all-important Castel Sant'Angelo. In 995, Pope John fled the city.

Otto was just attaining his majority, and was eager to demonstrate his independence, especially at a time when imperial prestige was at a low ebb. He set off for Rome. The simple threat of German intervention was enough for Crescentius. Pope John was invited back to Rome, and Crescentius and all the senate pleaded for his forgiveness. They begged him to dissuade Otto from marching on the city. Before Otto could reach Rome, however, the Pope had died. Apart from his unpopularity with Crescentius' faction, little is known about John other than that he was the first Pope to have formally canonized anyone. The first saint to be officially declared as such by the Bishop of Rome was Bishop Ulrich of Augsburg, who had died in 973. Pope John canonized him in 993, at the request of his successor in the See of Augsburg. It was an act which commended the Pope to the German royal house, for Saint Ulrich had been an active supporter of Otto who had been crowned Holy Roman Emperor in 962.

Otto III heard of John's death when he was in Ravenna. He acted much as he would have done had he been in Germany rather than Italy: he appointed someone to the vacant See. The man he chose was his own cousin, Bruno, who was a monk and chaplain to his court. He was only 24 years old. In Germany, the Church and the State were very much intertwined. Churchmen became great landowners by virtue of their office and established themselves as feudal lords. It was generally recognized that the Church had the authority to dissolve the feudal oaths that cemented society. It was important, therefore, that the men appointed to high positions in the Church should be those whom the King could trust. Bruno might have been expected to understand King Otto's position.

He was born, possibly in the village of Steinach not far from Salzburg, the second son of the Count of Wormsgau. He was educated at the cathedral school in Worms, and there made a special study of the fathers of the Church. He was particularly fond of the writings of Pope Saint Gregory the Great, so much so, that when he was consecrated Pope on 3 May 996 he chose the name Gregory for himself. A fortnight later, Pope Gregory V anointed his cousin Otto III as Holy Roman Emperor.

If Otto had expected a compliant pope, he was disappointed. Remembering that he would have to live in Rome after the Emperor had withdrawn,

Opposite: *A thirteenth-century window in Chartres cathedral, donated by the furriers, depicts scenes from a legendary life of Charlemagne. The stories may have been concocted to account for the presence in the Abbey of Saint Denis of relics of Christ's Passion. In the episode shown here Charlemagne, on his way home from capturing Jerusalem, is greeted at the gates of Constantinople by the Emperor Constantine, who is later to give him the relics.*

Gregory determined on a policy of reconciliation towards Crescentius. He did this against Otto's advice, and after Otto had condemned Crescentius to exile. Pope and Emperor also clashed over the Bishop of Prague. Adalbert of Prague had fled to Rome to take refuge there from opponents in his own diocese. When Otto arrived he wanted to make Adalbert part of the imperial entourage. Gregory objected. Pope John XV had earlier ordered Adalbert to go back home. If Gregory were to allow his predecessor's instructions to be overruled by the Emperor, there would be no reason why those he himself issued should not be similarly set aside. And so, much to Adalbert's distress and Otto's irritation, Pope Gregory insisted that his predecessor's orders should be obeyed.

When the Emperor left Rome, he committed the protection of the papacy to the Counts of Tuscany and the Dukes of Spoleto. Gregory soon had to flee to the safety of Spoleto as Crescentius once more rallied the Roman nobility. Crescentius then chose John Philagathos, the Archbishop of Piacenza, as an anti-pope; Gregory immediately excommunicated the intruder into his See, but his position was a difficult one. Bishop John was a personal friend of Otto, so the Emperor's attitude could not be relied upon. To further complicate matters, the anti-pope had the indisputable advantage of having been acclaimed by the Roman people, and not simply appointed by a German king.

In the event, Otto decided to back Gregory. His decision may have been influenced by a move of the Crescentius faction to call upon the Byzantine Emperor for support against the German one. Whatever Otto's motives, he marched back to Rome and, after only minor skirmishes, re-entered the city on 20 February 998. That very same day, Gregory was enthroned as Pope for the second time.

Crescentius had locked himself away in his stronghold of Castel Sant' Angelo. It was besieged, he was captured and beheaded, and his body thrown from the walls. His anti-pope, John XVI, suffered in some ways an even more terrible fate. He was blinded, his mouth, ears and tongue were mutilated, and he was then imprisoned in a monastery. He was brought out of prison for the synod which deposed him. One by one his papal garments were stripped off. He was sent back to the monastery sitting facing backwards on a donkey, holding its tail in his hands. On his head was a mock papal mitre. The crowds that had once acclaimed him Pope now jeered at his downfall.

Otto thus dominated Rome. In order to fill all papal and civil offices left vacant by the fall of Crescentius and his supporters, the Emperor brought back the house of Theophylact. The Pope was not consulted, it seems. Gregory's self-will had brought him to the point of destruction. It was not to happen again, the Emperor decided. The papacy must be reduced in status to a part of the Imperial household. When Gregory died in February 999, Otto appointed as Bishop of Rome a man who would be more obedient to his wishes.

Gregory had been the first German to become Pope; Gerbert of Aurillac was the first Frenchman. He was also one of the first popes who would have become famous as a scholar even if he had not been Pope. He was born near Aurillac in about the year 945. He studied widely and travelled extensively at the expense of wealthy and influential patrons, and eventually became secretary to the Archbishop of Rheims. He was brought to the attention of Otto II, who made him abbot of Bobbio, the monastery which, more than any other, was renowned for the size of its library. As an abbot he was a disaster. He fled back to Rheims only to become embroiled in a conflict even greater than the one he had provoked at Bobbio.

The King of France had died and the Archbishop of Rheims had secured the election of Hugh Capet, Count of Paris, to the throne. But Duke Charles of Lorraine also had a claim to the throne and, after the death of the Archbishop, he put his own nephew in charge of the See. This was unacceptable to Hugh, who deposed Charles's nephew and appointed Gerbert in his place.

Gerbert now found himself in a difficult position. For the most part, the monks in France sided with Charles of Lorraine and the Pope against Hugh. But Gerbert was himself a monk. Although for a time he upheld an anti-papal line, when Pope John XV declared in 995 that Gerbert's appointment was illegal, he capitulated. Under Pope Gregory V, Gerbert was appointed Archbishop of Ravenna by the Emperor, who endowed him with lands which, in the eyes of the Pope, were part of the Papal States. His tenure of office at Ravenna was brief. On Otto's instructions he became Bishop of Rome on Easter Sunday 999. He chose to be called Sylvester II.

Problems at Bobbio and at Rheims, and the troubles of his predecessor, seem to have convinced the new Pope that Church and State had to work closely together. The rational order of the world could be maintained only as long as the government rested upon a firm imperial base. The theory naturally commended itself to the Emperor. He rewarded the Pope with grants of lands, but the lands were to be his personal property, reverting to the Empire on his death. It was an entirely different notion to the one enshrined in the legendary Donation of Constantine made to the first Pope Sylvester, but Sylvester II acquiesced in the Emperor's attempt to turn the papacy into a feudal lordship. It is little wonder that a document of the period criticizes the Donation of Constantine as a forgery, and attacks the whole idea of there being any such thing as 'a Papal State'. This criticism, however, played no part in the subsequent history of the legend.

Too many people were alienated by the threat to the independence of the Church lands. The house of Theophylact and also that of Crescentius, the one promoted and the other humiliated by Otto, rose in revolt in 1001. The following year the Emperor died, aged 22. In 1003 the Pope died. For almost half a century to come, appointments to the papacy were to be in the control of one or other of these two families.

Sylvester's rule was too brief for him to achieve a great deal. He extended the papacy's influence into new corners of Europe, supporting Stephen, the first King of Hungary, and appointing Poland's first archbishop. He was in correspondence with King Olaf I of Norway, who was forcibly converting his subjects to Christianity, and persuaded him to drop the Runic script in favour of the Roman one.

It is as a scholar rather than as a Pope that Sylvester is chiefly remembered. On a visit to what is now Spain, he had learned how to calculate in Arabic numerals, and helped to encourage their use throughout Europe. His contact with the Arabs brought the philosophy of Aristotle, which they had preserved, to his notice. This he studied, as well as the many Latin writers who were in danger of falling into oblivion. He was a model-builder too, constructing machines for his students to teach them the relative positions of stars and planets. So wide and deep was his learning that legends later attributed it to magic, or to the devil.

As Pope, Sylvester had tried to improve the moral standards of the clergy, denouncing simony (the offence of buying or selling offices in the Church), nepotism and impurity. But his reign was too short for him to achieve lasting reforms. As the toy of the Roman nobility, the papacy once more went into decline after his death. It reached such an appalling state that one Roman priest seems to have bought the office from Benedict IX – a member of the house of Theophylact – in order to reform it. But this Pope, Gregory VI, though a great improvement on those who had gone before, could not free himself from the taint of simony. Henry III of Germany intervened. Gregory was deposed, and retired with good grace. There were two other short papacies – those of Clement II and Damasus II – and then the Emperor chose Bruno, Count of Egisheim and Bishop of Toul, as Pope. He took the name Leo IX.

Bruno was born in June 1002, his body covered, so the legends relate, with tiny crosses. At the age of five he was put in the care of the Bishop of Toul.

Above: *Suitgar, Count of Norsleben and Bishop of Bamberg, was appointed to the bishopric of Rome by the Emperor Henry III at the end of 1046. He took the name Clement II. Pope Clement immediately embarked upon a campaign of reform, but he died in October 1047.*

By 1026 he was a deacon, and commanding the troops which the diocese of Toul had to provide for the Emperor Conrad's expedition into Lombardy. His career as a warrior was cut short by the death of the Bishop. He was called home to head the diocese himself, which he did for 23 years with considerable success, and with great dedication to the reform of clerical, and particularly of monastic, life.

Bruno was related to Henry III. He was an obvious choice for the papacy, but he would not accept it without the approval of the people of Rome. He entered the city as a barefoot pilgrim and was hailed as 'a most strong Pope, whom the Lord has sent to free us from our enemies'. Such enthusiasm did not last long. When his attempts to reconcile the warring factions among the Roman nobility by peaceful means failed, he resorted to brutal force. The lands of the Crescentii and the Theophylacts were laid waste, their towns destroyed and their vines uprooted.

He was equally ruthless with churchmen. One of his first acts was to call a synod for the week after Easter 1049, to depose simoniacal bishops. One prelate, trying to defend himself from the crime of simony by committing the crime of perjury, fell dead in the midst of the gathering, and this was taken as a sign that God was on the side of the reformers. Clerical concubinage was also to stop. But Leo was a practical man: something had to be done for all those women who were dependent on the clergy. Those in Rome became servants in the papal palace.

Many of the advisers with whom Leo surrounded himself were from France or Germany. Hitherto, the papal entourage had mainly been composed of Romans, now it began to represent all the Churches of Europe. When the Council of Rheims declared him 'Universal Primate' in 1049, some reflection of that universality could already be found among his staff. He sent them as legates (his personal representatives) to other Churches and rulers the length and breadth of Europe, but he also travelled a good deal himself, holding reforming synods wherever he went, though not always with success. In 1053, the armed followers of disenchanted bishops set about the Pope's own bodyguard outside the building in Mantua where a meeting was taking place.

Failure also marked the Pope's dealings with the Normans, who were now busy dividing up southern Italy among themselves. They constantly harried the Papal States to the south of Rome, and so an army was mustered against them. They were anxious not to go to war with the Pope, and offered to retreat, but Leo's counsellors suggested he could win better terms than

Opposite: This statuette of the Emperor Henry IV decorates the side of the sarcophagus of Charlemagne, shown on page 77. Henry, who came to the throne in 1056 at the age of six, died in Liège, in present-day Belgium, in 1106. In 1076 he broke his agreement with Pope Gregory VII over the investiture question, and for the rest of his life was at odds with the papacy except for a very short period after the reconciliation at Canossa. He also had strained relations with most of the German nobility, including his own sons.

Right: Bruno, Count of Egisheim, was to become Pope Leo IX in 1049 at the request of his cousin, the Emperor Henry III. Towards the end of his life he led, disastrously, what he called a 'holy war' against the Christian Normans of southern Italy. Some have seen in this war the remote origins of the Crusades. Leo died in 1054, and was immediately revered as a saint.

S. LEO IX. PONTIFEX CLIV.
ANNO DOMINI MXLIX.

Right: *In 1077 Pope Gregory VII, fearing that the Emperor Henry IV was about to attack him, took refuge in the castle of the Countess Matilda at Canossa. But Henry had come to make his submission to the Pope. After standing in the snow for three days he was reconciled to the Church by Gregory, as Federico Zuccari (c. 1540-1609) somewhat fancifully shows here. The submission, however, was only a political maneuver, and three years later Henry was once again excommunicated.*

those being proposed, and battle was joined. The papal army was routed. For two days, Leo prayed over the bodies of the fallen, and ordered a church to be built as a memorial. He was then led away as a captive to be kept for eight months in the city of Benevento.

In 1054, the Pope sent a legation to Constantinople, headed by Cardinal Humbert, in an attempt to win Byzantine support for an alliance against the Normans. But there were also other problems to be sorted out. In southern Italy, the liturgy, the monastic life, the style of architecture and decoration of the churches, were still Byzantine, but the Patriarch of Constantinople feared a gradual extension of Latin influence in the area. He closed the Latin churches and monastic houses in the Eastern capital, and claimed that the Western practice of using unleavened bread at Mass was uncanonical.

The mission was a complete disaster. Both Cardinal and Patriarch were intransigent, and on 16 July 1054 the papal legate slapped a decree of excommunication against Patriarch Cerularius on the altar of the great church of Sancta Sophia. The Patriarch retaliated in kind against the Pope. The excommunication was of symbolic rather than of real importance, for the two Churches had for long drifted apart from each other, but it was a sad end to a pontificate which had begun so well. By the time the excommunications were issued, Leo was dead, which robbed the Roman one of any strict legality, but relations between the Eastern and Western Churches had deteriorated beyond legal niceties. The events of 1054 marked the definitive break between the two.

Among the many outstanding men who surrounded Leo there was one of particular ability. His name was Hildebrand. He was born about 1020. Little is known about his early life except that, despite his German-sounding name, he was an Italian, and may have been a monk in Rome. He served the papacy under Gregory VI, and went into exile with him after his deposition for simony. Leo IX brought him out of retirement, and under Leo's successor he headed the papal chancery – the civil service which ran the Church. He had a hand in the election of at least two of the popes, and one of them, Nicholas II, created him a deacon.

Hildebrand was unusual among the reformers. Unlike him, the majority of them were foreigners living in the middle of a great number of unreformed Italians, and their chief problem was one of security. There were two things to be done: to provide a satisfactory way of carrying out papal elections in an orderly manner, and to protect the electors. Robert Guiscard, the Norman Duke who now ruled southern Italy, became a vassal not of Pope Nicholas II personally, but of Saint Peter. That took care of security for the electors. The other requirement was met by the election decree of 1059.

There were other provisions of the synod of 1059. The impediment, no longer observed, to a bishop becoming pope was officially removed, and the laity was forbidden to attend services led by clergy living in concubinage. But it was the election decree which was most important. It laid down that, for the future, cardinal bishops were to nominate a candidate for the papacy, lesser cardinals were to approve him, and the clergy and the people of Rome were to accept him. The choice was to be made from among the clergy of the Roman Church, and the Emperor was to have no more than a formal right of approval. The election was to be in Rome, but if the city proved unsafe, then it could take place anywhere. It was to be the election itself and not the enthronement which empowered a new pope to act with papal authority.

The decree was a valiant effort by the reformers among the Roman clergy to free the papacy from political interference. But it also signalled the establishment of the cardinals as a corporate body of electors, and as advisers to the pope. They were to operate like the ancient Roman senate, but the name given to a gathering of cardinals, a 'consistory', was taken from Byzantine rather than Roman practice.

Hildebrand was undoubtedly one of the moving forces behind the decree, but in 1073 it was not put into practice. Hildebrand was acclaimed as Pope by the people of Rome. He accepted, and chose the name Gregory VII.

In personal appearance, the new Pope was undistinguished. He was short in stature, lacking in dignity, and weak in voice. By training he was a bureaucrat, with a civil servant's conviction that, no matter how revolutionary his ideas might seem to others, he was really always acting according to precedent. He was utterly convinced that only through a complete separation of Church and State could the Church rid itself of the ills which afflicted it. And the most blatant sign of State interference in the Church, he believed, was the problem of investiture.

When a bishop was appointed to a See, the local civil authority, who was frequently the Emperor, gave him as symbols of office his ring and staff. They symbolized the 'temporalities' – the property and income – of the diocese, and all the this-worldly responsibilities that the office of bishop carried with it. In February 1075, Gregory issued a decree forbidding the lay investiture of clerics.

The German King, and future Holy Roman Emperor, Henry IV, was already at odds with the papacy because of the papal alliance with the Normans in Italy. He was not at all pleased with the decree against investiture. Gregory, however, chose just this moment to alienate the support of the Normans as well. Afraid of a too-powerful vassal to the south, he switched his allegiance to the Lombards, investing one Lombard prince with the city of Benevento as a buffer against Norman expansion northwards.

Nor was the vigorous attack on concubinage, simony and lay investiture popular with many of the clergy. They felt that he was subverting the natural and established order. Certainly, many clerics in the early eleventh century had taken wives because they believed such behaviour was perfectly acceptable. Just how revolutionary the Pope's actions were was demonstrated in Milan when the people, with his support, rose against the nobility – who were on the future Emperor's side – and against the archbishop appointed by Henry.

In the torrential rain of Christmas Eve 1075, Gregory VII was attacked by a pro-Imperial group as he said Mass at Santa Maria Maggiore. The Pope's supporters were victorious in the ensuing battles in the city, and the leader of the Imperial party fled and took refuge with Henry IV.

Henry called a synod at Worms. The bishops of Germany condemned Gregory's actions and declared him deposed. Gregory excommunicated Henry in return, forbade him to use his royal powers, and absolved his subjects from their oaths of allegiance. Civil war broke out in Germany, and the bishops deserted Henry. The future Emperor could have their support, they said, only if he obtained the Pope's pardon. Gregory, meanwhile, had offered his support to the rebellious princes, and had promised to travel to Germany to preside over the trial of the future Emperor

But as the Pope travelled north, Henry came south. Thinking he was coming to do battle, Gregory took refuge in the castle of the Countess Matilda at Canossa. It was surrounded by three walls. Just inside the outermost of them, Henry came and stood barefoot in the snow, and asked Gregory's forgiveness. After three days of waiting, he was absolved from his excommunication. It seemed to mark the triumph of the spiritual over the temporal power in the Empire. In reality, the Pope had been outmanoeuvred.

Gregory had no wish to forgive Henry. He did not trust him, and with reason. He had, moreover, promised his support to the German princes at war with Henry. But if popes were first and foremost the pastors of souls which reformers always claimed them to be, then absolution could not be denied by him.

It was not long before Henry returned in arms against the Pope, arriving outside Rome early in 1081. He did not stay, but retreated, to return again the following year. This war of attrition succeeded in arousing opposition to Gregory among the Roman clergy, who decided, in May 1082, that while

Church property might be mortgaged to relieve the poor, redeem captives, or maintain church services, the money raised must not be used for the payment of soldiers. There was no longer any money to fight Henry, and the Countess Matilda was reduced to melting down the treasures of Canossa to supply the Pope with funds. The Roman clergy finally deserted Gregory in 1084. They went over to the anti-pope, Clement III, whom Henry had appointed. The city fell, Henry was crowned Holy Roman Emperor by Clement, and Gregory was besieged in Castel Sant'Angelo.

Gregory appealed for help to Robert Guiscard of Normandy. When the Normans arrived they found only a small German garrison remaining, but even so the devastation they wreaked in the city was enormous, greater even than the destruction caused by the Saracens in 846. They did not linger in the pillaged city, and fell back to the south, taking Gregory with them. He died at Salerno on 25 May 1085. 'I have loved righteousness and hated iniquity,' he said as he lay dying, 'therefore I die in exile.'

He was a victim partly of his own political incompetence in having made enemies simultaneously on two fronts, and partly of his zeal for the ideals in which he believed. He has left a memorandum in the form of headings for 27 chapters of a collection of canon law, which outlines his position. It is preserved among the papal registers, the first complete set to have survived, which record his correspondence, at the rate of some two letters a week, on a whole variety of topics to a great diversity of people. The Roman Church, Gregory held, had never erred, nor could it ever err. The Bishop of Rome could judge all, and be judged by none, could summon general councils and had the duty of approving decisions taken by synods of bishops before they became binding. He was Universal Bishop, with the right of intervening in important matters anywhere in the world. He could depose bishops, and release subjects from their oaths of allegiance.

Gregory had wanted someone to succeed him who would espouse these policies. His immediate successor, Pope Victor III, survived only a year, and then the small group of cardinals who had not sided with the anti-pope chose Odo, Cardinal Bishop of Ostia. Odo had been born at Chatillon-sur-Marne about the year 1042. His father, Eucher, had belonged to the newly emerging class of knights. Odo had been at school in Rheims, and had then entered the Benedictine Monastery at Cluny. When Gregory had asked his great friend the Abbot of Cluny for able men to assist him in Rome, the Abbot had sent Odo. The Cardinal Bishop's sympathies had been entirely with Gregory, who had used him as a legate in both France and Germany.

Odo was installed as Pope Urban II on 12 March 1088 at Terracina. The Emperor was still in Italy, and Rome remained in the hands of the anti-pope. Urban could not enter it in triumph until 1097, and even then he needed the armed support of the Countess Matilda, and had to bind the local nobility to him by feudal oaths. Though he did not control Rome at his accession, Pope Urban had much to his advantage. Within the city itself there had been a reaction in favour of the Gregorian ideals, and among the Normans there was growing dissension following the death of Robert Guiscard. Urban seized the initiative by the brilliant stroke of preaching a Crusade.

Holy war to aid the struggle of the Byzantine Empire against the Turks had been considered by Gregory VII, but he had never acted upon the idea. In March 1095, an emissary from the Eastern Emperor, Alexius I Comnenus, had appealed for help at a synod of French, German and Italian bishops in Piacenza. In November that same year, after a council held at Clermont in France, Pope Urban had preached a sermon calling upon people to go to the assistance of the Emperor. It is not clear what it was that Urban had in mind: helping the Emperor to stave off the Turks, or recovering the Holy Land from the Moslems. In the event, Jerusalem became the goal, and with crosses on their clothes, thousands flocked to join the Crusade.

It was preached throughout Europe by Urban and his delegates. The Pope himself travelled through France for eight months, whipping up religious fervour among the peasant class, and channelling the bellicosity of the emergent knightly class away from Europe and into the Middle East. The moral authority of the Pope, as the instigator of this holy adventure, grew enormously, because all those who 'took the cross' became part of the papal 'family', and as this made them temporary churchmen they were exempt from secular law, and a moratorium was placed on all their debts. There were spiritual advantages to be gained as well. Notorious public sinners were allowed to commute the penance imposed upon them by the Church into a promise to take part in a war to liberate Jerusalem.

Urban has been given the title of 'Blessed' by the Catholic Church, a term marking a step towards the recognition of his sainthood. He was a monk, and a particularly ascetic one. He encouraged the growth of a new movement in the Church which brought men and women together to live lives dedicated to God in village communities, without the formal structure of religious vows. He lifted the ban on the Eastern Emperor in an effort to reconcile East and West. He called a council at Bari to discuss the vexed question of the *filioque*, a term now part of the creed of the Western Church but rejected in the East, as it still is. One prelate whose advice was asked by Urban during the council at Bari was Anselm, Archbishop of Canterbury, who had come to Italy to seek the Pope's help in his struggles with the King of England, William II.

The Pope died on 29 July 1099, just a fortnight after Jerusalem had fallen to the Christian army. He had restored the image of the papacy, but his Roman power-base remained weak. The city was divided among warring noble families, each with a stronghold set inside an ancient ruin. Even Anselm was not immune from attack. He was set upon by some partisans of the anti-pope, Clement III, as he made his way from the Lateran to Saint Peter's. The aristocracy was no longer having it all its own way, however. There was another class growing up within the city which did not belong to the nobility but which owned property. Its members were excluded from political life in Rome, and their aspirations required an outlet. This was provided by Arnold of Brescia.

As a preacher of great power, he combined an attack upon the evils he saw in the papal Curia and the scandal of Church involvement in secular affairs with a plea for the grievances of this new 'middle class' to be heard. Even before he arrived in Rome, the people had risen in revolt and established a commune. After his arrival, they expelled Pope Eugenius III from the city, condemned the Donation of Constantine as heretical, and turned for help to Frederick Barbarossa, the new King of Germany. But Barbarossa's aim was to assert imperial rights in Italy, and an alliance with the Pope – who was to crown him Holy Roman Emperor – was ultimately more to his advantage. The commune had also reckoned without Nicholas Breakspear.

Breakspear was to be the only non-Italian pope to hold office for the 137 years between 1124 and 1261, and the sole Englishman ever to hold the office, though some others have come near to it. He was, in all probability, born in a house on the site of the present Breakspear Farm at Abbot's Langley in England, early in the twelfth century. His father, a minor royal official, became a monk at Saint Alban's Abbey, his mother and a brother survived long enough to know that he had become Pope.

That must have come as something of a surprise. He had left England about the year 1120 without any qualifications, possibly not even able to read. He had joined a religious community near Avignon, and had eventually become Abbot. As Abbot he had attracted the attention of the Pope, and by January 1150 had become Cardinal Bishop of Ostia. From then on a great deal was heard of him.

He travelled widely on papal business for Pope Eugenius III, especially in Scandinavia, where he was responsible for setting up an archbishopric with

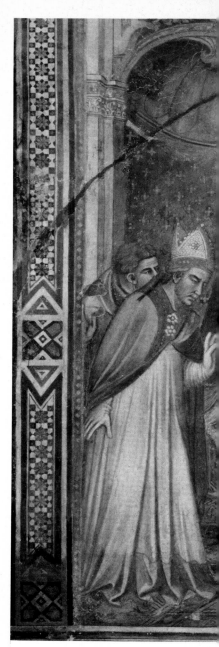

ten dependent sees for the Norwegian Church. Some of the new dioceses were in the Orkneys and Faroes, in Iceland and Greenland – an indication of how far the influence of the Bishop of Rome had reached by this time. Nicholas was a consummate diplomat, and persuaded the Swedish Church to join England in paying Peter's Pence, a tax paid to the pope.

Thanks to the preaching of Arnold of Brescia, when Nicholas Breakspear was elected as Pope Hadrian IV on 5 December 1154, his control of the city of Rome was limited to the Vatican area. The greater part of Rome was dominated by the commune. On his election he paid the sums of money to the citizens of Rome which they had come to expect as part of the election celebrations, but this made no difference. Then, when one of his cardinals had been attacked, Hadrian acted vigorously. He placed the whole city under an interdict, still a new enough tactic to be effective. All Masses, funerals and other services ceased, and Hadrian refused to lift the ban until Arnold had been banished. Arnold fled – straight into the arms of Frederick Barbarossa's advancing troops. He was handed over to the Prefect of the City for execution.

Above: In 1408 Aretino Spinello, assisted by his son, painted a series of frescoes in the Palazzo Publico in Siena depicting the struggle between Pope Alexander III (1159-81) and the Emperor Frederick Barbarossa. It is the scene of the Emperor's submission to Alexander, which took place in Venice in July 1177, which is pictured here.

Hadrian had used spiritual sanctions against the Romans; Frederick now employed physical ones. When he refused to make payments to the citizens, as was customary when a new Emperor was crowned, and closed the Leonine city to them during his coronation as Holy Roman Emperor, the Romans rioted. The riot was brutally suppressed. But the commune itself survived, and Frederick showed little interest in the other problem over which Hadrian needed his help: the Norman incursions into the southern Papal States.

The Pope therefore turned once more to the Byzantines, who, together with the Saracens, had finally been driven out of Italy and Sicily in the early years of the 1070s by the Normans. An alliance was formed with the Byzantines, and the Normans immediately offered terms. But Hadrian's advisers argued that the terms were not good enough. Battle was joined, the papal forces defeated, and Hadrian was captured. Even so, the victorious Normans offered the Pope very favourable conditions: the Kingdom of Sicily was to be granted to King William (he already ruled it in any case) and in return he would swear honour and allegiance to the Pope. He would also give both military and financial help in suppressing the Roman commune. Hadrian found himself allied with his former enemies, and at odds with the Emperor.

He sent legates to see Frederick. One of them read out a letter from the Pope which was mistranslated, perhaps intentionally, by the interpreter. It greatly angered the Emperor. The Pope was made to sound as if he believed that Frederick held the Empire as a fief from the papacy. Such an idea may not have been far from the Pope's mind. Since the early ninth century, it had been customary during Imperial coronation ceremonies for the Pope to hand a sword to the Emperor, picking it up from the altar in Saint Peter's in very much the same way as the pallia were handed to bishops. This gesture was intended to emphasize papal power over the Emperor. In the twelfth century, Saint Bernard of Clairvaux had supported such papal claims by basing his argument on a passage from Saint Luke's Gospel (Chapter 22, Verse 38): 'They said, "Look, Lord, here are two swords". And he said to them, "It is enough".' He argued that the pope possessed two 'swords', the first one representing spiritual strength and the second temporal power. The second he handed over to the Emperor to be used on behalf of the papacy. But even if Hadrian had such high-flown notions of papal monarchy, he did not put them into the letter which so angered Frederick.

The Emperor claimed that his authority came directly from God, and that his coronation, like that of the Byzantine Emperor's, was a mere recognition of an accomplished fact. But Carinal Bandinelli, one of the legates, asked rather undiplomatically from whom the title of Emperor came if it did not come from the pope. The legates were rapidly despatched back to Rome, and Frederick himself arrived in force the following year. He annexed part of the Papal States, abolished the communes in the north, and demanded that Italian bishops do him homage. He was now ready to negotiate with the Roman commune if the papacy refused to capitulate. Hadrian's problems were all the greater because some of his cardinals did not approve of his alliance with the Normans, but it was not a dilemma he was required to solve. He died in September 1159, leaving the conflict with the Emperor to be coped with by his successor.

The conflict between Church and Empire dominated Hadrian's reign, but he deserves to be remembered for much else besides. He was an able administrator, and chose his servants well. He reorganized the papal patrimony and restored papal lands, never hesitating to use force if need be, but not minding particularly how strong his vassals were as long as they were obedient and recognized his overlordship. He remained a pragmatic Englishman, even while ruling Rome.

He never forgot his native land. The Abbey of Saint Alban's benefited greatly from his pontificate, and their patron saint's feast day was extended to the whole of England. According to the Donation of Constantine, the

islands of the West belonged to the Pope: he bestowed the lordship of Ireland on King Henry II of England, and blessed his invasion of that country, just as an earlier Pope, Alexander II, had blessed William the Conqueror's invasion of England.

At the beginning of his reign, Hadrian had reason to complain that papal justice was ineffective in England, but after John of Salisbury, later Bishop of Chartres but then a clerk at Canterbury, returned from visiting the Pope, cases started to flow in until the extent of papal jurisdiction in England came to pose a threat to the monarch's control of affairs.

The law was playing an increasing part in the life of the Church. Not long before Hadrian died there was published the 'Concordance of discordant canons', or the *Decretum* as it came to be known. It attempted to bring together the various sorts of legal provisions, the statements of theologians, the decisions of councils and so on, into a coherent body of law. One of the first of many scholars to write a commentary on the *Decretum* was Roland Bandinelli, the cardinal who had so angered Frederick Barbarossa by his undiplomatic question. On Hadrian's death, Bandinelli was elected to succeed him, with the title of Alexander III.

The Bandinellis were a wealthy family, prominent in the affairs of their native city of Siena. Roland was born in the early years of the twelfth century. He earned a reputation for learning, taught canon law and theology in Bologna, and then became canon of Pisa. It is not clear how he came to the attention of the Pope, but he had written on both canon law and theology, and his well-thought-out hierarchical scheme for the Church, together with his broad notion of what fell within the competence of the Church courts, must have commended him. By the end of 1150 he was a cardinal deacon, the following year he became a cardinal priest, and by 1153 he had been appointed papal chancellor.

He was well known for his support of Hadrian's policy of committing the

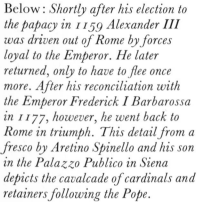

Below: *Shortly after his election to the papacy in 1159 Alexander III was driven out of Rome by forces loyal to the Emperor. He later returned, only to have to flee once more. After his reconciliation with the Emperor Frederick I Barbarossa in 1177, however, he went back to Rome in triumph. This detail from a fresco by Aretino Spinello and his son in the Palazzo Publico in Siena depicts the cavalcade of cardinals and retainers following the Pope.*

Roman Church to an alliance with the Normans rather than with the Emperor. After his election, one of the pro-German cardinals, Octavian of Monticelli, tried to tear the papal cloak from Bandinelli's back, but when that failed he produced another one which his servant had thoughtfully brought with him. Octavian put it on back to front, a chronicler recounts and had to take it off again. Sartorial problems notwithstanding, Octavian was acclaimed in Saint Peter's and consecrated Pope, while Bandinelli had to be hurried out of Rome. The Emperor opted for Octavian, who became an anti-pope – the first of four to reign between 1159 and 1180. Most other monarchs sided with Alexander III. Thus the Church was in schism.

England was one country that supported Alexander, but Henry II presented a problem. He was at odds with Thomas Becket, Archbishop of Canterbury, because of Becket's opposition to interference in elections to bishoprics, and to the King's attempts to restrict both clerical immunity from prosecution and their right to appeal directly to Rome. Becket considered that such actions contravened the customs and traditions of the English Church, and ran counter to the Gregorian reforms. Alexander sympathized with the Archbishop, but could not afford to alienate the King. The murder of Becket solved some of the Pope's problems. Henry gave way on most points and, after some hesitation, Thomas Becket was declared a saint on 21 February 1173 when evidence of miracles at his tomb had been provided.

Alexander was careful about canonization. He had agreed readily enough to canonize King Edward the Confessor in 1161, but he refused to canonize Anselm, and had the miracles attributed to Thomas Becket investigated with care. He told the King of Denmark that no saint could be publicly venerated until he had been approved by the Roman Church. This was all part of the increasing centralization and legislation of the Roman See, much of the lawmaking being contained in the 4,500 or so letters Alexander wrote to kings, bishops and abbots all over Europe.

In 1179 bishops, abbots and other heads of religious orders met in council in the Lateran basilica. After all the confusion of the last papal election, the Lateran Council determined that the pope was to be elected by a two-thirds majority of the cardinals, without reference to the clergy or people of Rome, and without consultation with the Emperor. It laid down a rigid division between Church and State: no laymen were to own churches, instead they were to become patrons of livings (for which the Latin word was *advocatus*, and from which the term 'advowsons' is derived), no cleric was to be or-dained unless there was money to support him, and none was to be promised a benefice unless it was already vacant. The clergy were not to take on secular occupations, and were to live chastely – neither of which provisions was observed – and schools were to be established in cathedrals for their educa-tion. Among the decisions which directly affected the laity was the prohibi-tion of tournaments.

Before the council met, the Emperor had abandoned his anti-pope and recognized Alexander. He was troubled, or at least his clergy were, by the threat to the validity of their ordination by continuing in schism, and Frederick Barbarossa found himself threatened by too many enemies at once. After the reconciliation, the Pope's troops were active in and around Rome, reducing castles to papal obedience. One nobleman who lost his fortress to the Pope was a certain Gandulf, who gave his name to Castel Gandolfo.

Alexander had not been back in Rome for more than a couple of years, after a decade's exile, when there was another reaction against him, and the election of yet another anti-pope. Again, he fled the city. He died on 30 August 1181 in Civita Castellana as he was making his way back to Rome, disguised as a pilgrim. When his body was brought to the Lateran, the Roman crowd showered his coffin with stones and dirt, demonstrating their deep resentment of his failure to assert his authority as Pope.

Above: *Pope Alexander III badly needed the support of the English King Henry II (1133-1189) who is pictured here, in his struggle with the Emperor Frederick Barbarossa. But the conflict between Thomas Becket, the Archbishop of Canterbury, and the King soured relations between the papacy and the English monarch.*

PP. III.

✠ INNOCENTIVS EPS SERVVS SERVORV DI. DILECTIS FIL

SPECV BEATI BENEDICTI REGLARE VITA SERVANTIBVS IN. P PA

VIRTVTV NVLLV MAGIS EST MEDVLLATV. QVA QD OFFERTVR A

CARITATIS. HOC IGIT ATTENDENTES. CV OLI CAVSA DEVOTIONIS ACCE

VBE TVE BEATVS BENEDICT SVE CONVERSIONIS PRIMORDIO CONSECRAVIT. E

INSTITVTIONE IPIVS LAVDABILITER DNO FAMVLANTES: NE PROTEPOR

SPIRITVALIS OBSERVANTIE DISCIPLINA TORPERET. APOSTOLICV VOBI

IMPENDENDV. SPERANTES QD IDE BEATISSIM BENEDICT NRE DEVOTI

THE ZENITH OF PAPAL POWER

The thirteenth century has been called the greatest of all the centuries. This is certainly true where scholarship is concerned, for it saw the first flowering of a new kind of higher educational institution: the university. Bologna, Paris and Oxford Universities may have existed before the century began, but in the 1200s they were adorned with an astonishing array of scholars. And though theology may still have been the 'queen of the sciences', philosophy, especially the philosophy of Aristotle, began to establish itself as a separate area of study. But there was another academic discipline which was attracting increasing attention. As the bureaucracies of the emerging nation-states grew ever more complex, rulers had need of men who were expert in administration and learned in the law. Two great popes dominated the thirteenth century: one at the beginning, the other at the end. Both were renowned for their knowledge of the law.

Lotario dei Conti was only 37 when he was elected to the throne of Saint Peter as Pope Innocent III. That his predecessor, Celestine III, was over 90 when he died may have had some bearing on the cardinals' choice of the youngest of their number for the office, but it was an obvious one: the papacy ran in Lotario's family. Lotario was the youngest of four sons. His father, Trasimondo, Count of Segni, was married to Claricia Scotti, and Claricia's brother, Paolo, had been Pope Clement III. One of Lotario's nephews was to become Pope Gregory IX, and another nephew was to father the future Pope Alexander IV.

Lotario had studied law at Paris and Bologna. He had been a pious student, and while in Paris had made a pilgrimage to the tomb of Saint Thomas at Canterbury in England. He had become a cardinal deacon during the pontificate of his uncle, Clement III, and had written a pious work on how the world should be despised. Even on so serious a subject he had managed to be amusing, just as he managed the occasional witticism as he sat three times a week in his papal court as the supreme judge on earth of Christian men.

He was a man of outstanding intelligence and broad vision, but he was not a good judge of character. He made some bad decisions over the succession to the office of Holy Roman Emperor, but his failings often arose from his inability to understand that men acted often from base rather than from noble motives. But he was no dreamer. Good lawyers cannot be dreamers. He may have been deceived by Otto, then by Frederick, and finally by King John of England, but within his limits he was an able administrator. He streamlined the papal Curia, he appointed his own judges to run the city of Rome, and after the death of the Emperor Henry IV he replaced the German administrators of the Papal States with his own nominees. Though he was never guilty of falling into nationalist sentiment himself, he made great use

Opposite: *This fresco of Pope Innocent III (1198-1216) is in the 'Holy Cave' at Subiaco, the spot where Saint Benedict was reputed to have lived in the early sixth century when he first retreated from the world. While Innocent was Pope, a monastery was built around this cave, with the Pope's support and assistance.*

of it, and of the rising tide of anti-German feeling in Italy. He employed members of his own family to tie together the various titles by which the papacy held rights to land.

Though of noble descent, Innocent III was not from a rich family. As Pope, however, he could call upon great sums of money to buy, and to bribe, back the lands he believed belonged to the Roman See. And if, by using his family and their allies to staff and administer the Papal States he enriched them in the process, it was at least a practical way of ensuring loyalty in a society which was increasingly bound together by ties of blood as well as by feudal oaths.

The papacy became wealthy during his tenure of office, but Innocent was always ready to disburse money, as well as to demand it if it was his due. He rebuilt the Lateran and Vatican palaces; he made rich gifts to the Roman churches; he provided the impoverished Archbishop of Ravenna, whose predecessors had been great rivals to the Bishop of Rome, with liturgical vestments. He founded a hospital for orphans after having dreamt that newborn children were being dredged up out of the Tiber, and once a year he and his cardinals gathered outside the hospital to distribute money to 3000 paupers and 300 inmates.

He could be generous, but he was also tough. On being elected, a pope was traditionally expected to hand out money to the citizens of Rome in return for their good behaviour. Innocent refused to do this immediately. He first determined just how little he could safely pay, and distributed that amount. Riots broke out, which he put down; but he could not afford to let Rome occupy too much of his time. There were other important matters which demanded his attention.

Innocent had been elected in January 1198. Less than six months before, the Emperor Henry VI had died suddenly. Henry had been King of Germany, King of Sicily, King of Italy and he had hoped to become King of Jerusalem. But so long as the security of the Roman See remained a priority, no Bishop of Rome could happily contemplate the same military power holding territory to both the north and the south of the city. Sicily, moreover, was a region to which the papacy itself had long laid claim. Innocent, therefore, was relieved to find a variety of claimants to the titles which Henry had united in himself.

The dying Emperor had put his son, Frederick Hohenstaufen, under papal protection and, had the Imperial title been hereditary, then Frederick would undoubtedly have been the rightful heir. But no pope was going to concede that the title was indeed hereditary. Innocent himself revised the Imperial coronation ritual to include the pope's girding the sword on to the emperor, as a sign that it was the papacy which gave the emperor his temporal authority. In any case, Frederick was too young. The choice really lay between Henry's brother, Philip, and the head of a rival dynasty, Otto IV.

Innocent took his responsibility for the Empire very seriously. He even ordered a separate register to be kept for all his letters on Imperial matters so that he could refer to them more easily. He called a secret consistory of his cardinals, and drew up a careful document outlining the reasons why Philip should not be chosen. The reasons looked convincing enough, but there is no doubt that behind the choice of Otto lay the conviction that he would listen to the Pope more willingly, and would interfere less in Italian affairs than would his rival.

Otto was the nephew of King Richard I of England, and had English support. But the English were at odds with the King of France, and so Philip had French support and, moreover, seemed to be winning the civil war which raged in Germany between the two factions. Innocent thought it politic to change sides. He had scarcely done so, however, when Philip was assassinated, and so Innocent wrote immediately to the German princes and pointed out to them that heaven had eventually come down quite clearly on the side of Otto.

Otto arrived in Rome for his coronation as Holy Roman Emperor. The event was accompanied by battles between Romans and Germans, and Otto blamed the Pope for the deaths which ensued. He also made it clear that he had designs on Sicily, and on other lands that the papacy claimed as its own. And so ten years after espousing the cause of Otto, Innocent found himself excommunicating him and absolving his subjects from their oaths of allegiance. He ordered the German princes to elect another emperor, and switched his support to Frederick Hohenstaufen. It was to prove a costly mistake, but the resultant problems were to arise only after Innocent's death, and at his coronation, Frederick made what appeared to be very generous promises to the Church.

Otto, meanwhile, continued to fight with the aid of King John of England, but was decisively defeated by the French at Bouvines, and left the English King at the mercy of his barons. The battle for the Empire, therefore, had an indirect effect on the signing of Magna Carta.

In the early years of his pontificate, Innocent had been at odds with King John. In the course of a dispute over an appointment to the Archbishopric of Canterbury between King John and the monks of Canterbury, Innocent had intervened to instruct the monks to proceed with the election of Stephen

Langton, an old friend of his from their student days at Paris. Langton had stayed on at Paris after Innocent had left, and had gone on to become one of the University's most respected scholars – he is credited with having divided the Bible into the chapters we use today. In 1206, Innocent made Langton a Cardinal, and at the same time commended him to the monks as their next Archbishop.

But King John would not accept the Pope's choice, and so in March 1208 Innocent put the whole of England under an interdict. Such spiritual penalties had little effect on the King. Four years later, the Pope had to issue another bull absolving all John's subjects from their allegiance, excommunicating anyone who had dealings with him, and handing the whole country over to the King of France who promptly made active preparations to invade. John, unable to trust his own barons, gave way.

There were no half-measures with the English King. Not only did he accept Langton as Archbishop of Canterbury, he also handed the whole country over to the Holy See, receiving it back as a fief of the papacy. He and his successors were to be the pope's liegemen. Innocent was completely taken in, as he had been by Otto and Frederick: from then on, King John could do no wrong. When Langton's name appeared at the head of those who had forced Magna Carta on the unwilling King, Innocent suspended his old friend from the office to which he had appointed him, and dispensed John from having to fulfil the provisions of the Charter.

The papal vassalage to which John had committed England was by no means unique. Such was the prestige of the papacy under Innocent that monarchs hurried to embrace this theoretically servile status. Bulgaria became a papal fief, and so did Aragon. Portugal and Castile already held that status, and renewed their feudal contracts. Together with Navarre, these Iberian kingdoms formed an alliance to drive the Saracens out of Spain, an alliance which would scarcely have been possible had the papacy not provided the unifying force. The alliance won a major victory at Navas de Tolosa, and Innocent was soon involved in establishing ecclesiastical administration in the newly liberated areas of Spain.

Innocent was ready enough to intervene where there were no feudal ties. He was consulted about the succession to the crowns both of Norway and Sweden. With the agreement of Otto, he raised Bohemia to the rank of a kingdom. When the King of France wanted to repudiate his wife, a Danish princess, in order to marry Agnes of Meran, the Pope refused to let him do so, though he legitimized the children whom the King had had by Agnes. Influential people were related both to Ingebiorg, the King's wife, and to Agnes, his mistress, and the Pope did not want to offend any of them. Alliances were in the balance.

The great disaster of Innocent's pontificate, though it did not seem so to the Pope at the time, was the Fourth Crusade. He was obsessed with the crusading ideal, and preached or authorized six of them during his reign. He made valiant efforts to pay for them by taxing the whole Church, but despite his careful preparations he did not always have much success. By the time the Fourth Crusade had gathered at Venice in 1202, it had run out of money. Eventually, the Venetians agreed to transport the crusaders to Constantinople in return for their capturing a Christian town on the Dalmatian coast. The Pope explicitly forbade the attack by crusaders on fellow Christians, but it happened nonetheless and the soldiers were then sent on to the capital of the Byzantine Empire.

At first, the army camped on the outskirts of the city, but quarrels between Greeks and Latins finally flared into open warfare. The crusaders laid siege to Constantinople and it fell after two months, in April 1204. Constantine's Christian city was then sacked by Christian soldiers, supposedly on their way to recapture Jerusalem in the name of Christ. Precious objects, priceless works of art and noble buildings were destroyed, but the credulous Westerners

took special care to preserve objects they considered relics: the Crown of Thorns (Saint Louis of France was later to sell it to the Venetians), Christ's baby clothes and one of his teeth, a tooth of John the Baptist, an arm of Saint Stephen, and the entire body of Saint Andrew.

Count Baldwin of Flanders was crowned as Constantinople's Latin Emperor. He then invaded Bulgaria to force its submission, and was captured. Innocent, trying by diplomatic means to reunite Bulgaria with the Holy See, was reduced to pleading for Baldwin's life.

Above: *This painting by Delacroix shows the crusaders' entry into Constantinople. The Fourth Crusade, preached by Innocent III in 1202, led to the disastrous sack of this Christian city by Christian soldiers, supposedly on their way to recover the Holy Land.*

Right: *Much of Church law was contained in decretal letters, answers by popes to particular questions, usually from bishops. In 1230, Gregory IX (1227-41) instructed that the whole body of the law be rearranged in a logical order. Raphael's fresco in the Vatican shows the Pope handing over the completed volume to a Church lawyer.*

But the fall of Constantinople held out great hopes for the papacy. The Roman Church had tried to establish its primacy over the Patriarch of that city for 900 years: this now seemed to have been achieved, as did the reunion of the two Churches. Innocent expressly recognized the validity of Orthodox ordination, but insisted that all future ordinations should be performed in accordance with the Latin rite. He maintained the structures of the Orthodox Church, but wherever there was a Greek metropolitan (a head of an ecclesiastical province, ranking between archbishop and patriarch) he intruded a Latin archbishop alongside him. The Pope warmly welcomed the opportunities for reunion which, he believed, the fall of Constantinople held out, but it had been no part of the original purpose of the Crusade. In 1213 Innocent called for another expedition to the East, to take place four years from then. He made detailed and meticulous preparations for it, but before it could set out the Pope was dead, and nothing came of his plans.

Crusades were not limited to wars against the Moslems. In 1204 the Pope called upon the King of France to take up arms against a Christian heretical sect which was gathering strength in the south of France, in return for the same sort of spiritual benefits which would be his were he to go to the Holy Land. Heresy, he said later, was to be treated with a knife, as a doctor treats a wound.

The heretics in this instance were Albigensians, members of a sect which believed that all matter was evil. The 'perfect', or full members, sometimes took this belief to the extreme of fasting until death. The less extreme members lived by a rigorous regime which included sexual abstinence, as well as abstinence from certain sorts of food. They were also very critical of the worldliness of the Church.

The 'crusade' against the Albigensians, led by Simon de Montfort, Earl of Leicester, was conducted with horrifying cruelty. It eventually became as much a dynastic war as a religious one, as the nobility of northern France struggled to subdue the south of the country. The Church made little attempt to temper the brutality of the armies it had called into being. The Abbot of Cîteaux, who was also Archbishop of Narbonne and a leader of the Catholic forces, was asked in the course of one massacre how the soldiers should distinguish Catholics from heretics. 'Kill them all,' he replied, 'God will recognize his own.' The story was repeated by a German monk: whether the Abbot really did make the remark is unclear, but it has gone down in history as epitomizing the spirit of the crusade. Innocent, who could be gentle with individual heretics, was unbending when it came to entire sects.

The Inquisition was one of the results of the crusade against the Albigensians. To be fair, it was the invention not of a pope but of Frederick II, who gave his secular officials the task of hunting out heretics, a task which Innocent's nephew, Gregory IX, was to take over on the Church's behalf. The starting point for the Inquisition, however, was the handing over to papal officials of the right to make all enquiries into the beliefs of the people of southern France. Hitherto such enquiries, if they had been made at all, had been the responsibility of local bishops; now Innocent transferred jurisdiction over heresy to his own legates, who could enforce their will by excommunication or interdict. Any cleric who opposed these legates could be removed from office without right of appeal.

Popes of later generations were to use as inquisitors members of a new sort of religious order, which also sprang into being during Innocent's pontificate. Members of the older orders were supposed to live out their lives in one place; members of the new ones, the friars, wandered about Europe preaching, with no special commitment to any single house of their order. The Albigensian crusade played its part in the foundation of one of the new orders of friars.

Dominic de Guzman, sub-prior of the Cathedral of Osma in Spain, decided that he would attempt to persuade the heretics of the error of their ways by example, as well as by preaching. He gradually gathered about him a group of like-minded missionaries who developed not only a particular manner of life, but a special style of preaching. Although the group became known as the Dominicans, after the name of their founder, Saint Dominic, their official title was, and remains, the Order of Preachers. They wore a white religious habit, but when preaching they put on a black cloak, and so the 'black friars' have left their name on the streets or areas of many towns where their houses used to stand.

It was not until after Innocent's death that the Dominican Order was formally recognized. Before he died, however, he had given his approval to another group, who took their name from Saint Francis of Assisi. The Franciscans, or Greyfriars, were to have a chequered history, as it proved increasingly difficult to live out Saint Francis's ideal of absolute poverty. The extreme views of some members of the Order were eventually declared heretical, but Saint Francis's inspiration still lives on in the rule of life followed by the largest religious order in the Catholic Church today.

Both Franciscans and Dominicans faced a crisis very early in their history when the Fourth Lateran Council, called by Innocent to meet in 1215, decided that no new religious orders were to be founded. The Franciscans evaded this prohibition by claiming that Innocent's approval of Saint Francis's primitive rule in 1209 had established them before the ban was issued. The Dominicans, however, had to accept an already existing rule, that of Saint Augustine, and adapt it to their own needs.

This great reforming Council, which in terms of numbers attending it had no equivalent until modern times, was one of the great triumphs of Innocent's pontificate. The reverses the Pope had suffered had in no way dimmed his energy, and he gathered together the first genuinely universal council of the Western Church. There were assorted patriarchs, over 400 bishops and more than 900 abbots, heads of religious orders, representatives of princes and other delegates. The Archbishop of Amalfi was suffocated in the crush.

In three solemn sessions in November 1215 the Catholic faith was defined against the heresies of the Albigensians and others, the Byzantines came under attack, and Constantinople, Alexandria, Antioch and Jerusalem were subordinated – in that order of precedence – to the primacy of the Roman Church. Faced with a decline in religious practice, the Council insisted that the faithful should go to confession once a year, and to communion at Easter. Secret marriages were condemned, so was the abuse of the granting of indulgences, and simony. Against the pretensions of monarchs across Europe, the Council demanded that elections to bishoprics be canonical and free from interference. There were to be schools for the clergy attached to cathedrals, and the parish clergy were enjoined to preach regularly and administer the sacraments carefully. Rules about the granting of benefices to the clergy were tightened up, and all religious orders were instructed to hold a general council, or chapter, every three years.

It was characteristic of Pope Innocent that among the decrees of the Lateran Council a demand for a four-year truce among Christian princes was included, to allow time for a Crusade. But, as previously mentioned, the Crusade was never to take place. Innocent III died on 16 July 1216, when still only in his mid-fifties. Despite his comparative youthfulness, he had been Pope for over 18 years. As Vicar of Christ – a title he was the first pope to adopt – he had made and unmade kings and emperors. He had, or so he thought, reunited the Greek and the Latin Churches. He had been the inspiration behind two Crusades to the Holy Land, although the first never reached there, and the second never even set out. He had refounded the Papal States, streamlined the papal bureaucracy, and held one of the most important reforming councils in the history of the Church. He had put into practice the ideals which popes since the days of Saint Gregory the Great had held, but had been unable to implement. His pontificate marks the high point of the papacy.

The degree to which he had dominated Europe could not be sustained. When his nephew, who became Gregory IX, lay dying in August 1241 there was a good chance that divisions within the College of Cardinals would prevent them reaching agreement on a successor, thus leaving the way open for the Emperor Frederick II to appoint someone sympathetic to him. Gregory recalled what an English teacher of canon law had once said to him: if the cardinals failed to elect a pope they should be locked up until they did so. Gregory called Matteo Rossi Orsini, senator of Rome and the city's leading layman, to his bedside to make plans. After Gregory had died, Orsini arrested all the cardinals he could find and immured them in the Septizonium palace, together with the coffin of the Pope, to speed up the process of election. He subjected them to all sorts of discomforts. One cardinal complained that whenever he lay down to sleep a soldier stuck a spear up through his mattress. Not surprisingly, one cardinal died, and this

gave the remainder an idea. They chose the extremely ill Bishop of Sabina, who died within three weeks of his election as Celestine IV. But in those few days the cardinals were able to escape from what was, in effect, the first proper conclave to elect a pope. They gathered together again at Anagni in 1243 without the constraints imposed by Orsini, and chose Sinibaldi Fieschi, cardinal-priest and Bishop of Albenga, as Innocent IV.

Like his namesake at the beginning of the century, Innocent was a lawyer. Indeed, he was possibly the most academically gifted pope in a hundred years. As a politician, he was tough and perhaps even worldly, but he had a

Above: *Giotto's painting of a medieval dream sequence attributed to Pope Innocent III (1198-1216). The basilica of Saint John Lateran is shown toppling over, but Saint Francis of Assisi holds it up. This was said to have persuaded Innocent to approve the foundation of the Franciscan Order.*

Above: *A sixteenth-century French school portrayal of the coronation of the reluctant Pope Celestine V. As a simple peasant, he had been living a hermit's life before he was chosen as a compromise candidate after a conclave lasting over two years. He was elected in July 1294, but his unsuitability for the office brought about his resignation in the December of the same year.*

well-developed appreciation of the value of sanctity in the life of the Church. He staffed his Curia with highly capable men, whom he then sent out to serve in ecclesiastical offices throughout Europe. Many of these papal appointees came to England, and the 'provision' of foreigners, who sometimes could not even speak the language, to English benefices became a major grievance against the papacy.

By the time Innocent became Pope, the Emperor Frederick II dominated Italy as well as his native Germany. To be free of him, the Pope had to flee Rome, first to his home town of Genoa, and then on to France, where he took up residence in Lyons. He summoned a council to meet there, at which he deposed the Emperor and outlined the theory that the papacy could 'translate' the Empire to whomsoever it wished, but it was not until after Frederick's

death in December 1250 that Innocent could risk returning to Rome. Even then his position remained weak.

Four years later, Innocent himself died in Naples. His successor Honorius III was elected in the same city, for in order to discourage the election of anti-popes Innocent had ruled that the conclave was to take place wherever the pontiff had died. He had also ruled that no cardinal could vote for himself.

He was an ambiguous character. Innocent III had spoken, on at least one occasion, as if Crusades were intended to compel Moslems to become Christians. Innocent IV, while defending the right of Christians to go to war to recover the Holy Land, property which, he said, was rightfully theirs, had insisted that unbelievers had rights in natural law, and that wars of conversion were unjust. On the other hand, he was the first Pope to allow the Inquisition to use torture to extract confessions. His pontificate also saw the Christianization of Lithuania and the crowning of its ruler as king, and the departure of missionaries, especially Franciscans, for the Far East. Their work had little permanent effect, which was perhaps a sign that the Pope's attention was wholly devoted to his conflict with Frederick II over Italy, a conflict which did a great deal to lower the prestige of the papal office in people's eyes.

Yet if the papacy suffered from too much worldliness under Innocent IV, it was to suffer from the opposite failing under Celestine V. The curious circumstances surrounding his election in July 1294 began two years earlier with the death of Pope Nicholas IV. Ten days after Nicholas's death the conclave gathered, as it should, in the palace near Santa Maria Maggiore, though it soon transferred to the new Dominican church of Santa Maria Sopra Minerva. There were only 12 electors, half of them being Romans, and the Romans were equally divided between the Colonna faction – Nicholas had been a Colonna – and the Orsinis. Fighting broke out in the city between supporters of the two factions, the civil war was followed by plague, and so the cardinals were forced to retire from Rome, first to Rieti and then to Perugia.

It is not entirely clear what happened early in July 1294 to break the deadlock between the rival groups. It seems that a letter arrived from a hermit, Pietro da Morrone, urging the cardinals to come to a swift decision for the good of the Church. He was proposed as a compromise candidate, perhaps in jest, and was elected pope even though his qualifications for the post were negligible. He had certainly founded and directed a small congregation of Benedictine houses, in which the monks lived out a life of extreme asceticism. However, he had left the congregation to retire to a hermitage on Monte Morrone – from which he took his surname. He was almost illiterate. He came from among the peasants, and his lack of sophistication may have appealed to them, but his ignorance of the workings of the Church, and his language, peppered as it was with naive obscenities, scarcely made him a suitable candidate for the office of pope.

In the event, his term of office lasted less than six months. He was under the influence of King Charles II of Naples, under whose protection he had placed himself, and from whose territories he never strayed. Much of the papal business was conducted by the King, who nominated all but three of the cardinals whom Celestine appointed. The Pope's own interests lay elsewhere – with the extreme religious groups in the Church. He endowed his own Congregation of Benedictines – now known as the Celestinians – with enormous privileges, and even made over to them the great monastery of Monte Cassino. He was a patron of Jacapone da Todi, one of the outstanding religious poets of the Middle Ages. His interest, however, was not in the Franciscan's poetry, but in his desire, which the Pope indulged, to live out a life of strict poverty outside the houses of his order. Celestine himself decided, even as Pope, to try to recapture something of the severity of a hermit's life by shutting himself in a tiny cell and committing the government of the Church to three cardinals. As it became increasingly difficult to approach the

121

Pope, the cardinals decided that something must be done. The possibility of his abdicating was discussed and then agreed. At a consistory of cardinals held on 13 December 1294, Celestine read out his speech resigning the office of pope. As he read, he stripped off the papal vestments. After the statutory ten-day interim period laid down, the cardinals once again met in conclave. They quickly agreed on the choice of 60-year-old Benedict Caetani, who became Pope Boniface VIII.

The Caetani were middling nobility, though little is known of them before Benedict's father, Roffred. His mother, Emilia, was ecclesiastically very well connected: she was the niece of one pope (Alexander IV) and a great-niece of another (Gregory IX). Benedict may have been born at Anagni, where in 1275 his Uncle Peter became bishop, but scarcely anything can be learned about his early life beyond the fact that he went to Bologna to study law.

His story really begins when he accompanied a papal legate to France, and then went over to England to support King Henry III against his rebellious barons. He was in England for nearly three years and had the experience of being besieged in the Tower of London. Afterwards he was to serve for a time as a papal tax collector in France before being made a cardinal deacon in 1281. As a cardinal he was constantly employed on diplomatic missions, both for the pope and for Charles of Anjou – the Angevins having replaced the Hohenstaufens as Kings of Sicily.

All the while, Benedict was amassing enormous wealth. When Innocent IV lay dying he is supposed to have said to his grieving relatives, 'Why do you weep. Have I not made you rich enough?' The relatives of Boniface VIII would never have reason to complain on that score. But despite the riches he accumulated as a cardinal, he and his family still had some social climbing to do before the Caetanis could rival the Colonnas and Orsinis.

In 1296 he married his great-nephew, Roffred, to a middle-aged and somewhat disreputable widow, whose lover was reputed to have murdered his wife for love of her. The widow was thought to be wealthy. When this proved not to be the case, Boniface coolly remarked that he had not known she was already married (he chose to regard her lover as her husband), granted Roffred an immediate divorce, and married him off to an eligible Neapolitan heiress with little delay.

The Colonnas had supported Boniface at his election, but as he set about acquiring lands for his relatives, the interests of the two families clashed. One Colonna, Stephen, seized a train of papal mules carrying treasure into Rome to finance yet more purchases of land. It was a stupid act, and the Colonnas offered to return what had been stolen. They were not, however, prepared to hand over Stephen to the Pope for punishment. Boniface summoned the Colonna cardinals to see him. They fled to a family stronghold. There they published a manifesto against the Pope, questioning the legitimacy of Celestine's abdication, and therefore of Boniface's election. The Pope replied by deposing the cardinals, and excommunicating the whole Colonna family, down to the fourth generation. They came of evil stock, he declared, and Rome could not be safe so long as they survived. He granted crusading privileges to all who went to war on his behalf against the Colonnas. The Colonnas fled. According to the poet Petrarch, who was a friend of the family, some even travelled as far as Egypt, Persia and Arabia. But several came together at the court of the King of France, an ever-present threat to the Caetanis' security.

Another threat was the retired Pope, Celestine. So long as he survived, he was a symbol around which opposition could gather. Even before leaving Naples for his splendidly extravagant coronation, Boniface had cancelled all Celestine's appointments, and invalidated all his grants of benefices or privileges unless they were confirmed within a definite interval. The measures were draconian, but at least they cut through the tangle which his

Above: *Pope Boniface VIII (1294-1303) had an exalted sense of his own authority. This splendid bronze statue from Bologna admirably captures his imperiousness.*

last two predecessors had bequeathed him and cleared the way for him to make his own appointments. He summoned Celestine to Rome, but the ex-Pope fled to his old mountain haunts to be given an ecstatic welcome by the peasants who flocked to see him. When he was at last captured he was trying to make his way to Greece. He was brought back to Anagni, working miracles, it was said, on the way. Boniface imprisoned him in the castle at Fumone, where he died in May 1296. Years later, Boniface was accused of having starved him to death, but as the former Pope was nearly 90 years of age there seems no reason to blame his successor.

Though he earned an evil reputation, and Dante committed him to hell in his *Divine Comedy*, there was much that Boniface did which improved the condition of the Church and of the Papal States. His legal training encouraged him to codify and rationalize both the civil law of the territories controlled by the papacy, and the canon law of the Church. He added to the existing five books of the Church's law a sixth called, unimaginatively, *Sext*.

In 1300 he proclaimed a Jubilee Year, the first of the 'Holy Years' held at regular intervals ever since. Special indulgences were attached to visiting Rome and making the rounds of the churches and shrines. Pilgrims poured into the city, so much so, one eyewitness claimed, that at any given time there were 200,000 strangers in town. Even if that figure is an exaggeration, the numbers must have been immense compared with the total population of Rome, thought to be some 40,000 in the Jubilee Year. And money flowed in. Two clerics stood with rakes near the altar of Saint Paul's Outside the Walls, pulling in the coins left by pilgrims.

Boniface paid the Jubilee very little attention. He was away from Rome more than ever in the year in which it took place. The point of the whole exercise was to raise money, for the papal policy in Sicily cost Boniface's treasury a third of its revenue during his pontificate. Finance was a subject close to his heart. Early in 1296 he issued his bull *Clericis Laicos*, complaining, in the language of Saint Jerome, of the laity's hostility to the clergy. In future, he decreed, the clergy were not to pay local taxes without the express permission of the Holy See. All who insisted on payment, and all who paid what was demanded, were to be excommunicated. King Philip of France retaliated by forbidding the export from his country of all moneys and other negotiable valuables. It was a shrewd move.

Boniface blamed the King's evil counsellors, and complained that the King's action inhibited legitimate trade with which the papacy, with its international contacts, was very much bound up. But eventually the Pope had to concede defeat, at least as far as France was concerned. In an emergency, said the Pope, even the clergy could pay taxes to the King, and he even left the King to define an emergency. Elsewhere, however, he insisted on a strict observance of *Clericis Laicos*, which put England at a distinct disadvantage in its war with France.

The Pope's problem was that he needed French help to pacify Italy. When they failed to achieve results, Boniface reversed his policy. He recognized the right of the Crown of Aragon to rule in Sicily, which until now had been under the control of the Angevins, and accepted the German Albrecht of Hapsburg as Emperor-elect. As he wrote in his bull in which he declared his intentions, the papacy was to the Empire as the sun to the moon: the moon has no light of its own, it all comes from the sun. The imperial electors may claim to make kings, but it was the papacy which had transferred the Empire from the Greeks to the Germans. This powerful statement of the claims of the papal monarchy was followed by a letter urging all subjects of the Empire to throw off allegiance to France. Philip responded by calling what was in effect the first *Parlement* of all three estates: the nobles, the clergy and commoners. His chancery had prepared 29 charges against the Pope, to be considered by the *Parlement*, and then taken back by the deputies to every corner of France.

Even before the *Parlement* met, an emissary had been despatched to Italy to arrange a *coup* against the Pope. The plotters included the Colonna exiles at Philip's court, an Orsini cardinal, and even some of the families under the patronage of the Caetani. They found Boniface at Anagni, and at first had little trouble in arresting him, but then the inhabitants of Anagni, afraid of being accused of complicity in this scandal, suddenly turned against the invaders. They fled empty-handed. Boniface returned to Rome with an Orsini escort, but he was a broken man. He died on 11 October 1303, just a month after his capture.

He was buried in the chapel he had prepared for himself. During the rebuilding of Saint Peter's, his coffin was opened and as his body was found largely incorrupt, a description was made. He had been fairly tall and stoutly built with strong features, rather prominent ears and a bald head. He was splendidly dressed – he had been a patron of the arts, including embroidery from England. The tomb itself has for the most part disappeared, but it represented one of the earliest works in Rome in the Gothic style. Arnolfo di Cambio, who designed it, has also been credited with sculpting for Boniface the great bronze statue of Saint Peter, the foot of which is kissed by countless numbers of religious pilgrims and visitors as they enter the basilica which bears his name.

Boniface was also something of a patron of learning. The mystical theologian Meister Eckhart benefited from his generosity, and the Pope encouraged several universities, and founded the one in the city of Rome. He was well aware of the intellectual currents of the day. He knew that they were opposed to the high doctrine of the papacy which had flourished in the thirteenth century. Successive popes tried to forbid the study of Aristotelian philosophy for, as they clearly perceived, the philosophy of a pagan could only lead to a view of the world in which Christianity had little part. Even the synthesis between Aristotle and Saint Augustine achieved by Saint Thomas Aquinas was for a time condemned, or at least some of his views were, in 1277—three years after his death—by the Bishop of Paris. Eleven days later, the Archbishop of Canterbury issued a similar condemnation.

And just as popes struggled in vain to forbid the study of Aristotle, so they fought to prohibit the study of Roman law. That, too, was outside the Church's control because it came from a society in which the Church had played no part. The combined effect of Aristotelian philosophy and Roman law made the king into an absolute sovereign. Thus there was no place for the emperor, and certainly none for the pope.

Against this new view of the world, exemplified in the life of King Philip IV of France, the Pope produced a new synthesis of the old doctrine. In *Unam Sanctam* he restated it as formally as he could, attempting to command the assent of Christians where he knew he could scarcely persuade. This bull appeared in November 1302. It was a careful statement of papal claims to ultimate and absolute sovereignty. Outside obedience to the Pope, it ended, there is no forgiveness of sin, or final salvation. It was the first papal bull to be published on a theological rather than on a legal issue, and it marks the end of the medieval papacy. Its implications have worried people ever since, but it is not altogether clear that Boniface himself really believed what he wrote down under the guidance of Giles of Rome, his theologian.

He was not a religious man. In the posthumous trial to which he was committed by the French King, he was accused of not believing in the presence of Christ in the Eucharist, or the resurrection from the dead. And as for his morality, a shoemaker recalled that when he was a boy of 17 and living in Padua, the then Cardinal Caetani had tried to seduce him. 'There is no more wrong with living with a boy or with a woman', one witness reported him as saying, 'than there is with rubbing one hand against another.' Even the Pope's cook turned accuser. He had been ordered to buy so much meat during Lent, he complained, that his activities had given rise to scandal.

As one historian has written recently, while Innocent III was a man who could not know disillusionment, Boniface VIII was a man whose essence was disillusionment. Perhaps it was because, with his high intelligence and understanding of the world, he had realized that the ideal of a papal monarchy holding sway over emperors and kings, which he had propounded in *Unam Sanctam*, was out of date even before he had committed it to paper. Certainly the world which Clement V faced after his election in 1305 was a very different one from that over which Innocent III had so serenely ruled a century before.

PAPA · EVGENIVS · QVARTVS ·

EXILE AND SCHISM

Pope Boniface VIII's immediate successor, Benedict XI, died less than nine months after his election, and so in 1304 a conclave had to gather again. The cardinals met in Perugia. They were evenly divided between pro- and anti-French factions. After almost a year of intrigue and behind-the-scenes bargaining, the compromise choice was Bertrand de Got, not himself a cardinal, but the Archbishop of Bordeaux and an influential figure at the court of the King of France.

He was of noble birth. His father was Lord of Villandraut and many other places besides, and it was at Villandraut in the Gironde that Bertrand was born. The date of his birth is unknown. He studied canon and civil law at Orleans and Bologna, and his ecclesiastical career began with a canonry in the Cathedral of Bordeaux. Eventually he also became a canon of the Cathedral of Lyons, where his brother was Archbishop. He served his brother as chief assistant, and clearly accomplished his duties well, for in 1294 he was entrusted with a diplomatic mission to England and the following year was made Bishop of Comminges. In 1299 he became Archbishop of Bordeaux. As Pope, he chose the name Clement V.

He was crowned at Lyons. The place was not of his choosing. He would have preferred Vienne, but Philip IV of France wanted to put Pope Boniface posthumously on trial, and the only way Clement could buy time was by granting the King's wish that the coronation should take place on French soil, for he was deeply concerned about the damage which such a trial would do to the power and prestige of the papacy.

The new Pope was a strange mixture. He was no match for the French King, but when dealing with other princes he could be brusque and imperious. He was an invalid, suffering from what seems to have been a cancer of the stomach, and during the periodic bursts of intense pain he would become a recluse. Yet at other times he was pleasant and affable, a patron of the arts as well as of learning. He founded universities at Orleans and Perugia, and established chairs of Hebrew, Arabic and Syriac at Paris, Bologna, Oxford and Salamanca. He added a seventh book, the 'Clementines', to the body of Church law, the last to be officially added to the *Corpus Iuris Canonici*.

His family was his failing. He made no less than five of his relatives cardinals. In his will he left 200,000 florins to relatives, friends and members of his household, and another 300,000 to a nephew to lead 500 knights on a Crusade. There were other substantial benefactions, and all that was bequeathed to his successor was a treasury of 70,000 florins.

Clement had a never-ending need for money, both for himself and for the officials of his growing court. Greed was unrestrained: anyone who wanted to see the Pope had to tip even the man at the door. To provide

Opposite: *Pope Eugenius IV (1431-47) was a man of great asceticism who had been a member of a religious order. Consequently, he interested himself in re-establishing branches of 'strict observance' within the other orders in the Church – the Dominicans, the Benedictines and the Franciscans. Eugenius twice issued bulls concerned with the Franciscans, one of whom is seen here kneeling before him. Four days after his coronation he attempted a reform of the Friars Minor, and a year before his death he gave a large measure of autonomy to the Observants. In this picture from the Vatican Library he is shown on a throne surrounded by cardinals. His papal coat of arms is shown beneath the picture.*

Above: *The Palace of the Popes at Avignon in southern France was begun under Pope Benedict XII (1334-42) and continued under his successor, Pope Clement VI. The popes lived at Avignon, with one very brief interval, from 1309 to 1376.*

adequate income for his servants he had to increase his control over the appointments to bishoprics throughout Europe, to allow the same individual to hold several benefices, and to permit such a person to draw a variety of incomes from different sources. This 'pluralism' was harmful to the spiritual good of the Church. So was the appointment of people who had no intention of carrying out the duties attached to the benefices they acquired.

Clement's policy was determined by his attempts to free himself from the King of France's influence. He therefore cultivated the friendship of the King of England and of the King of the Romans, Henry of Luxembourg.

As Archbishop of Bordeaux he had been the vassal of King Edward I of England which may have affected his attitude towards the English King. He freed Edward from all the promises he had been forced to make to his barons, and when the Archbishop of Canterbury opposed the King the Archbishop was summoned to the papal court, suspended from office, and had his revenues confiscated. When Robert the Bruce stirred up trouble he was excommunicated. Clement also played a large part in arranging the marriage between Edward's son and a French princess, and although Edward II first took sides against the Pope, when he, too, fell out with his barons he turned to Clement for support.

Henry of Luxembourg was elected to the title of King of the Romans, and Clement announced that he would crown him Emperor in Rome in 1312. But first Henry had to re-establish control over Italy, and win back Rome for the Pope, from the hands of Robert, the Angevin King of Naples. But by the time the Emperor-elect had taken Rome, he and Clement had fallen out. Clement made it clear that he considered the Emperor subject to the Pope. Not surprisingly Henry thought otherwise. When the time for the coronation came, therefore, Clement was still in France, and the ceremony had to be performed in the Lateran basilica by the Cardinal Bishop of Ostia. Clement heard the news with equanimity, and indeed it scarcely mattered: Henry died from a fever little more than a year after his coronation.

Philip of France, irritated at not winning the title of Emperor for his brother, demanded a high price in his relationship with the Pope. Clement had to have removed from the papal registers all Pope Boniface's acts, and those of his immediate successor, which were judged to be against French interests. In addition, Celestine V was to be canonized, a saintly victim of Boniface's atrocities. Clement was forced to agree, but canonized Celestine under his name of Pietro da Morrone. The implication was that Celestine had every right to resign his office, something which the French, with the support of the Colonna cardinals, strenuously denied.

The final price which King Philip demanded from the Pope was the suppression of the Knights Templar. This was a religious order, part monastic, part military, whose purpose was to protect pilgrims and guard the routes to the Holy Land. The Order had been founded on the site of Solomon's temple two centuries before, and its early history had been a distinguished one. But by the beginning of the fourteenth century it had become little more than an enormous banking organization which even ran the royal treasury of France. The gossip was that because they controlled so much wealth the Templars must be wealthy themselves, but that appears not to have been true. There were other accusations against them, including sorcery and dealings with the devil.

Philip arrested all the Templar knights in his dominions in 1307, acting, he claimed, at the request of the Inquisitor General of France. These 2,000 or so knights were formally charged with denying Christ and spitting on the crucifix during the initiation ceremony into the Order, of practising sodomy and encouraging others to do likewise, of leaving unsaid the words of consecration at Mass and worshipping an idol. Torture made the majority confess to these crimes.

On hearing this, Clement instructed all monarchs to seize the remaining knights. But then many withdrew their confessions. The Pope ordered all judicial proceedings to be suspended, and said he would handle the affair himself. On his own authority he decreed the suppression of the Knights Templar, but he never condemned them. On Philip's instructions, however, many died at the stake.

The French King's motives have never been entirely clear, but as he had already despoiled the Lombard bankers and the Jews, the most likely explanation is that he was after the Templars' alleged riches. But if greed were his motive, then he was to be a little disappointed, for Clement tried to make over such property and money as they possessed to the other military orders. But Philip did manage to get his hands on the lion's share.

All these preoccupations had kept Clement in France. By the time they were over he was too ill to go to Italy, which was, in any case, largely under the hostile control of the Emperor Henry VII. So the papal court was still at Avignon when Clement died in 1314. It remained there until 1376.

The period between 1308, when Clement decided to establish his court at Avignon, until the return to Rome under Gregory XI has become known as the 'Babylonian captivity'. The French kings wanted to keep the popes 'captive' within their own sphere of influence, and there were a great many French cardinals, created by Clement and his successors, who had a marked distaste for living in Italy.

But it was no novelty for the papacy to be located elsewhere than Rome. Between 1100 and the death of Clement's predecessor in 1304, the popes had spent only 82 years in the city of which they were nominally the bishops. The oddity of the 'captivity' was not that the Curia was established outside Rome,

but that it was outside Italy. Avignon was not, strictly speaking, French territory. When Clement settled there it belonged to the Kingdom of Naples, but the Angevin princes of Naples were so busy fighting off Aragonese claimants to their title that they were too preoccupied to bother the Pope. In any case, technically they were his vassals.

The country surrounding Avignon was part of the Papal States, and in the middle of the fourteenth century the pope purchased the town from Naples. It was a convenient place to live, especially after Pope Benedict XII had built the great palace which still dominates the town. It had rapid sea and land connections with Italy.

Yet whatever reasons may be used to justify Clement's establishment of the Curia in the south of France, in the long term it did untold damage to the Church. It was no wonder that in his *Divine Comedy* an Italian patriot such as Dante should have put Clement, along with Nicholas III and Boniface, into hell.

Clement had been something of a compromise candidate, and so was his successor. The conclave held in May 1314 was attended by a large group of Gascon cardinals, and a slightly smaller one of Italians. There were also a few French or Provençal cardinals and they were more likely to side with the Gascons than with the Italians. There was so much trouble between the servants of the two main groups that the Italian cardinals had to flee for their lives, but they were all united again in the Dominican house at Lyons by the Count of Poitiers. He sealed off the house with troops to ensure a quick decision, and made it clear that his own preference was Jacques Dueze, Cardinal Bishop of Porto. He was not a popular choice, but at 72 he was unlikely to live long. On 13 August 1316 he became Pope John XXII.

There is a legend that Pope John was a cobbler's son, but in fact he came from rich middle-class parents living in the town of Cahors. He went to school there, and then moved on to Montpellier. He was successively Bishop of Frejus, of Avignon, Cardinal-Priest of San Vitale and Cardinal Bishop of Porto. As Bishop of Frejus he had served Charles II of Anjou as Chancellor, and this had given him an insight into the machinations of politicians. Their antics caused him frequent amusement, often to their discomfiture. He had a lively mind, a gift for repartee, and a rather peremptory, imperious manner. Like his predecessor, he was disposed to show too much favour to his relatives, but popes of the day needed friends around them whom they could trust, as events at the beginning of John's reign were to demonstrate.

The Bishop of Cahors had been found guilty of simony, and was awaiting sentence. He decided to murder the Pope by putting arsenic in his food and drink. Not trusting natural poisons, however, he employed sorcery as well. He practised first on a wax figure of the Pope's favourite nephew, who conveniently died, giving the conspirators – there were several people in the plot with the Bishop of Cahors – confidence enough to commission three more figures. One was labelled with the name of the Pope, and all three were 'baptized' in the chapel of the Bishop's palace at Toulouse. The figures and the poisons were hidden inside loaves of bread, which the conspirators then tried to smuggle into the papal palace. They were caught, they confessed, and the Bishop of Cahors was burned at the stake.

The Bishop's fear of Pope John's anger over the charge of simony was typical of the Pope's reign. He was zealous in the extreme over what he took to be the Church's spiritual good. He tried to ensure that the Inquisition never abused its power, but he was equally determined that it should operate with the utmost efficiency. He used the Templar money to found new military religious orders to fight the Moors in the Iberian peninsula. He overrode opposition to his plans to reorganize large dioceses in France and Spain into smaller, more effective ones, and he abolished the right of prelates to hold several benefices at the same time, which had been tolerated and even encouraged by his predecessors.

IOANES QVONDAM PAPA
XXIII OBIIT FLORENTIEA
NO DNI MCCCCXVIIIIXI
KALENDAS IANVARII

He had inherited an almost empty treasury, and so he promptly set about righting this by establishing a new fiscal system which, in time, brought him enormous wealth. In addition, because he was a man of frugal habits and cut down extravagance in the papal court, he was also able to bequeath an ample treasury to his successor.

The tendency of the fiscal system to centralize control was enhanced by the ascendancy John achieved over appointments to bishoprics. Having almost abolished the election of bishops by cathedral chapters, the Pope could appoint men who had deserved well of him, or men who, in his opinion, would govern their dioceses well. This also meant that princes who wanted to reward one of their own servants had to win the Pope's favour. And so he had political as well as spiritual power.

John XXII was in a strong political position at the outset of his reign. The Emperor's early death had left the Powers in some disarray. In Italy the local nobility were striving to establish small regional states, while succession to the Imperial title was disputed between Frederick of Austria and Louis of Bavaria. For a while the Pope remained neutral, but then the Visconti in Milan seemed on the point of constructing a power-bloc in central Italy which would have presented a threat to papal interests. Unfortunately for the Pope, he finally chose to back the wrong man. He favoured Frederick of Austria, who was shortly afterwards defeated in battle by Louis of Bavaria. Louis promptly laid claim to the remnants of Imperial power in Italy. In January 1328 he entered Rome. The city was under an interdict, but Louis brought a number of excommunicated Franciscan clergy with him, and they were prepared to say Mass.

These Franciscans were another of Pope John's problems. A mystic called Joachim of Fiore had preached a curious theory that the Church's period of power was about to end, and another era, that of the Holy Spirit, was at hand. In this new era the priesthood would be replaced by new monastic orders which would lead all men back to true Christianity. Joachim's teaching had a great influence on one group of Franciscans who became known as the 'Spirituals'. They adopted extreme positions, refusing to accept decisions taken by the Order's authorities. They, and the associations they had founded, had been encouraged by Pope Celestine. Pope John dissolved their associations. They took him to be Antichrist , and felt justified in allying themselves with his enemies.

The clash with the Spirituals was only the beginning of the Pope's troubles with the Franciscans. A large number of them, with the support of the General of the Order, came to believe that Christ and his Apostles owned absolutely nothing and did not even hold property in common. This view, too, was condemned by Pope John, and the Franciscan General was summoned to Avignon and imprisoned. He escaped and, like so many of his subjects, went over to the side of Louis of Bavaria.

Another Franciscan at Louis' side was the philosopher, William of Ockham, whose surname was derived from his English birthplace. He is studied today for his philosophical theories, but in his own day it was his political theory which made him famous. He wanted a radical separation of the Church from the State. He insisted that the authority of the Emperor came from God, and not through the pope but through the people. In cases of emergency the pope might enjoy political authority, but if a pope was acting heretically, the Emperor had both the right and duty to depose him. William, of course, believed that John was behaving heretically when he condemned the Franciscan views on poverty.

The most radical version of this sort of political theory was propounded by Marsiglio of Padua in his *Defender of the Peace*. Not only did he deny that the pope had any authority over the Emperor, but argued the opposite point of view: that the Church was subordinate to the State. It was the Donation of the Emperor Constantine, not the primacy of the Apostle Peter, which gave the papacy its prerogatives. Even in strictly ecclesiastical matters the supreme authority was not the Bishop of Rome, but a general council of the whole Church, in which laymen had a place alongside the clergy.

These theories proved useful to Louis. There was no pope in Rome to anoint him as Emperor, so he called a meeting of the people of the city on Capitol Hill. A bishop on Louis' side called upon the crowd to hail Louis as Emperor, which they obediently did. Although he was anointed in Saint Peter's by two bishops, the diadem was put on Louis's head by a layman, in the name of the people.

Pope John could not tolerate such abuse of his authority. He excommunicated the new Emperor, and condemned the *Defender of the Peace*. Louis' response was to declare the Pope deposed, and Marsiglio, whom Louis had made imperial vicar of the city of Rome, persuaded the clergy of the city to choose a new bishop. They elected one of the Franciscan dissidents, who took the name Nicholas V. He was crowned Pope in 1328, and Louis was re-crowned Emperor by him.

Nicholas was not a success. He had a reputation for running after honours and women, while keeping up a pretence of asceticism, and his life-style proved too expensive for Louis, who abandoned him. He thereupon submitted to Pope John, and spent the remainder of his days in comfortable imprisonment in the palace at Avignon.

John XXII died in December 1334. He is sometimes credited with adding the third coronet to the papal tiara – the second had been put there by Boniface VIII. Such a symbol of the plenitude of papal power would have suited his conception of his office. But his theories of the papal monarchy were an anachronism. People were no longer prepared to believe that the office of emperor was in the pope's gift, or that oaths taken to emperors who did not enjoy papal approval were null and void. Pope John was upholding a medieval doctrine as the world about him, and indeed his own administration, was moving ahead into the Renaissance understanding of government and authority.

There was a dichotomy between theory and practice. Papal administration in Italy was gradually reorganized on lines employed elsewhere in the peninsula. The papacy was prepared to grant 'vicariates' over territories to a family already well established within them, as long as the family recognized that the ultimate title to the territory belonged to the pope. In the middle of the century a constitution was drawn up for the Papal States which was so forward-looking that it remained in force until the eighteenth century, and became a model for other states.

As the papacy gradually regained control in Italy, it became possible for the popes to think about returning. Pope Urban V went back in 1367, but returned to Avignon to die in December 1370. He was succeeded by Pierre Roger de Beaufort, who took the title Gregory XI. He was the last Frenchman to be elected Bishop of Rome.

He was a nobleman, the son of Guillaume de Beaufort and Marie de Chambon, and was 42 at the time of his election. He owed his rapid rise to both his ability and his connections. By the time he was eleven he was a canon twice over, and had been made a cardinal by his uncle, Pope Clement VI, when still only 19. He was a trained canon lawyer, of high moral character and had a cultivated mind. He was personally charming, and of a pious disposition. He was also a man of taste, and ordered the restoration of the Roman palaces to prepare for the papacy's return.

He had told Edward III of England that to go back to Rome was his dearest wish. At the time of his election this seemed an immediate possibility, as the papal armies reported a string of victories in Italy. But this did not last, and there were problems with the European powers as well as a shortage of money (Gregory had to pawn his jewels to pay for the return journey); the final obstacle was the rise of Florence against the Pope.

Florence had many grievances, in particular the refusal of the Papal States to sell grain to Florence during a famine, and in an increasingly nationalistic Italy there was strong resentment against Papal States being ruled by French popes and administered by French rectors. The Florentines inscribed 'Liberty' in letters of silver on their red banner, confiscated Church property, pillaged the offices of the Inquisition, and outlawed the clergy.

The only Italian town where the people did not rise against their papal governors as the revolt spread outwards from Florence was Rome itself. Encouraged by a visit from the saintly mystic Catherine of Siena, Gregory decided to risk the journey back. Guarded by 2000 mercenaries he entered Rome in January 1377, to be mobbed by cheering crowds. Less than a month later, the English mercenary captain, John Hawkwood, coming to the aid of a cardinal besieged in Cesena, massacred most of the town's inhabitants in a single day. By nightfall, 4000 people lay dead in the streets.

This horrific event shocked Florence into suing for peace. The Pope had put them under an interdict which forbade other Christians from having dealings with them. Their allies deserted them, and their trade slumped. And so a great peace conference was called, but before it could meet, Gregory XI had died. He died in the new papal palace of the Vatican, which from now on replaced the ancient palace of the Lateran as the pope's official residence.

His death occurred on 27 March 1378, and there followed one of the most bizarre, and ultimately most tragic, of papal elections. Before Gregory was buried the people were on the street demanding an Italian pope. The cardinals went in fear of their lives as the mob blockaded the roads out of the city, and immobilized the boats on the Tiber. Bonfires were built to burn the cardinals if they did not give the Romans what they wanted. One cardinal actually made his will.

It all proved a needless concern. The unanimous choice of the conclave after only one day was Bartolomeo Prignano, Archbishop of Bari, and Chancellor of the papal Curia under Pope Gregory. But Prignano was not himself a cardinal, and therefore not present when a mob forced its way in past the troops guarding the entrance. To distract their attention, the cardinals dressed up their oldest colleague (who was an Italian) in papal robes, and put him on the papal throne. The diversion was enough to allow time for the rest of the conclave to make an undignified exit.

No doubt the swiftness of the election had been in part the result of fear of the Roman mob. But Prignano, or Urban VI as he chose to be called, had the support of an influential group of electors, and the French cardinals themselves had been divided on the advisability of choosing yet another French pope. The morning after the election, Urban interviewed the cardinals one by one and asked them whether they regarded the ballot as free and canonical. All agreed it was, and signed a letter saying so. The choice seems to have been widely welcomed. John Wycliffe, the English theologian and reformer, saw new hope in Urban for the reform of the Church, and the saintly but practical Catherine of Siena called upon him to create enough Italian cardinals to redress the balance against the French. Even the King of France, who had most to lose, seemed reasonably content at first.

Wycliffe was right: Urban had nursed a burning desire to reform the Church throughout his term as Chancellor. But if his intentions were good his methods were disastrous, and he rapidly dissipated the good will which greeted his election. He had an extraordinarily exalted idea of his own authority. Reminded on one occasion that he could not excommunicate someone without first having warned that person three times, he shouted 'I can do anything if it is my will and judgement.' Two weeks after his enthronement he denounced two of the cardinals present as simoniacs, and called one of them a half-wit. He even tried to attack two other cardinals physically, and had to be restrained.

He also lost the good will of civil rulers. One who had lent money to Pope Gregory asked for it back. Urban refused to pay it, saying there was no evidence that it had been spent on the needs of the Church. He insulted an

official of the Queen of Naples and asserted that Naples (from which he came, though his family's roots were in Pisa) was being badly administered, since it was being run by a woman.

The French cardinals were the first to desert Urban, and others followed. They claimed that because the cardinals had been in fear of the mob at the election it had not been free, and they set up a new conclave. The choice this time was Cardinal Robert of Geneva, who took the title Clement VII in 1378. The Great Schism of the Western Church had begun.

Naturally, the French King sided with Clement. The two men were cousins, and so the anti-pope went back to Avignon to live. Equally naturally, England, being an enemy of France, came down on the side of Urban, and put pressure on Portugal to do likewise. Spain and Scotland opted for Clement too, and so in the first instance did the Italian states, but he soon antagonized them into opposition.

Urban, who occasionally led his armies himself, promised crusaders' indulgences to all who took up arms against the French, and special indulgences for those who did not take part themselves but sent fighting men. Clergy were allowed to desert their benefices to take part in the wars. Support for Urban against the French was taken up enthusiastically in England, but the one major battle that was fought near Ypres in 1382 had no influence on the outcome of the schism.

The Pope appointed new cardinals to replace those who had deserted him, but alienated even them by his rages. A group considered deposing him, but when Urban discovered the plot he had five of the cardinals tortured and then killed – although the one English cardinal he let go free. Yet when Urban died in Rome in October 1389 the remaining cardinals, instead of accepting the Pope in Avignon as the legitimate Bishop of Rome, promptly elected a successor to Urban.

The Catholic Church has always accepted the 'Roman obedience' (Urban VI and his successors) as the rightful line, rather than the 'Avignon obedience' (the followers of Clement VII), or the later 'Pisan obedience', but the issue was not a simple one. If Urban's election were not free, then he was not canonically elected, and the cardinals were justified in choosing someone else. And if Urban were insane, and his behaviour certainly calls his sanity into question, the cardinals might have been right to depose him, just as they would have been had he been a heretic. (The dissident Franciscans had used Pope John XXII's supposedly heretical views on the resurrection of the body as a reason for supporting their anti-pope, Nicholas V, though John made it plain that he was speaking as a private person.)

At first, the leading Church lawyers tended to side with Urban rather than with Clement, though some believed from the very beginning that the only solution was to call a council of the Church. The difficulty with this solution was that many also believed that only the pope himself could call such a council. Much influenced by the prevailing political thought, a theory eventually emerged according to which authority in the Church came from God, but through the people. Authority resided in the people as a whole, though for practical reasons it might have to be exercised by the people's representatives, the pope and the cardinals. In emergencies, the Church might have to meet in council to sit in judgement upon its representatives.

This theory, called conciliarism, enjoyed a great vogue at the time, and posed a question about authority in the Church which has not been satisfactorily resolved. Many of those who talked of the 'congregation of the faithful' as the final seat of authority on earth thought of the Church primarily in terms of those holding office within it, together with those who held office in the State. But even if in practice the 'congregation of the faithful' were an oligarchy rather than a true democracy, the theory had too many democratic overtones to appeal for long to the nobility of Europe, challenged as it was at this time by the rising power of the middle class.

Left: *John Huss (c. 1369-1415), pictured here, was born of a Bohemian peasant family and he came much under the influence of the writings of the Englishman, John Wycliffe. The anti-pope, John XXIII, condemned him as a heretic, and he went to the Council of Basle under a safe-conduct from the Emperor Sigismund to plead his case. At Basle, however, he was put on trial and burned at the stake.*

In any case, even a council was no real solution. Unless the popes could be persuaded to resign, there was a danger that further schisms might be created. For that reason when Angelo Correr was elected Pope Gregory XII in November 1406 at the age of 80, he, together with all the other cardinals of the Roman obedience, had already sworn that they were ready to resign, should that seem to be the only way forward. He had also promised to work only for the reunion of the Church, and not to create any new cardinals to perpetuate the schism. He wrote to the Avignonese Pope to inform him of this, but he eventually went back on his promises, announcing that he could not voluntarily renounce the papacy. He created several new cardinals, who were anti-French, and anti-conciliarist.

These actions created a storm. Dissident cardinals from both camps set up a general council of the Church at Pisa. It began in 1409, and attracted a

Opposite: *In 1431 Aeneas Sylvius Piccolomini, the future Pope Pius II (1458-64) entered the service of the Bishop of Fermo and in his entourage went to the Council of Basle where he worked for other bishops and for Cardinal Albergata, one of the legates of Pope Eugenius IV. Later on in the history of the Council he became an active opponent of the Pope. Pinturicchio (c. 1454-1513) was employed towards the end of his life to paint ten scenes from the life of Pius II for the Piccolomini Library of the cathedral at Siena. This one shows the young Aeneas on a white horse in the foreground on his way to the Council of Basel.*

wide representation of churchmen and lay leaders. Both Popes were commanded to present themselves for judgement, and when they refused to do so both were deposed and a third one chosen. He soon died, however, poisoned, some believed, by his successor, the anti-pope John XXIII.

John XXIII was supported by Sigismund, King of the Romans, and as a price of his support Sigismund demanded that John confirm that another council would be called, to meet this time at Constance, in Sigismund's dominions. All three Popes were afraid they would be asked to resign, and John was forced to agree to do so, should those of Rome and Avignon do likewise. He made this offer at the beginning of March 1415. On the twentieth of the same month John organized in Constance a spectacular tournament for Sigismund and others attending the Council. Under cover of the confusion surrounding the affair he fled the city. On 6 April the Council of Constance passed a decree, known as usual from its opening words as *Haec Sancta*, declaring that the Council's power came directly from Christ, and was superior to that of the pope. In the light of this decree John XXIII, now a prisoner of Sigismund's, was deposed.

The 'Roman' Pope Gregory XII now agreed to recognize the authority of the Council, though he first of all had it reconvened in his own name. Having ensured his own future, and the future of all those whom he had appointed to office, he then resigned, to spend the last two years of his life as Cardinal Legate in Ancona. This left only the Pope of the Avignon obedience, Benedict XIII. He refused to abdicate, and was subsequently deposed. On 11 November 1417, after the former Gregory XII had died, the Council elected Cardinal Oddo Colonna as Pope Martin V.

The Great Schism was not yet entirely over. John XXIII had no successors, and died in 1419 after being reconciled to Martin, but Benedict XIII lived on in his great fortress of Peniscola until his death in 1423, when he was succeeded by Clement VIII. Six years later, however, Clement VIII was bribed to repudiate his claim, and a solemn conclave of his cardinals earnestly elected Oddo Colonna once again as Pope Martin V.

Despite the major role which the Colonna family had played in papal politics for half a millenium, Oddo was the only member to become pope. He was born at Genazzano in 1368, and like so many popes of the period had studied and then taught canon law. He had been employed by his patron Urban VI in the Roman courts, in diplomacy and as an administrator. In 1405 he became a cardinal deacon, and the following year was appointed archpriest of the Lateran basilica and vicar of Rome. After John Huss, the Bohemian religious reformer and disciple of John Wycliffe, had come to Constance – under a safe-conduct from Sigismund – Oddo played a major part in his trial and condemnation to death at the stake for heresy.

It was three years after his election before he could return to a devastated Rome. Martin V was the first Roman magnate to become Bishop of Rome since Boniface VIII, who had tried to destroy the Colonna fortunes. Martin began to rebuild them. He lived in one of his family's palaces while the damaged papal palaces and city churches were restored. He employed several Tuscan painters to decorate them, including the great Florentine artist, Masaccio.

The Council of Constance had been a reforming Council, and Martin set up a commission of three cardinals charged with implementing reforms in the Church. As the Council had requested, he made the College of Cardinals into a more internationally representative body, introduced new rules to guarantee his control over its members and to govern the details of their way of life and even of their dress.

He never accepted all that the Council had decided, in particular the decree *Haec Sancta*, but he took care not to alienate the conciliarist party too much. A month before he had been elected the Council had passed another decree, called *Frequens*, which laid down that there were to be further councils at regular intervals. Martin accepted its terms unwillingly, but

considered it unwise to reject it utterly. The first of the councils, at Pavia in 1423, met on time. The second was scheduled for Basel in 1431, but Martin died on 20 February that same year, before it could begin.

The cardinals who gathered in conclave in the church of Santa Maria Sopra Minerva agreed that whoever was elected was to have a free hand in reforming the Church, but could reform the papal Curia only with the consent of the college. Half of all papal revenue was to go to the cardinals. Cardinal Gabriel Condulmaro signed this agreement on 3 March. He was later to reconfirm it as Pope Eugenius IV on the day of his own coronation, 12 March 1431.

The date of Eugenius' birth is unknown, but it must have been about the year 1383. His father Angelo was a wealthy Venetian merchant, and the family had close links with the Church. One of Gabriel's uncles became Gregory XII, and his only sister – he had two brothers as well – married Nicholas Barbo and became the mother of Pope Paul II.

Though he began his ecclesiastical career early – he was a canon of Verona at 15 – he took his duties seriously. He lived in Verona for a while, but then went back to Venice to join a newly-founded religious order, the Canons Regular of Saint Augustine. He thoroughly enjoyed being a monk, but had little time to savour the pleasures of prayer and contemplation. Before he was 25 he had become Bishop of Siena, and the day Gregory XII's cardinals deserted him to go to Pisa, he was appointed to the College and put in charge of Ancona.

As Pope, Eugenius was immediately faced with a revolt by the Colonnas, who were afraid of once again losing their newly-recovered wealth. He had to hire mercenaries, and ally himself with the enemies of the Colonnas. All this required money, which Eugenius did not have. He attempted to raise taxes in Rome, and the people rose in revolt. The Pope had to flee the city, first to Pisa and then to Florence where, more by accident than design, he had a hand in bringing Cosimo de' Medici back to power and thus restoring stability and prosperity to the great banking and commercial centre of Italy.

Below: *The tomb in the basilica of Saint John Lateran of Pope Martin V (1417-31). It is attributed to the sculptor Isaia of Pisa, of whom very little is known. Isaia was working in Rome for Pope Pius II from 1462 to 1464. Pope Martin was a member of the Colonna family, and the family's emblem, a column, can be seen to the right of the picture, just above the papal tiara.*

At the time of Eugenius' arrival, Florence was the home of artists of genius. Masaccio had just died, but della Robbia and Donatello were at work, and so was Fra Angelico, whom Eugenius was later to summon to Rome to work in the Vatican. Ghiberti was designing the doors of the Baptistery, and he was engaged by Eugenius in later years to produce a sumptuous tiara, one of the few luxuries which the otherwise ascetical Pope permitted himself.

Eugenius moved on from Florence to Bologna, and then to Ferrara. The Council which the decree *Frequens* had demanded should meet at Basel was still in session, and, despite protests from a rump which remained behind, he managed to transfer it to Ferrara. So it was to Ferrara that the Emperor of Constantinople came in March 1438, looking for support from the West in his struggle against the Turks who by now were threatening the capital of the Eastern Empire. The Emperor was followed a few days later by the Patriarch, and after problems of protocol had been settled, leaders of East and West sat down to discuss reunion.

The debates dragged on for over a year, though plague and the Pope's financial difficulties forced the Council to move to Florence. On 5 July 1439 a Bull of Reunion was signed by the Emperor of Constantinople, by all the Greek bishops present save two, and then by Eugenius and the Latins.

Part of the agreement was that Eugenius should come to the aid of the Eastern Emperor, and encourage other European princes to do likewise. A papal fleet was sent into Byzantine waters, and an army was despatched, only to be defeated at Varna in 1444. Opposition to reunion had shown itself among the Greeks as soon as the negotiators had returned home, and the failure of the Western forces put an end to hopes. Union between Rome and Constantinople survived Eugenius' death in February 1447, but only just. No more was heard of the question of union after the fall of Constantinople to the Turks in 1453.

Eugenius had begun his ecclesiastical career as a member of a religious order, and he never forgot the fact. He lived modestly, even parsimoniously, partly from choice and partly because he was, for much of his reign, desperately short of money. But he was well able to appreciate beauty, and, as mentioned, brought Donatello, Fra Angelico and also Pisanello to Rome to improve the city and its churches. There was a great deal to be restored and rebuilt, and this he encouraged, but he forbade anyone to remove stones from the ancient pagan monuments in the city to help with the rebuilding, as had so often happened, thus preserving for future generations many of the fine works of an ancient – albeit pagan – past.

After his return to Rome in 1443 he brought his old religious order to the city to serve in the rebuilt Lateran basilica. He was active in the reform of the papal Curia, and of the lives of the clergy throughout the Church. He vigorously opposed clerical concubinage, and firmly refused all requests from princes to approve as bishops candidates who were below the approved age laid down in the canons.

Many of Eugenius' enterprises ended in failure. The agreement with the Greeks reached at Florence was followed by reunion with other Christian Churches of the East, but none of this endured. The Council of Ferrara-Florence, however, had established the principle that differences in 'rites' (the way the liturgy is performed) do not necessarily mean a difference in belief. It is a fundamental principle, yet Christians are only just coming to appreciate some of its implications.

For most of his reign, Eugenius' position seemed weak, yet he survived an attempt by the rump Council of Basel to depose him and elect the Duke of Savoy in his place. At Ferrara and Florence he managed to assert his authority over the Council, and the conciliarist movement faded away as a serious attempt to govern the Church.

The Renaissance papacy was about to replace the experiment with democracy within the Church, just as Renaissance princes in Italy had already replaced the experiment in communal government.

POPES OF THE RENAISSANCE

One of the unlooked-for consequences of the conciliar movement had been the growth of a consciousness of national identity. For administrative reasons, students at the medieval universities had long been grouped together as 'nations', though these units often bore only a distant relation to what would now be understood by the term. At the Council of Constance there were initially four nations: the French, the English, the Italian and the German; a fifth nation, the Spanish, was added later. To bring back the unity which the Church was seeking, major decisions had to be accepted by all five nations.

This was fine in theory. In practice, however, it was an implicit recognition that the universality to which both Church and Empire aspired was fast disappearing. Pope Martin V had given further impetus to the development of the idea of nationhood when he had agreed 'concordats' or treaties with individual rulers over the appointment of bishops and other ecclesiastical matters. So, too, had the changing function of papal nuncios; from being occasional ecclesiastical envoys they had become permanent resident ambassadors of the Holy See.

The nuncios represented the temporal power of the papacy as much as its spiritual authority, perhaps more so. The universal spiritual authority of the papacy was at a low ebb but, like other European rulers, the popes were committed to building up a well-financed, efficiently run and firmly controlled state. The splendour of the Renaissance papacy was a sign of its recovery of confidence within its own territorial domains. But as temporal princes, the popes had one great disadvantage. Their office was elective. No matter how dissolute his life, no pope ever presumed that one of his family could inherit his title in the way, for example, that the Habsburgs had made the title of Emperor their own. Popes could, and did, make their relatives cardinals, but they could not guarantee the succession. Instead, many Renaissance popes promoted family interests outside Rome, and none more so than Rodrigo de Borja as Pope Alexander VI.

The Borgias ('Borgia' is the Italianized form of the Spanish name) have a lurid reputation. It is not entirely undeserved, but some of its more colourful detail owes a great deal to the envy of the Romans at the undoubted success enjoyed, at least for a time, by Alexander VI and his children.

The Borgias began as modest aristocrats in the service of the court of Aragon. Rodrigo was born in 1431, the son of Jofre de Borja and Isabella. Isabella's brother Alonso became the compromise pope Callistus III in 1455 when the Colonnas and the Orsinis could not agree. Before becoming a cardinal, to which rank he had been promoted as a reward for speeding the departure of the anti-pope Clement VIII, Alonso had been Bishop of Valencia. His promotion meant that he went to Rome, leaving the episcopal

Opposite: *Pope Alexander VI and two of his illegitimate children – a hostile portrayal of the Borgia family by the nineteenth-century painter Dante Gabriel Rossetti. The Pope and his son Cesare are whispering to the lovely Lucretia Borgia, who was used by them to further the family's ambitions.*

Right: *A portrait of the second Borgia Pope, Alexander VI (1492-1503). He was endowed with remarkable gifts, highly intelligent, boundlessly energetic, enormously ambitious, and utterly unscrupulous. From 1456, when he was created a cardinal by his uncle, Pope Callistus III, he set about amassing riches, and built up the Borgia family fortunes at the expense, in particular of the two great Roman families, the Orsinis and the Colonnas.*

palace in Valencia empty. After his father's death, therefore, Rodrigo moved into the palace from the family home in Jativa.

Rodrigo began his studies in Valencia, and then, in about 1449, he went to Rome and on to Bologna to study law. In 1456 his uncle Pope Callistus made him a cardinal, and sent him to pacify the March province of Ancona, which task he performed with remarkable skill. On his triumphant return to Rome the grateful Pope made him Vice-Chancellor of the Church, and Commander-in-Chief of the papal armies.

He now began to accumulate enormous wealth. He was endowed with Spanish bishoprics, Italian abbeys, and benefices in and around Rome. They were not gathered indiscriminately. Rodrigo so contrived his endowments that they gave him command of the routes into the city of Rome and control over much of the Roman Campagna, the traditional haunt of the Colonnas and the Orsinis.

These acquisitions brought him a large income, but most of this he spent, building in Rome the most splendid palace of the day in the whole of the Italian peninsula. In 1472 he departed in great style for Spain to pave the way for the marriage between Ferdinand and Isabella, and thus bring about a united kingdom of Castile and Aragon. On his return to Italy he engaged once again in a frenzy of building activity – a palace in Pienza (now the Palazzo Vescovile), fortifications at Subiaco, a carved high altar for the church of Santa Maria del Popolo in Rome. His mistress Vanozza commissioned frescoes for one of the side chapels in the same church.

Vanozza de' Cataneis was already 31 years old when she and Rodrigo became lovers. She was a woman of outstanding beauty, intelligence and business sense, and was the proprietor of three hotels in the city of Rome. She was married three times in all: once before, once during, and once after her relationship with Cardinal Borgia. The future Pope had four children by her, but he had already had three other illegitimate offspring. In all, he was to father ten illegitimate children by four mistresses, although the name of only one mistress other than Vanozza is known: Giulia 'la Bella' Farnese. Giulia had married Orsino Orsini in 1489 when she was 19. The ceremony had taken place in the Borgia Palace, and she became Rodrigo's mistress shortly before his election to the papacy in August 1492.

The choice of Rodrigo as Pope was a surprising one, and there were soon to be accusations that he had bought the papacy. But it seems unlikely that there was any direct bribery. It would not have been necessary. No one attending the five-day conclave could have been unaware that in divesting himself of the Vice-Chancellorship of the Church, and of his many lucrative benefices, the new Pope would have much to give away to those whom he favoured.

In any case, in 1492 he presented quite a different image to the one by which he is remembered. There was no reason to think then that he would openly flaunt a young mistress in the Vatican palace, nor leave papal administration in the charge of an illegitimate daughter while on a tour of inspection of newly-conquered territories. It is true that stories about his way of life had been circulating in Rome long before his elevation. In 1460, for example, he was reproved by Pius II for a party he had given in Siena. Pius had heard that ladies had been invited with instructions to leave husbands or brothers behind. 'We leave it to you to judge,' wrote the Pope, 'if it is becoming in one of your position to toy with girls, to pelt them with fruits . . . and, neglecting study, to spend the whole day in every kind of pleasure.' But it soon became clear that the stories had been exaggerated, and only a few days later the Pope was writing to apologize.

Although Rodrigo was renowned for the ostentation of his public life – during processions he would cover the streets with tapestries, and fill them with flowers – in private he was frugal to the point of being parsimonious. In later days, cardinals might avoid dining with him for fear of being poisoned, but earlier it had been the quality of the food set before them that they feared.

Alexander VI was reported to have seized hold of the papacy with an almost childlike enthusiasm. His coronation was so grand an affair that it proved too much even for him. He fainted twice. He lost no time in promoting the interests of his family. Cesare Borgia, his son by Vanozza, was made a cardinal together with Alessandro Farnese, the brother of Giulia 'la Bella'. Cesare was only 18 at the time. Lucrezia, another of Vanozza's children, was married to Giovanni Sforza, Lord of Pesaro, in a splendid Vatican ceremony. Alexander's favourite son Juan, who had inherited the Duchy of Gandia from his half-brother in 1488, was married to the cousin of the King of Castile, and to promote the interests of the dukes of Gandia in the curious division of the world into 'spheres of influence' that Alexander was called upon to make, he gave the greater share to Spain, to the detriment of Portugal. (The fourth Duke of Gandia—Rodrigo's great-grandson, Francisco de Borja—became a member of the Society of Jesus and eventually head of the Order. His canonization has somewhat redressed the balance of the Borgia reputation.)

Apart from the choice of Cesare, the first group of cardinals was on the whole impressive, and they represented all the major states. This internationalizing of the Curia annoyed the Italian contingent. Cardinal Giuliano della Rovere, Alexander's chief opponent in the conclave, had already fled and now others joined him in support of Charles VIII of France who was pursuing a claim to the throne of Naples. Charles captured Rome in December 1494 on his way south through Italy, and passed through it again on his way back to France. But it was a Pyrrhic victory; it left him weakened and his cardinal supporters exposed. The Pope determined to tame them.

The Sforza Lord of Pesaro was now of no help to Alexander in his plans, and Lucrezia was bored by life in a provincial town. She was therefore granted a divorce on the grounds that her marriage had never been consummated (a charge which her husband at first indignantly denied), and married to the illegitimate son of the King of Naples. Cesare renounced the cardinalate and married a sister of the King of Navarre. The new King of France asked the Pope for permission to divorce his wife to marry Anne of Brittany. This was granted, and in return the King promised to help the Borgias in their plan to subdue the Roman nobility. The only proviso made was that Cesare should first help the French to recover Milan, and this part of the bargain was rapidly fulfilled. The French troops were now at the disposal of the Borgias.

Cesare was the model for Machiavelli's *The Prince*. He was remarkably handsome, intelligent and charming, if utterly unscrupulous. He was also a brilliant general and a perspicacious administrator. The papal 'vicars' who ruled the Papal States in the name of the papacy, but who more often than not behaved as princes in their own right, were excommunicated by Alexander and then swiftly put to flight by his son. The Romagna was so united under Cesare that it seemed it might survive as a duchy in his charge even after the death of Pope Alexander. So strong were the Borgias that Colonna lands could be seized, and Orsinis put in prison. But the d'Estes of Ferrara were another matter. They could only be won by marriage.

Two hundred thousand people crowded into Saint Peter's Square to receive the Pope's Easter blessing in the Jubilee Year of 1500. In July the Pope's son-in-law, Lucrezia's husband, was attacked on the steps of Saint Peter's. He was carried half dead to a room in the Vatican where he was cared for by Lucrezia until, in August, one of Cesare's lieutenants broke in and strangled him. Lucrezia was now free to marry again, and was betrothed to Alfonso d'Este, heir to the Dukedom of Ferarra. She married him by proxy at the end of December 1501, and went to live with him early the following year. On the Halloween before she left, Cesare gave a farewell party for her. Fifty courtesans were invited. They danced naked with the servants, picked up chestnuts from the floor with their teeth, and were competed for by the men present. It was a scene well in keeping with the Borgia legend, but there is nothing to suggest that it was typical. Indeed, Lucrezia did little to merit the horrendous reputation with which she has been saddled. She was a dutiful daughter to her mother in later years, and to her father in his diplomatic entanglements. She was an affectionate sister, an attentive wife to at least two of her three husbands, and a tender nurse, it seems, to her second husband, for whom she genuinely grieved. In Rome she lived under the shadow of her father and her brother. In Ferarra she could live her own life. She seems to have had an affair or two, indulged her passion for singing and dancing, looked after the Duchy in the absences of her husband, and spent the final years of her life in decent piety. In other circumstances one might have said she was a credit to her father.

The Borgias were a close-knit family. Being Spanish, they were perhaps too demonstratively affectionate towards each other to suit the Italian taste of the day. When Juan, the second Duke of Gandia, was stabbed nine times and his body thrown into the Tiber, his father was deeply affected. He would have given seven papacies, he said, to have Juan restored to him, and looked

CAES·BORGIA·VALENTIN

upon his son's death as a judgement by God upon his own life. He even went so far as setting up a commission to look into the whole question of Church reform. The commission reported that a general council was needed, and that doomed it to failure. With memories of Constance, Basel and Florence still so recent, no fifteenth-century pope could look with equanimity upon the possibility of another outbreak of conciliarism.

Alexander lavished much of the wealth he amassed upon his children. He put a good deal of what remained to practical use. He fortified Castel Sant' Angelo to withstand a three-year siege, and other Borgia castles outside Rome received similar treatment. At the Vatican he added the medieval Torre Borgiana, and a fountain in Saint Peter's Square. The bull motif of the Borgias can still be seen on the new ceiling he added to Santa Maria Maggiore, gilded with the first of the plunder to arrive from the Americas. The Vatican's 'Borgia apartments' he had painted by Pinturicchio, and the way was cleared for the Via Alessandrini, which cut through from the river up to the Vatican palace.

Popes did not usually baptize their own children or officiate at their marriages, and no one could claim that Alexander VI, who did such things, was an admirable man. But neither was he as bad as legend has made him out. Only two of the cardinals who elected him were non-Italian, and much of the antipathy to the Borgias sprang from their Spanish origin. It is not surprising then that for his own safety he should advance so many of his own family, and put Spaniards in charge of the newly conquered territories of the Romagna. Of course, such actions only added to his unpopularity with the Italians, and they were ready to put the worst possible interpretation on his death in August 1503. A week earlier he had been at a supper party with Cesare, who was also taken ill. Rumours rapidly spread that either the two Borgias chose the same occasion to attempt to poison each other, or that Cesare had poisoned his father and taken a little himself to escape suspicion. The truth is probably quite simple: it was a sultry summer in Rome, both Borgias were struck down by fever, and the younger man survived.

Cesare's illness prevented him from being in a position to ensure the election of another Spaniard as Bishop of Rome, although he was able to seize what remained of his father's wealth. Pius III, the Pope who succeeded Alexander, lasted less than a month. He in turn was succeeded by the arch-enemy of the Borgias, Cardinal Giuliano della Rovere, who took the name Julius II. Cesare was arrested, and won his freedom only by agreeing to surrender his control over the Romagna, after which he fled Rome. He died in 1507, fighting for his brother-in-law in an obscure battle in Spain.

The new Pope had been born in 1443. His father, Raffaello, was a brother of Pope Sixtus IV who had been General of the Franciscans, and Giuliano had studied with the Franciscans in Perugia. When his uncle became Pope in 1471 Giuliano was made Bishop of Carpentras. He went on to acquire seven more bishoprics, one archbishopric (that of Avignon) and a multitude of other benefices. He served as legate in France for two years, and shortly after Alexander VI's election he fled to the court of Charles VIII. There was a short reconciliation with the Borgias, during which he helped to arrange Cesare's marriage, but then Cesare attacked the Duchy of Urbino. Giuliano's nephew was in line of succession to it and so the Cardinal thought it politic to flee to France once more.

In the confusion which followed Alexander's death the papal territories tried to escape from the strong, though largely benign, rule Cesare had imposed on them. Julius determined to win them back. The Emperor Maximilian and the French helped him to recover Faenza and Rimini from the Venetians, but fearing French ambitions in Italy he then turned on them and their main Italian ally, Ferarra. Julius enjoyed the excitement of war. He led his own army out of Rome, and during the siege of Mirandola he grew

impatient when a small breach had been made in the walls. He drew his sword and scrambled through at the head of his soldiers.

But then came disaster. In April 1512 the papal army under the command of Cardinal Giovanni de' Medici was defeated by the French at Ravenna. The defeat put Rome itself in jeopardy, and Julius was on the point of flight when news came from Giovanni de' Medici through his cousin Giulio that French losses were enormous, and included their young and brilliant commander. In Giovanni de' Medici's opinion, which proved to be correct, the French would be unable to take advantage of their victory. Julius took heart, and after Giovanni had made his escape from his French captors the grateful Pope helped him to win back Florence, which had risen against the Medici family in 1494.

Julius was the most martial of popes. But he was also a patron of the arts and the inspiration of Renaissance Rome. In April 1506 he laid the foundation stone of the new Saint Peter's. 'Noble edifices', Pope Nicholas V is reported to have said in a remarkably lucid deathbed speech in 1455, 'combining taste and beauty with imposing proportions would be immensely conducive to the exaltation of the chair of Saint Peter'. There was little left of taste, beauty, or imposing proportion in the rickety basilica of old Saint Peter's. Julius went ahead with demolition, and Bramante was employed for the building which was to rise in its place.

Until Bramante's time, architectural style in Rome had been largely determined by the classical models to be seen in the ancient ruins of the city.

Above: *A bull surrounded by sheaves of wheat is the emblem of the Borgia family. It figures largely in the decorations of the apartments built by Alexander VI in the Vatican, a detail from which is shown here. The Borgia Apartments were painted by Pinturicchio, and in a curious amalgam of pagan and Christian motifs the Borgia bull is related to the Apis bull, sacred to the ancient Egyptians.*

Now Rome was to have a new style, one that was to fit the taste, and the pretensions, of the Renaissance papacy. The project lasted a century and cost Julius and his successors a million and a half ducats, but it set the tone for the whole of the new Rome.

It seems quite likely that in Julius' mind the basilica was simply the setting for his own tomb, and for this he employed Michelangelo. The enterprise was never completed, however, and only the statue of Moses remains as an indication of the magnificence that was intended. Michelangelo was also put to work designing the uniform for the Swiss Guard – still worn today – which Julius was busy organizing, and completing the painting of the Sistine Chapel, which was already resplendent with the work of Boticelli, Ghirlandaio and Roselli.

The renewed vigour of the papacy, and its links with the past, was to be celebrated by Raphael's frescoes in the Vatican palace. In the Stanza d'Eliodoro the frescoes are allegories of the events of Julius' pontificate. One shows Attila before the gates of Rome, a reminder of the delivery of the papacy from the threat of the French after the disaster at Ravenna. The same theme of delivery recurs in the picture of Saint Peter being freed from his chains – the significance being that Julius had been Cardinal-Priest of San Pietro in Vinculo, which translates as 'Saint Peter in Chains'. The papal pretensions were given visible expression in a way in which they had not been since the reigns of the first Leo and the third Sixtus over a thousand years before.

Such an assertion of papal power, whether in Rome itself or in the Papal States, was welcome neither to the cardinals nor to the Roman nobility. In 1511 Julius was faced with a revolt by the Roman barons, and the defection of many of the cardinals to the side of the French. The dissident cardinals and the French summoned a reforming council. Julius responded with his own Lateran Council, the fifth of that name, which began in 1512. The Council was a political move, a successful bid to undercut the French initiative, for Julius had little interest in Church reform as such. He issued bulls forbidding an appeal to a council against the Pope, and made a brief, but significant, incursion into English history by granting Prince Henry (Tudor) a dispensation in order to marry Catherine of Aragon, the young widow of his deceased brother Arthur.

Julius bequeathed the consequences of the Lateran Council to his successor, for he died in Rome in February 1513. The man chosen to follow Julius as Bishop of Rome was the commander of the papal troops at the battle of Ravenna, Cardinal Giovanni de' Medici.

He had been born in 1475, the son of Lorenzo the Magnificent. Shortly before his birth, Lorenzo's wife, Clarice Orsini, had dreamed she was giving birth in Florence Cathedral to a large but docile lion. Florence was the foremost city of the Renaissance, and the Medicis its leading family. As a child, Giovanni had about him men of the calibre of Marsilio Ficino who had translated the whole of Plato into Latin for Cosimo de' Medici.

At the age of 13 Giovanni became the youngest cardinal ever, at the instigation of his father, though the embarrassed Pope insisted that his elevation be kept secret for three years. Those three years he spent at Pisa studying theology and law. In 1492 he went to Rome, taking with him a letter from his father written to him as a warning against the corruption of the papal city. Lorenzo had every reason for his jaundiced view. During Mass in the Cathedral in Florence one day in 1478, there was an attempt on the life of Lorenzo and his brother; it happened while the Host was being elevated. Lorenzo survived, his brother did not, and the man behind the conspiracy turned out to be Pope Sixtus IV. Despite his distrust, Lorenzo decided he would have to keep a closer watch on events in Rome, and so despatched his son. Cardinal Giovanni tried at first to remain on friendly terms with everyone, but the intrigue proved too much for him to bear. He moved back to Florence.

Above: *In the later Middle Ages Swiss mercenary soldiers served many rulers. Early in the sixteenth century Pope Julius II organized them into a special papal army, and Michaelangelo designed a uniform for them. Though they now play a purely ceremonial role, the Swiss Guard still exist. They come from the canton of Lucerne, which makes an exception in favour of the Vatican to the law that its citizens may not fight for foreign countries.*

Above: *The Dominican friar
Girolamo Savonarola (1452-98)
was a preacher of great power. His
influence upon the people of Florence
between 1490 and 1494 helped to
bring about the expulsion of the
Medicis from that city, after the
family had dominated it for 60
years. But his political entanglements hastened his own downfall,
and he was hanged.*

But Florence was no longer a safe place for the Medicis. They fled
before the advancing army of Charles VIII, leaving the French King
and Savonarola, the fiery Dominican reformer, in control of the city.
Savonarola's powerful words accused Alexander VI, with some reason, of
simony, lechery and nepotism. To the Pope this sounded dangerously like
the charges he was hearing from Cardinal Giuliano della Rovere in the
French camp, and he excommunicted Savonarola. The crowd was fickle. It
turned against the friar, and he died at the stake.

This did not reopen the gates of Florence to the Medicis. Giovanni and
his cousin Giulio travelled abroad, disguised as mendicant friars, and only
after their return and offer of service in the armies of Julius II, did the Pope
help them to win back their native city in a bloody campaign.

Giovanni de' Medici had not seemed a likely candidate in the conclave
of 1513. Indeed, at one point he seemed about to die, and his possible early
demise may have persuaded his rivals to give way. He took the name Leo X.
The coronation on 19 March was a somewhat shabby affair, but the procession to Saint John Lateran, which he postponed for almost a month, was
particularly grand. 'God has given us the papacy', he is reported to have
said, 'let us enjoy it.'

He pursued a far more peaceable career than had his predecessor, but
otherwise his achievements built on, and strengthened, many of those of
Julius II. The Lateran Council remained in being until 1517, though in
terms of reform its achievements were small. Leo's sympathies lay more
with the artistic inheritance bequeathed to him. He favoured Michelangelo
in particular, and sent him off to Florence to beautify the family church –
which is why Julius' tomb remained unfinished. In Raphael's picture of
Attila at the gates of Rome, originally undertaken at the instigation of
Julius, it is Leo's portrait, rather than that of his predecessor, which appears.
Leonardo da Vinci, who had served as a military engineer to the Borgias,
was invited to Rome but by this time he was a very old man.

Erasmus dedicated his translation of the New Testament to Leo, and in his
'School of Athens', glorifying Greek philosophy, Raphael was paying a grace-
ful tribute to a man who had been brought up in a humanist household.
Indeed, Leo was much more a patron of learning than Pope Julius who had
used the funds of the University of Rome to finance his wars. He hired dozens
of new professors, created new faculties, encouraged the study of Greek and
set up a press for printing Greek. To that extent he had much more in common
with Alexander VI, also a patron of learning, than with Julius. But, like
Alexander, he also dedicated himself to the promotion of his family. He
succeeded in making Medicis into dukes of Florence, of Urbino and, ultimately, granddukes of Tuscany. His grandniece, Catherine de' Medici,
married a man destined to become King of France. His dynastic ambitions
provoked a plot against his life in 1517, led by a cardinal whose brother had
been deposed at Siena in favour of the Medicis. The plot was discovered, the
ringleader strangled, and the two other cardinals who had joined him fined.
Part of the reason for the cardinals' disaffection may have been Leo's
creation of eight new members of the College. Together with all the other
electors in the conclave of 1513 he had promised not to appoint any cardinals,
and had gone back on his word. After the plot, however, he went on to
create 31 more, all of them supporters of the Medicis. He was doing his
best to ensure that Medici family interests would be served by any future
papacy, as well as in the dukedoms of Italy.

The conspiracy no doubt occupied much of his attention in 1517, but
events in Wittenberg that same year, news of which slowly reached him,
were ultimately to affect the Church deeply and to divide it more decisively
than had the Great Schism of the fourteenth century. Whatever lay behind
the movement which has come to be known as the Protestant Reformation,
the events which precipitated it had begun in 1507 and reached their climax
a decade later.

In 1507 Pope Julius II had granted a plenary indulgence to help to pay for the rebuilding of Saint Peter's. This grant was renewed by Pope Leo, and trade in indulgences had been stepped up to offset the costs of the war in which the Medicis captured Urbino. The plenary indulgence for the rebuilding of Saint Peter's had not been preached in that part of Germany where Martin Luther, a very able young professor at the University of Wittenberg, was working. This was partly because the Elector of Saxony had a remarkable collection of relics in his castle at Wittenberg and did not want competition, Leo having approved in 1516 the granting of an indulgence to anyone who, for a small fee, visited the Elector's display. Wittenberg was under the jurisdiction of Archbishop Albrecht of Mainz, and he had eventually prevailed upon the Pope to allow the plenary indulgence to be preached in his province. He needed money, and would get half the proceeds. A Dominican preacher was appointed in January 1517.

The theory behind indulgences was, and still remains, confused. The basic understanding is that an indulgence is a remission of the penance imposed by the Church for some serious sin which has been confessed and forgiven. When Martin Luther wrote to Archbishop Albrecht on the last day of October 1517 he already had his doubts about the whole idea of indulgences, but he restricted his criticisms to the traffic in them. Only when the Archbishop failed to reply did Luther publish his *Ninety-five Theses* (a 'thesis' is a statement of position), marking the start of the Protestant Reformation.

Below: *Savonarola, the Dominican friar and reformer condemned to death under Alexander VI, was executed in Florence in 1497. This anonymous painting illustrates three episodes from the execution: sentence being passed on him and two supporters; the condemned men being led to the gibbet; their execution by hanging. The fire beneath them was to consume their bodies after death.*

Albrecht complained to Rome. There was little to upset the Pope in Luther's theses, but his explanations revealed strong doubts about papal primacy. Joachim di Fiore's prophecies had first been printed in 1515 in a book dedicated to Giulio de' Medici. He had foreseen the coming of Antichrist. Now Luther began to wonder if the Pope was Antichrist. On 15 June 1520 the bull *Exsurge Domine* called upon him to recant within 60 days. In the same month Luther published *On the Papacy at Rome*, arguing that the Pope was only a symbolic figure of unity and that the true Church was invisible, being the community of all believers. At the Diet of Worms, presided over by the new Emperor Charles V in 1521, Luther stood firm and refused to recant anything he had written. The Protestant Reformation had truly begun.

On his way back from the Diet of Worms, Luther was seized and imprisoned by the Elector of Saxony. Immured in the castle of Wartburg and with only Erasmus' Greek and a Hebrew Bible, he translated the New Testament into German in 10 weeks.

Pope Leo entirely misunderstood the nature of the crisis with which he was faced. He underestimated the strength of Luther's beliefs, seeing in them simply a quarrel between the Augustinian Order, to which Luther belonged, and the Dominicans who were preaching the indulgence. He also underestimated the hostile feelings aroused in Germany by the extra taxes he was trying to raise for a crusade against the Turks. The German princes believed that too much money was already in the hands of the Church, or was travelling to Rome in the form of bribes. They saw the papacy as very much a secular power, and some of them were ready to oppose it.

Leo's patronage of the arts and learning, his carnivals, the elaborate hunting expeditions of which he was so fond, all plunged the papacy deeper and deeper into debt. When he died on 30 November 1521, banks failed, businesses closed down, and the artistic community fled from Rome. The cardinals chose a saintly man as his successor, rather than someone of noble birth. The ascetical Adrian of Utrecht became Pope Hadrian VI and was the last non-Italian to be elected until 1978; he was also the only Dutch pope. But within two short years Hadrian had died, and the cardinals were once again in conclave.

Although more than half the electors at the conclave of 1521 had been appointed by Leo, it was not until 18 November 1523 that they chose the man he had intended should follow him – his cousin Giulio de' Medici.

Giulio was the illegitimate son of the Giuliano de' Medici who had been assassinated in Florence Cathedral at the instigation of Pope Sixtus IV. Lorenzo had brought up his nephew as his own son, and destined him for a military career, enrolling him in the Knights of Rhodes. Giulio had, however, expressed a preference for the life of an ecclesiastic, and attached himself to his cousin Giovanni. But Giulio had still not made up his mind by the time of Giovanni's election as Leo X: he rode in the procession as a Knight of Rhodes, although shortly afterwards he opted finally for the Church. This decision posed a problem. His illegitimacy effectively barred him from advancement in the Church. At first Leo simply dispensed him from the impediment, but when that caused offence he set up a commission to examine the question. Not surprisingly, the commission decided that his father had been married to his mother, and so there was no problem. Thus Cardinal Giulio de' Medici could take up his new post as Archbishop of Florence with a quiet mind.

When Lorenzo, the last of the legitimate Medicis, died in 1519 Giulio was sent to look after the city of Florence. He commissioned a memorial for the dead man, who had despised him, and for his own father. Michelangelo was employed to build a magnificent tomb. The latter was never finished, but the sculptor's portrayal of the dead Lorenzo de' Medici, which is commonly known as 'Il Pensoroso' (The Thinker) from the pose of the

subject, must surely be one of the most frequently reproduced works of art.

Giulio, who took the name Clement VII at his election, was perhaps even more of a connoisseur than his cousin had been. Leo could sit for hours listening to music, contemplating the tapestries from Flanders and the painting of Michelangelo with which he had adorned the Sistine Chapel. Clement was less flamboyant, but could just as readily appreciate the exquisite jewellery of Benvenuto Cellini as the grandeur of Michelangelo's statuary, or the design for the Last Judgement scene for the back wall of the Sistine Chapel, one of the last things he commissioned. His favourite artist, Giuliano Romano, was engaged to decorate the Vatican apartments. The theme he was given was the life of the Emperor Constantine. In 'The baptism of Constantine' Clement is portrayed in the guise of Pope Sylvester. It was another assertion of the outdated papal ideology.

Clement had been elected for his supposed political skill. It was thought that he was too adroit to be manipulated by anyone. But dynastic interests dictated that he take the side of Francis I of France. This was a mistake. Francis was defeated at the Battle of Pavia in February 1525 by the Emperor Charles V. Clement's response was to put together a league of the defeated French, the English who were too far away to be effective, and those Italian states who felt themselves threatened by the power of Charles (as Emperor, Charles V already ruled Austria, Spain and the Netherlands, and he had a claim on Naples). This league was another mistake.

In September 1526 Cardinal Pompeo Colonna, of the pro-Imperial party, invaded Rome. Clement had to flee to the safety of Castel Sant' Angelo while Colonna troops pillaged the papal palace. The price of his freedom was secession from the league he had set up. But scarcely was he free than papal troops retaliated against Colonna strongholds, and the Colonnas themselves were stripped of all titles.

That was Clement's third political mistake. The following year Colonna soldiers and German troops, many of them Lutherans, together with a Spanish contingent, marched on Rome. On 6 May 1527 the city was captured and Clement had to flee along the corridor which Alexander VI had prudently constructed between the papal apartments and Castel Sant' Angelo. From the windows the Pope could see members of the 40,000-strong army butchering clergy and laity alike, and the following day Rome was so ruthlessly sacked that even Cardinal Colonna suffered remorse. Charles V ordered mourning, and the Pope grew a beard as a sign of his grief. Clement's bitterness was complete when he heard that Florence had once again declared itself a Republic.

He fled disguised as a gardener to Orvieto, and it was there that the English envoys found him when they came to seek an annulment of King Henry VIII's marriage to Catherine of Aragon. Clement temporized, giving the English King's emissaries the impression that he would be prepared to grant what they asked, provided that he could obtain freedom of action. But the Pope had little alternative but to come to terms with Charles V, and as the Emperor was Catherine of Aragon's nephew there was no likelihood of the annulment being granted.

In the Summer of 1529 Clement allied himself with the Emperor and with Francis I of France to bring the newly proclaimed Republic of Florence back under Medici control. It fell to the papal army in August 1530 after a ten-month siege, and a year later Alessandro de' Medici was proclaimed Duke. In December 1532 Clement and Charles met at Bologna where, nearly three years before, Clement had crowned the victorious Charles as Emperor. A marriage between the Emperor's natural daughter, Margaret of Austria, and Alessandro de' Medici had already been arranged; now the Pope wanted approval for a marriage between Catherine de' Medici and Henri de Valois, Duke of Orleans. This was given, and the Pope travelled to France to perform the service in October 1533. It was the highpoint of

Medici dynastic ambition. Much had been sacrificed to this ambition, including the allegiance of England to the Bishop of Rome.

The Emperor was demanding a price for his support of Clement. Lutheranism was by now widespread in Germany. It had become a political issue because some princes adopted it and others rejected it. Charles was convinced that there was no way of overcoming the disunity within his Empire except by a council of the Church to initiate the reforms the Protestants were demanding. The cardinals had had a brief taste of what reform might mean under the short pontificate of Hadrian VI, and they did not like it, but by now Clement had no choice. It was over a decade, however, before the council could meet.

Clement was never to see it. After a protracted illness he died on 25 September 1534, at the comparatively early age of 57. His remains, and those of his cousin Leo X, were laid to rest in the church of Santa Maria Sopra Minerva. He died hated by the people of Rome. They never forgave him for the sack of 1527.

Left: *Perhaps the best-known portrait of Martin Luther. It was painted by Lucas Cranach (1472-1553) who came to live in Wittenberg in 1505, three years before Luther was appointed to a lectureship in the university there. Cranach's portraits have helped to form our image of Luther's circle of friends.*

THE REFORM
OF THE
CHURCH

When Alessandro Farnese was elected Pope Paul III on 13 October 1534 he was 66 years of age, and the last surviving cardinal of those created by Alexander VI. Had his predecessors Clement VII and Leo X still been alive, he would have been ten years older than Clement and seven years older than Leo. He therefore belonged to the same generation of Renaissance popes. He was perhaps even more in love with the spirit of ancient Roman culture than his immediate predecessors – at least, with that spirit as he conceived it.

He rebuilt the ancient Roman Capitol, the Campidoglio. That was a sign not only of his respect for Roman civilization, but was also a symbol of the complete dominance which the papacy had achieved over the life and culture of sixteenth-century Rome. He revised the city's street plan, he strengthened its defences against both the Turks and the Imperial armies, for the Emperor Charles V delighted in alarming papal officials with talk of another sack. But the fame that Pope Paul III was to achieve owed most to his success in bringing together a council to reform the Church.

That the Church was in dire need of reform was recognized by most of the Renaissance popes. Even Alexander VI had had his reform commission. Julius II had summoned the Lateran Council, Leo X had kept it in being, and Clement VII, admittedly under pressure from the Emperor, had been persuaded of the need to call the Church together to discuss the challenge presented by Luther. Paul III, however, managed to get under way one of the most important general councils in the whole history of the Church. That it met only towards the very end of his pontificate, and that it had to be suspended before he died, was no fault of his.

He had been born on 29 February 1468 at Canino. His family owned extensive lands around the shore of Lake Bolsena, not far north of Rome, and had played a major role in Italian history since the twelfth century. He began his education in Rome and continued it in Florence as a member of the Medici household, where he began to develop a close friendship with Giovanni de' Medici, the future Leo X.

He was elevated to the College of Cardinals in 1493, at the same time as Cesare Borgia, with the title of Cardinal-Deacon of Saints Cosmas and Damian. Because he owed his appointment to his sister Giulia 'la Bella' he was unkindly known as 'Cardinal Petticoat'. His morals were no better than those of some of his more notorious contemporaries, and he fathered four illegitimate children, though two were later to be declared legitimate by Julius II. He particularly doted on one of his children, Pierluigi. He became Duke of Parma, Piacenza and Castero, married Girolama Orsini, and was assassinated, to his father's great grief, in 1547. Paul's daughter Constanza married Boso II of the house of Sforza, and shortly after his election the Pope was

Opposite: *Paul III (1534-49), the pope who approved the founding of the Society of Jesus (1540) and summoned the great reforming Council of Trent in 1545. A great patron of the arts, he employed Michelangelo as architect, painter and sculptor at Saint Peter's, and in the Vatican.*

able to raise two grandsons, Alessandro Farnese and Ascania Sforza, to the rank of cardinal: Alessandro was 14 at the time, his cousin just two years older. Paul was later to bestow the same honour on another of Pierluigi's sons when the boy was only 15. Paul's nepotism was well in the tradition of the Renaissance papacy.

Paul III had delayed becoming a priest until 1519, but from then onwards his moral life improved considerably. He expected to become pope after the death of Leo X, and again at the death of Hadrian VI. The choice of Clement VII particularly rankled. Clement, he was later to say, had robbed him of ten years of his papacy. Despite these disappointments he remained loyal to the Medicis, even when Pierluigi went over to the Imperial camp and took part in the sack of Rome.

Very soon after his election Paul III made it clear to the College of Cardinals that he was utterly convinced of the need to summon a council. The cardinals opposed the idea: such a council would be bound to threaten their vested interests. The Pope's response was to create a new group of cardinals who were in favour of reform. Two were Englishmen: John Fisher, Bishop of Rochester, and Reginald Pole. King Henry VIII executed the first a month after his appointment, and because Pole himself was out of Henry's reach at the time, executed the new cardinal's eighty-year-old mother instead. The Pope immediately excommunicated the English King, and put the whole country under an interdict.

Pole himself was an extremely devout man. At Viterbo, where he lived, he gathered a group of like-minded people around him whose concern for the reform of the Church, allied to the pursuit of their own sanctity, had just a suspicion of heresy about it. Despite this, Paul III chose him as one of the commission of cardinals who were to examine the state of the Church and suggest reforms. The commission reported in 1538, and its findings provided much of the agenda for the Council that was eventually to meet at Trent. Pole was appointed one of the Council's presidents.

Luther had called for a council as early as 1518, and two years later urged the German princes to take matters into their own hands if the Pope would not act. This resulted in the Diet of Nuremberg, during which a representative of Pope Hadrian VI read out a declaration of the culpability of the Roman Curia for the parlous state of the Church, but the Diet still went on to demand a council free of papal interference, consisting of Protestants as well as Catholics and laymen as well as clergy, which would meet on German soil.

Such terms were unacceptable in Rome. Clement VII was eventually browbeaten into agreeing to a council, and Paul III summoned it, but he wanted it to gather, not in Germany, but in Mantua. As far as the warring monarchs of Europe were concerned, this was neutral ground. The Pope had little reason to ally himself either with the Emperor Charles, who had an alliance with the Protestant princes of Germany, or with Charles' arch-enemy Francis I of France, who was in league with the Ottoman Turks. The Turks had invaded Italy in 1537 hoping, vainly as it turned out, for support for their invasion from French troops in the north.

The Pope's policy was to persuade Charles to take up arms against the Protestant princes and to encourage Francis to oppose the French Calvinists, or Huguenots as they were called. Charles despised the Pope. He could not understand the neutral role which Paul was trying to play. The Emperor agreed, however, to a marriage between the Pope's grandson, Ottaviano Farnese and his daughter Margaret of Austria, recently widowed by the murder of her husband Alessandro de' Medici. Paul wanted the Emperor to bestow Milan on Ottaviano, but that failed because the Pope gave Parma and Piacenza, to which Charles had a claim, to his beloved son, Pierluigi. This was no way for the Pope to win the Emperor's support for papal plans for the council. Once again, a pope's dynastic ambitions had interfered with the interests of the Church.

Neither Charles nor Francis was prepared to let their clergy go to a council at Mantua. Paul's alternative choice of Vicenza was equally unacceptable, so he made some effort to reform the Church without going to the lengths of a full-scale meeting. There were attempts made in Germany to reconcile Catholics and Protestants, but they came to nothing because neither Paul nor Luther would accept the compromises proposed. Charles lost patience with the delay, and appeared to be about to call a national synod of the German Church over which Paul would have had no control at all. The Pope was also alarmed because Lutheranism seemed at last to be making some progress in Italy, so he eventually gave in to the Emperor's demand that the proposed council should meet on Imperial soil. The place chosen was Trent, the modern Trento, in northern Italy.

Trent was acceptable to the Germans because it was just within the boundaries of the Empire, but it was also close enough to Rome for the Pope to hope he might be able to influence the course of the deliberations. In November 1544 the bull *Laetare Jerusalem* announced that the members of the Council should gather by 15 March of the next year, but the opening session had to be delayed yet again, until December 1545, and even then the Council of Trent began without the presence of Protestant representatives. The Pope did not give up hope of holding the meeting somewhere within his own Papal States. Using the excuse that a plague was raging in Trent he transferred it to Bologna, but the Imperial representatives refused to budge, and the Council was moved back again.

In his bull summoning the Council, Paul III had stated three objectives. He hoped the gathering would heal division in the Church, establish peace among Christian princes so they might make common cause against the Turks, and reform ecclesiastical life and administration. Trent failed in the first two objectives. Protestants and Catholics remained at loggerheads,

Above: *This sixteenth-century engraving shows three scenes from the life of the founder of the Society of Jesus, Saint Ignatius Loyola (1491-1556). In the first, and largest, part of the picture Pope Paul III is depicted confirming the Constitution of the Jesuits in 1540. The second scene shows Saint Ignatius writing the Constitution under divine inspiration, and the third portrays Ignatius blessing members of the Society as they set off to preach the Gospel in different parts of the world as the Constitution requires them to do.*

and though an alliance of Pope, Venice and Spain defeated the Turkish fleet at Lepanto in 1571, the victory had little practical effect. In its third objective, however, Trent succeeded triumphantly and moulded the shape of the Roman Catholic Church down to the present day.

The sessions of the Council were prolonged over five pontificates. For a time Lutheran representatives were present, but they demanded that everything discussed before their arrival be gone through again, required the abolition of bishops' oaths of loyalty to the papacy, raised the spectre of conciliarism, and refused to deal directly with papal legates. The military successes of the German Protestant princes, however, sent German bishops scurrying back to their dioceses, thereby bringing the session at which the Protestants were present to a sudden end.

Trent was also marked by the presence for the first time on the international scene of members of a new religious order, the Society of Jesus, or the Jesuits. Their rule had received official approval from Paul III in 1540. Members of the Society were typical of the new style of 'reformed' priests, not uncommon in the Church in the first half of the sixteenth century. They were cultured, devout, and at the service of the papacy, and were destined to play an enormous part in the education of Catholic Europe for more than two centuries. The missionary work of the Society spread swiftly to the Americas, to India and to the Far East, and in Europe itself Jesuits were to play a large part in winning back much of Germany from Lutheranism and, later, France from Calvinism. The Jesuits who came to Trent acted as the Pope's personal theologians and were to have considerable influence on the outcome of the theological debates, especially on the complex Lutheran doctrine of justification by faith alone, rather than by faith and good works as the traditional Catholic doctrine put it.

Trent had to resolve theological questions raised by the Lutherans as well as reform the Church. Charles V insisted that reforms be put high on the agenda, to show the Protestants that the Council meant business. Proposals for reform, and settlement of theological disputes went side by side.

Trent is often thought to have imposed upon the Catholic Church a very strict theological orthodoxy, from which no deviation would be allowed in future. It is true that, when confronted with the challenge of Protestantism, the Church was no longer able to afford to tolerate quite such a range of theological opinion as had been common in the Middle Ages. It had to close ranks for its own preservation.

On the other hand, the Council's teaching was not as cramping as is sometimes supposed. A theory of justification which might have been acceptable to some Protestants was rejected as inadequate, but it was not condemned. Luther's theory of 'consubstantiation', which accounted for Christ's presence in the Eucharist, was that the body and blood of Christ coexisted with the substance of the bread and wine. This was certainly condemned, but the alternative doctrine of 'transubstantiation' – that the sacramental bread and wine changed into the body and blood of Christ when consecrated in the Mass – was only tentatively put forward as the 'most suitable' way of understanding the Real Presence.

Reforms of ecclesiastical life did not have an easy passage through the Council. The requirement that bishops should reside in their dioceses was particularly hard fought. Only bishops were in future to have the right to choose clergy for their dioceses – hitherto lay patrons had exercised far too great a control over the appointment of parish priests. From now on, no priest was to be ordained unless he had a living to go to, and, once appointed, he had to reside within his benefice. Standards of clerical education were to be raised by the establishment of seminaries (training colleges for priests) in the dioceses, and priests were no longer to be allowed to live in concubinage. Either they conformed to the demands of celibacy, or they abandoned their benefices. To ensure that the Council's provisions were implemented there were to be regular diocesan and provincial synods.

Above: *The Council of Trent was convened by Pope Paul III in 1545 and met at intervals until 1563. Its chief purposes were to reform the Church, and to restate Catholic belief against the views of Martin Luther and other reformers. Titian's painting exaggerates the number of bishops who were present.*

This was Church reform on a massive scale. It was achieved too late to bring about reconciliation with the Protestants, but it gave a new shape to Catholic life, even if some countries were slow to adopt the reforms proposed. They were rejected in France, for example, because the King complained that they interfered with the ancient liberties of the Gallican Church (the name of which derives from 'Gaul', meaning France), the French kings having claimed far greater independence from Rome for the Church in their country than Christian rulers elsewhere. It was a legal requirement of the Church that the changes had to be formally published in a country before they became law there, and this held up the spread of the reforms to some extent. The decree *Tametsi* laid down the form of marriage which the Church would henceforth demand. As *Tametsi* was not published in England until the early years of this century, its provisions did not have the force of Church law here.

Pope Paul III was to see very little of all this. In a Roman carnival in 1545 he was portrayed as Androcles pulling the thorn of heresy out of the lion's paw. The classical image would have appealed to him. Although under his direction the Church was beginning to take on a new shape, Paul himself was more at home in the Renaissance world than in the tough modern world concerned to a great degree with missions to newly discovered lands, and theological controversies with heretics.

Paul resumed the work on Saint Peter's, and put Michelangelo in charge of it. He also commissioned Michelangelo to remodel the Capitol and the area around it, although all that was done at the time was to move the statue of Marcus Aurelius from in front of the Lateran to the square before the Capitol. The frescoes he commissioned for the papal apartments of Castel Sant' Angelo were criticized for their pagan motifs, but Paul lived long enough to unveil Michelangelo's magnificent *Last Judgement* in the Sistine Chapel on 31 October 1547.

He was as much a patron of learning as of the arts. Copernicus' *On the Revolution of the Heavenly Bodies* was dedicated to him. Ironically, half a century later it was put on the *Index of Forbidden Books*.

Pope Paul III died, aged 82, on 10 November 1549, after enjoying the longest pontificate of the sixteenth century. Despite the heavy taxes which he had had to impose upon the Papal States, and which led him briefly into war with Perugia and with the Colonnas, he was much mourned by the people of Rome. His monument in Saint Peter's, carved by a pupil of Michelangelo's, is one of the finest in the basilica.

The task of bringing the Council of Trent to a close, and of making provision for carrying out its decrees, fell to Pius IV, who had been born Giovanni Angelo de' Medici on 31 March 1499. His father, Bernardino, had been deeply involved in the party strife that afflicted Milan, and spent long years in prison. The family was not wealthy – they were not related to the great Medicis of Florence – and there was little money to pay for Giovanni's education. Somehow he managed to study medicine, philosophy and law at Pavia and Milan, and in 1525 emerged from the University of Bologna with a doctorate in canon and civil law.

He went to Rome, sent there by his brother for his own safety, and worked for a while in the papal Curia. He went on to serve his brother as a secretary, and that was the start of his rise to eminence. His brother, a soldier of fortune, married an Orsini, the sister-in-law of Pierluigi Farnese. That brought Giovanni to the notice of Paul III, who used him from 1534 as an administrator of the Papal States and then, six years later, as governor of Parma. He did not take Holy Orders until he was appointed Archbishop of Ragusa in Sicily in December 1545. Two years later he was made papal vice-legate for Bologna, and it was while fulfilling this office that he heard of the assassination of Pierluigi. His prompt action in hurrying to Parma was instrumental in holding that city for the Farnese family, and in gratitude Paul III created him a cardinal.

To reach that rank at the age of 50 was the sign of a steady but unexceptional career, a life marked more by loyalty than by brilliance. Nonetheless, for one of Giovanni's background it was a real achievement. Perhaps because he was of relatively modest birth, little is known about his private life. He was lively and friendly, and not over-scrupulous about the law of celibacy. There is a question mark over his life even as Pope, though nothing has been proved one way or the other, but before he took Holy Orders he had fathered two illegitimate daughters and a son.

The death of Paul III was followed by three fairly short pontificates, one of which was only 22 days long. The reign of Pope Paul IV from 1555 to 1559 caused Giovanni particular distress because of the Pope's anti-Imperial policy. Giovanni de' Medici was closely allied with Charles V, and the Emperor rewarded his loyalty in 1556 by the grant of the diocese of Foligno. Two years later Giovanni set off to visit his diocese, ostensibly to seek a cure for ill-health, but really it was as a protest against the policies currently being pursued by Pope Paul.

The conclave which followed the death of Pope Paul was a long one. It took three months of debate before the electors settled on Giovanni de' Medici as being someone acceptable to both the Spanish and the French. It was a popular choice.

The reign of Pius IV was nearly wrecked from the outset by his devotion to his family. After his election, no less than 28 of his relatives turned up hoping for some remuneration, but only one of them, the son of his sister Margherita, was appointed a cardinal with the title of Saints Vitus and Modestus in 1560. He was still only 21, and his name was Charles Borromeo. As Cardinal Archbishop of Milan he was to be one of the leading figures in the implementation of the decrees of Trent. He was to be canonized a saint in 1610 by Paul V.

Above: *The exquisite 'Casino' or summer house in the gardens of the Vatican palace was built by Pirro Ligorio (c. 1500-83) for Pope Pius IV (1559-65). Though it appears simple from the outside, its design and interior decoration made it one of the costliest buildings of its day.*

Opposite: *On 7 October 1571, the combined fleets of Spain, Venice and the papacy decisively defeated the Turks at the Battle of Lepanto. Though it did little to stem the Turkish advance, the victory greatly boosted morale in Europe.*
Giorgio Vasari (1511-74) painted a scene of the gathering of the more than 200 ships at Messina in Sicily on 24 August to be included among the other pictures of papal triumphs used to decorate the Sala Regia in the Vatican, where the popes met ambassadors of foreign powers.

Shortly after becoming Pope, Pius IV was faced with a crisis in the College of Cardinals. His predecessor's nephew, Cardinal Carlo Carafa, together with his brother and several others, was put on trial for the murder of his brother's wife. Pius had all the evidence read out to him, and condemned the Carafas to death, the Cardinal included. One other Carafa cardinal, Alfonso, had also been arrested, but he was found not guilty and released. He retired to his archbishopric in Naples, and soon died there, a man completely broken by the destruction of so much of his family. It was indeed a remarkably stern act for a generally easy-going Pope, but the Carafa attempt to establish, primarily on the basis of their papal connections, a degree of temporal power similar in nature to that which Alexander VI had won for the Borgias or Leo X for the Medicis, offended deeply against Pius IV's conviction that motives other than temporal aggrandizement had to prevail within the Church at its highest levels.

The Council of Trent was called together again at the beginning of 1562, after an interval of a decade. It closed finally on 4 December the following year with a string of decrees on the existence of purgatory, the veneration of saints, respect for relics and images, and the value of indulgences. In its decree on indulgences, Trent went back to where the Protestant Reformation had begun, and roundly asserted both the value of indulgences and the Church's authority to grant them. It was an act of confident defiance, a forceful reassertion of all that Protestantism most abhorred.

This renewed sense of self-confidence did not limit itself to theological expression. It was accompanied by a great flowering of Baroque architecture and music, issuing a challenge to puritan sensibilities. Pius IV commissioned a casino in the grounds of the Vatican which was one of the most costly edifices of the day. He also commissioned Michelangelo to design the Porta Pia, and laid the foundation stone himself. Michelangelo was also employed on the church of Santa Maria degli Angeli in the Baths of Diocletian, which now houses the Pope's tomb. It was completed in 1566, two years after the death of the great artist who did so much to renew the face of Rome under the not always welcome patronage of a succession of Popes. Pius wanted Michelangelo to be buried in Saint Peter's, but the artist's own wish was to be laid to rest in his beloved Florence. There was still one of Pius' plans for Saint Peter's that Michelangelo had no opportunity to carry out. It was the Pope, it seems, who first conceived the idea of surrounding the square in front of the basilica with a massive colonnade. It was left to Bernini to turn the idea into a reality.

Pius himself, despite his interest in the arts and in learning, was no humanist. But he supported, and was supported by, many who were and he raised a number of them to the rank of cardinal. Although he issued a new edition of the *Index of Forbidden Books* it was altogether more practical and less rigid than that published by his predecessor, Paul IV. He reduced the powers of the Roman Inquisition, which Paul III had founded, because he did not approve of the manner in which it conducted its heresy-hunting. His outlook was generally liberal, and in the interests of scholarship he struggled, yet again, to revive and re-staff the university of Rome, whose fortunes were at the mercy of the papacy.

Pope Pius took practical steps to see that the decrees of the Council of Trent became widely known. The Council's documents were of considerable length, so the Pope sponsored a catechism summarizing the main conclusions. He established a committee of cardinals to oversee the interpretation of what the Council had determined, and to implement its reforms. He issued a bull containing a 'Tridentine profession of faith' which must still, according to current Church law, be sworn to by anyone holding a benefice, or who is responsible for the care of souls, teaches in a seminary, or is being promoted in Holy Orders. The profession of faith explicitly rejects the positions held

167

Above: *Philip II (1527-98) became King of Spain on the abdication of his father, the Emperor Charles V, in 1556. As husband of Queen Mary Tudor ('Bloody Mary') he was instrumental in saving Mary's sister from the scaffold, and she eventually succeeded to the throne of England as Queen Elizabeth I.*

by Protestants, recognizes the Holy, Catholic and Apostolic Roman Church as the mother and teacher of all Churches, and includes an oath of 'true obedience' to the Roman Pontiff.

Pius died on 9 December 1565, 13 months after issuing this bull. The work of enforcing the decrees of Trent was left to his successors. But to do this effectively the Roman Curia needed to be reorganized. It was during the pontificate of Pope Sixtus V that the Curia took the shape which it has retained to the present day, with only the occasional change having been made since the sixteenth century.

Pope Sixtus was born Felice Peretti in December 1521. He later added the surname 'Montalto' after the town in the March of Ancona near the place in which he had spent the early years of his life. His father was a poor labourer, and he was looked after by an uncle who was a member of the Franciscans. Felice himself entered the same Order when he was 12 years old, going on to study in a variety of places, finally receiving his doctorate in 1548, the year after his ordination to the priesthood.

He soon won fame as a preacher, and especially as an advocate of reform in the Church. Cardinal Carpi, who looked after the interests of the Franciscans at the papal court, drew him to the attention of Paul IV. After he had spent five years in Rome, the Pope sent him in 1557 to the Venetian Republic as Inquisitor, a task he pursued with such zeal that on the Saturday before Palm Sunday 1559, 10,000 books were burned, to the fury of the booksellers and printers of the city. So great was the hostility which built up that he had to flee from the city, and its government informed the Pope that they did not want him back.

He went on to become General of the Franciscans with the rank of bishop, and in 1570 he was made a cardinal. During the long pontificate of Gregory XIII, his great enemy, he had little to do and so it was something of a surprise when 'the monk', as he was popularly known, was elected Pope on 24 April 1585.

The conclave had been short, but bitterly divided. There were the opposing parties of Alessandro Farnese and Alessandro de' Medici; there were those who favoured France and those who supported Spain. Many bargains had to be struck before the various groups could agree on Montalto, and perhaps one of the things in his favour, apart from his relative obscurity during the previous pontificate, was his apparent ill health; he had asked to be excused from the conclave because of it, and nearly collapsed entirely when informed that he was the intended choice. But the illness may have been a cunning pretence, for Sixtus V took office with what seemed to be quite remarkable vigour.

Within days of his enthronement (at which Japanese Christians were present, the first converts of the Jesuit missionaries), executions began as Sixtus strove to restore order in the Papal States, and within two years 7000 bandits had died. The Pope expressed his regret that the number was not higher. The death penalty was employed for incest, abortion, procuring, sodomy and adultery.

Financial measures, equally draconian, brought cash flooding into the papal treasury. Sixtus encouraged agriculture; the silk and wool industries were especially favoured, though he had little success with these. Like other rulers of Rome before and since, he undertook the draining of the Pontine marshes, again without much effect.

His ecclesiastical reforms, however, were more durable. He decreed that the number of cardinals should not exceed 70, a rule which remained in force until the reign of Pope John XXIII. In January 1588 he established 15 'congregations' or commissions of cardinals which were charged with overseeing the various aspects of the administration of both the Church and the Papal States. This provided the popes with the equivalent of modern government ministries, and by dividing the cardinals into the different congregations it effectively destroyed the corporate power of the College.

Sixtus imposed a tight control over the Church. The decrees of Trent were strictly enforced, firm discipline was required of the priests and students of Rome, and regular *ad limina* visits were once more expected of diocesan bishops. For all his zeal in defence of the Church, the Pope remained surprisingly cool when Henry of Navarre came to the throne of France and it seemed for a while that France might become Protestant. Sixtus accepted Henry's word that the King would safeguard the interests of the Church, and took no action. He was less circumspect where England was concerned. Much as he admired Queen Elizabeth's virtues as a ruler, he was determined to bring about her downfall. He promised a contribution towards the cost of the Armada being gathered by King Philip of Spain, but refused to pay his share when he heard that the Armada had been defeated.

Sixtus was an ascetical man, who continued to live according to the Franciscan rule of life even as Pope. But personal asceticism did not get in the way of public patronage. He improved the city of Rome with new streets and squares, commissioned Domenico Fontana to work on the Lateran and Vatican Palaces, restored the gigantic aqueduct Aqua Felice and gave it his name, consecrated the columns of Trajan and Marcus Aurelius to Saints Peter and Paul, and blessed the last stone to be inserted into Michelangelo's cupola over Saint Peter's. He was also responsible for the erection of the obelisk outside Saint Peter's, and for three other similar monuments elsewhere.

The new Vatican Library begun in his pontificate was a sign that his patronage extended to learning as well as to the arts. He encouraged Cardinal Baronius in the history of the Church which he was writing against the Lutheran interpretation produced by Protestant historians. Sixtus considered himself something of a scholar, and undertook a good deal of the editorial work on the new edition of the Latin Bible for which the Council of Trent had called. The edition proved so faulty that it was withdrawn a few days after the Pope's death.

Sixtus was no liberal. In 1587 he established an official Vatican press, which still exists, but he did so to combat the 'deceit of heretics and the

Below: *The word 'armada' simply means 'fleet' in Spanish, in this case the fleet of 129 vessels manned by 8,000 sailors and carrying 19,000 troops which Philip of Spain sent against England in 1588. After early skirmishes with the English fleet the Spaniards took refuge in Calais, but the English admiral despatched eight fire ships among them at night, as this engraving clearly shows.*

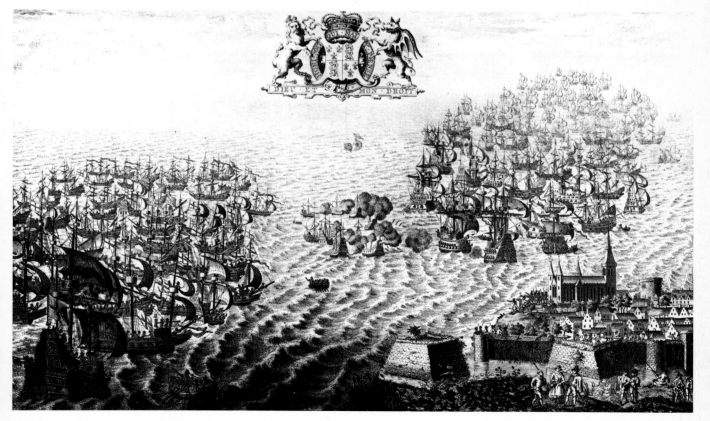

malice and ignorance of printers'. He had not greatly altered since his days in Venice as the Inquisitor. He ordered the preparation of a new and stricter version of the *Index of Forbidden Books*, which was even to include a work by the great Jesuit cardinal, Robert Bellarmine, eventually to be canonized a saint. Bellarmine was, the Pope believed, unsound on the extent of papal authority in temporal matters. Sixtus was not at all happy with the whole Society of Jesus, and considered revising its constitution and changing its name.

By the time of his death on 27 August 1590, Sixtus V had given shape to the new Rome as a centre of revitalized Catholicism, and determined the manner in which the decrees of Trent were to be implemented. To that extent he was a pope of reform. But he was also a pope of the Renaissance, not least in the way in which he had patronized his family, as well as the arts. A 15-year-old nephew had become a cardinal, two nieces had married into the greatest of Roman families. What distanced him from so many of his predecessors was the effectiveness of his control both of the Papal States and of the Church as a whole. The tremendous growth in the power of the Inquisition during his pontificate and his plans for a new *Index* were a warning of the way in which the Church was determined it was going to control thinking as well as behaviour in the future.

The problems to which such control would give rise was soon demonstrated. As previously mentioned, Copernicus' *On the Revolution of the Heavenly Bodies*, dedicated to Pope Paul III, was put on the *Index* in 1616. Only three years earlier, the mathematician and astronomer, Galileo Galilei, had publicly endorsed the theory that the planets revolve round the sun in his *Letter on the Sunspots*, and among those who wrote to congratulate him was Cardinal Maffeo Barberini.

Barberini had been born in Florance in April 1568, and at his mother's wish had been educated by the Jesuits, both in Florence and in Rome. Members of the Society were in the forefront of astronomical and mathematical studies, and many of them had eagerly adopted the theory proposed by Copernicus. Though Barberini was not himself a scientist – he took a doctorate in law from the University of Pisa in 1589 – he kept up more than a gentleman's interest in scientific matters.

An uncle brought Maffeo to the papal Curia. He prospered, was sent to Paris as papal nuncio, and created cardinal while serving there. In 1608 he was given charge of the diocese of Spoleto. Despite maintaining a large establishment in Rome, Barberini was active in his diocese, and was faithful to the decrees of the Council of Trent. He held a synod, built one seminary and began the construction of two more. He was a likely candidate in the conclave of 1623.

His time in Paris commended him to the French faction in the College of Cardinals, and they effected his election as Pope Urban VIII on 6 August. Galileo hurried to Rome in the hope that he could now have Copernicus' book removed from the *Index*. Many of those who sympathized with his determination realized that the problem was not as simple as he had supposed. His endorsement of Copernicus went beyond the then observable facts. There would have been less of a difficulty had he propounded his views as a working hypothesis, rather than as fact. Even so, there was still the stumbling-block of those biblical passages which seemed to require the sun to go round the earth. For these reasons Urban felt unable simply to remove the ban on Copernicus, but he encouraged Galileo to explain the system further in his writings.

In 1632 his *Dialogue on the Great World Systems* appeared, after something of a battle with the ecclesiastical censors. Its publication caused a storm, and particularly angered Pope Urban because he believed, probably erroneously, that he was being ridiculed in the person of Simplicio, one of the characters in the *Dialogue*.

Galileo was summoned to Rome, put on trial and, on 22 June 1633,

Above: *The Italian astronomer Galileo Galilei (1564-1642) espoused the Copernican theory that the earth went round the sun, and not vice versa, as had been the general view. The Roman Inquisition forced him to abjure these beliefs.*

required to abjure the opinion that the earth moved round the sun. He was also required to write nothing further on the Copernican system. He gave in to these demands, and suffered little other penalty. He lived until 1642, and was buried in the Florentine church of Santa Croce, near the tombs of Machiavelli and Michelangelo. The case of Galileo has become a *cause célèbre*, the archetype of all conflict between the Church and Progress, and it is easy to see why this should be so. To be fair to the scholars of the day, however, there existed at the time neither adequate critical apparatus for interpreting the Bible, nor satisfactory scientific theories to cope with all the problems to which the Copernican system gave rise. Nonetheless, the Galileo affair has left an enormous black mark against the history of Urban VIII's pontificate which otherwise, in the history of art and literature, was particularly distinguished.

Urban himself wrote elegant verse in Italian and Latin. He surrounded himself with poets and scholars, and revived an interest in humanist learning. He employed some of the finest architects. Among these was Gian Lorenzo Bernini who began work on the baldachino (canopy above the altar) in Saint Peter's shortly after Urban's election, and the basilica itself was consecrated, after it had been more than a century in the building, by the Pope on 18 November 1626. That same year Urban ordered work to begin on the construction of a summer residence at Castel Gandolfo.

There was some new project every year of his pontificate, and Bernini, whose genius was to dominate the artistic life of Rome for half a century, was kept busy. He reorganized the space under the dome of Saint Peter's to take a magnificent memorial to Urban VIII, which Bernini himself was to carve, and took charge of the Palazzo Barberini after the death of the Palazzo's chief architect, Carlo Maderno. The great flowering of high baroque art brought famous painters to Rome, but here Urban's taste was less sure. The arts had always had a part to play in the Catholic Reformation. In Urban's pontificate they continued to instruct and to edify, but they were also expected to delight the eye.

The Pope's skilful patronage of the arts had no counterpart in the political arena. The French faction who had supported his election as Pope had been right in thinking that he favoured France. When the Gonzaga family died out in Mantua, he supported French claims to the Duchy. But the Habsburgs also had their own claims. The Emperor plundered Mantua and seemed about to march on Rome. The threat of another sack of the city prompted Urban to raise a small army and to improve the fortifications of the Papal States. But when Cardinal Richelieu made a treaty between France and the Protestant Gustavus Adolphus of Sweden, the Pope soon found himself on the same side as the Emperor, even giving him modest financial support. Urban tried to prise Richelieu away from the Protestant alliance, but he was incapable of handling politicians of the calibre of Richelieu or his successor, Cardinal Mazarin.

As the Church's spiritual head, Urban was particularly interested in the problems of the missions. He enlarged the scope of the Congregation for the Propagation of the Faith, known from its Latin title as *Propaganda*. He set up new dioceses and missions, and to provide priests for these he founded a special college bearing his name. Gregory XIII had restricted the Far East to Jesuit missionaries only; Urban now opened China and Japan to all. He did so with the best of intentions, but the action was to have some unhappy consequences.

Urban VIII died on 29 July 1644. A year before, in the bull *In Eminenti*, he had condemned a book called *Augustinus*, written by Cornelius Otto Jansen, Bishop of Ypres, and published in 1641. In doing this, the Pope bequeathed to his successors a problem with Jansenism which was to trouble them for over a century, and was to play a part in the downfall of the Society of Jesus.

Opposite: *Bernini's statue in Saint Peter's of his great patron, Pope Urban VIII (1623-44). Shortly after his election to the papacy, Urban employed Bernini for the baldachino over the papal altar. This sculptor, architect and painter came to dominate the artistic life of Rome for the next half century.*

POPES AND KINGS

In the seventeenth century the Papal States could raise an army of some 50,000 men. By the time this chapter closes, on the eve of the French Revolution, the papal forces numbered only some 3000 or so, of whom one-tenth were officers. They were policemen rather than soldiers. They patrolled the papal territories to suppress banditry, not to fight off external aggression.

The popes were still territorial sovereigns, but the territorial basis of their authority was diminishing. Only the city of Rome itself was really important to them. There was a brief war in 1708-9 between pope and Emperor, but otherwise foreign monarchs marched and countermarched their armies across the Papal States in the eighteenth century with very little complaint from the States' nominal sovereign.

If the popes were to exercise any power at all, it had to be through a Church revitalized by the reforms initiated at the Council of Trent. The reorganization of the Roman Curia into congregations made it possible for the popes to influence the affairs of local churches in a way that had hitherto been difficult if not impossible. The newly established seminaries taught the faith as it had been laid down by the Council. The Congregation of the Inquisition and the *Index of Forbidden Books* ensured that the doctrine was kept pure. Local bishops were summoned to Rome to report on the state of their dioceses; strongly centralized religious orders with their headquarters in Rome – and fiercely loyal to the Holy See – reported back to the popes anything which they saw as diverging from strict orthodoxy. This renewed vigour in a strongly centralized Church was not at all welcome to the rulers of Europe, nor was it always welcome to the local bishops, either. The conflicts were most bitter in France, as the holy and competent Pope Innocent XI was to find out.

Innocent was born at Como on 19 May 1611, and baptized with the name of Benedetto. He was the fifth son of Livio Odescalchi and his wife Paola. Benedetto was first sent to a school run by the Jesuits in Como, but was taken away when still quite young to join his uncle's firm in Genoa, where he was to learn business affairs and administration. When a plague broke out in the region he fled for safety to Switzerland, although his mother stayed behind and died. He returned home for a time to Como but then, in 1635, went to Milan where he was appointed to the largely honorary task of commanding the urban militia. The following year he left for Rome.

He was still not certain whether he wanted to be a priest, but at the Sapienza, Rome's university, he began the study of canon and civil law. From Rome he went on to Naples. It was in Naples that he graduated, and in 1640 took the first steps towards the priesthood.

He returned to Rome and to a post in the papal Curia. Among the many

Opposite: *Benedict XIV (1740-58) was a liberal man of wit and culture. He is particularly remembered for his writings on the process of canonization. This portrait by G. M. Crespi shows the papal tiara on the table in front of him, and on his finger the Fisherman's Ring – the pope's personal seal which is broken at his death.*

who were using the Vatican's civil service to seek out fame and fortune, he was remarkable for the modesty, sobriety and retiring nature of his life. He rose quickly through the ranks, for his ability as an administrator soon attracted attention, and he was put in charge of collecting taxes in the March of Ancona. He accomplished this task to the satisfaction of the papal exchequer, but he also managed to do it with a great deal of compassion for the poor. The governorship of Macerata came next and, at the beginning of 1645, elevation to the rank of Cardinal-Deacon, with the title of Saints Cosmas and Damian. For the next three years he was a curial cardinal, engaged in the work of several of the Roman congregations through which the Church was governed.

There was famine in the Papal States in 1648. Remembering Benedetto Odescalchi's administrative skills, Pope Innocent X sent him as papal legate to Ferrara to cope with the situation there. He purchased grain, insisted on fair prices being charged in the markets, distributed free bread and gave money away to the poor. Not surprisingly, he became extremely popular with the citizens of Ferrara.

Two years later he was named Bishop of Novara, though he was still not a priest. Before the end of 1650 he was ordained, and was consecrated bishop the following year. As a diocesan bishop he took Saint Charles Borromeo as his model. True to the Council of Trent, he took great care over the education and the discipline of the clergy, and over the instruction of the laity. But he was not to remain long in his diocese. In 1654 he went back to Rome for an *ad limina* visit to report on the state of his See. Pope Innocent X made it clear that he wanted Benedetto to remain in Rome as an adviser, and after Innocent died in 1655 his successor, Pope Alexander VII, repeated the same request.

Benedetto became Pope Innocent XI on 21 September 1676. In the conclave preceding the election itself all the cardinals had agreed that whoever of them was elected would carry out a programme which firmly laid down the propagation and defence of the Catholic Church as the first duty of a pope.

It was a task to which the new Pope was very much attracted. He set about it with a will and concerned himself personally with all appointments to missionary dioceses. He set up new bishoprics in Brazil, and supported the Carmelite enterprise in Persia. He wrote to distant princes, urging them to accept the Catholic faith, and when a Jesuit-led embassy of Christians from Siam came to Rome he received them with great jubilation. When priests came back from their missions and visited Rome he asked to see them in order to learn at first hand something about the regions under their charge. He instructed the Congregation for the Propagation of the Faith to draw up a conspectus of missionary activity throughout the world. His concern was not only to spread the Gospel, for he was also interested in improving the way of life in missionary territory as well; he made an attempt to abolish slavery in Africa, though this had little success, and he established universities in Latin America and the Philippines.

As well as spreading Catholicism, he did what he could to counter the spread of Protestantism. Both the German Emperor and the Elector of Bavaria wanted to marry non-Catholic wives. He refused to give them permission in case Protestantism should get a foothold in otherwise Catholic territories. On the other hand, he was shrewd enough to advise King James II of England to moderate his attitude to those who did not share his Catholicism, but James chose to ignore this advice, to his ruination.

Innocent's major achievement was one in which religion and politics were combined. The French were still allied to the Ottoman Turks, and the Turks were threatening the very heartlands of Christianity. Papal diplomacy helped to bring about a league of the Emperor and King Jan Sobieski of Poland which inflicted a crushing defeat upon the Turkish army outside the gates of Vienna in 1683. Three years later a Holy League of the Emperor,

Above: *James II of England and VII of Scotland became King in 1685. Against the advice of the Pope he showed himself too favourable to those of his subjects who shared his own Catholic faith, and this hastened his downfall in 1688. He fled to France, where he died in 1701, still regarded by many as the rightful King of England.*

Venice and Russia once again defeated the Turks in the reconquest of Buda. Moslem expansion into Europe had been halted.

The Pope's problems with King Louis XIV of France were not limited to his support for the non-Christian Ottoman Empire. Louis was trying to increase his control of the Church within his own dominions. Kings of France had long claimed the right to enjoy the revenues from certain bishoprics when they were vacant. Louis now attempted to extend this right to all bishoprics. The French bishops appealed to Rome and Innocent protested to the King.

Louis' response was to hold two assemblies of the French clergy, the first in 1680, and the second two years later. The 1682 gathering approved the four Articles of the Gallican Church. For more than four centuries the Church in France, or the French kings on its behalf, had claimed a degree of independence from Rome greater than that exercised elsewhere. But never had their claims been so sharply formulated. The points that the assembly wanted to assert were:

1. The Pope has no power in secular matters, and kings cannot be subject to them on such issues. The Pope has no authority to release citizens from their oaths of allegiance to a king
2. A general council of the Church is superior to the Pope.
3. In France, papal authority is limited by the customs and traditions of the French Church.
4. Even in matters of faith, a papal decision is not binding unless it has the consent of the whole Church.

If the Pope had allowed relations between Rome and the Church in France to be governed by these Articles it would have paved the way for King Louis, and doubtless other monarchs elsewhere, to establish national Churches as had been done in England. Not unnaturally, therefore, Pope Innocent rejected the four propositions.

Louis' next step, which he took in 1685, was to revoke the Edict of Nantes. This edict had guaranteed religious toleration to the Huguenots. The King took this action partly to achieve religious uniformity in his country, partly to establish his own orthodoxy (or so he thought) in the eyes of the Pope, and partly as a bargaining counter: 'See what I have done for the Church,' he was saying, 'now it is time the Church did something for me in return.' But Innocent was unmoved. As the Huguenots fled the country or became Catholics against their will, the Pope denounced the policy of forced conversions. He singled out for special approval those French bishops who had condemned their monarch's actions.

Relations between Paris and Rome deteriorated further two years later when a new French ambassador arrived in Italy. He came with a squadron of cavalry, and claimed certain rights of jurisdiction around the French embassy in Rome. The rights had been repealed by the Pope, so when the ambassador insisted on them he was excommunicated, and the church where he went to Mass was put under an interdict. Louis retaliated by arresting the papal nuncio in Paris, by appealing against the Pope to a general council of the Church, and by occupying the papal estate at Avignon. Pope and King were still at loggerheads when, on 12 August 1689, Innocent died.

The process for his canonization was inaugurated shortly after his death, but had to be abandoned because of protests from the French. Eventually his cause reached the stage halfway to canonization in 1956, when he was 'beatified' – given the title of 'Blessed'.

His claim to sanctity rests partly on his overriding concern for the spiritual mission of the Church, but more important still was his own spiritual life. He had an heroic degree of detachment from things of this world, an attribute which, together with his particular care in financial transactions, had in addition the rather useful benefit of refilling the papal treasury.

Innocent's own asceticism seems to have affected the way he thought others should behave. Amid all the many problems with which France was presenting him there was also a conflict between the Jesuits and the rigorous sect within the Catholic Church called the Jansenists; they claimed to draw their inspiration from the writings of Bishop Cornelius Otto Jansen, which had been condemned by Pope Urban VIII. The Jansenists adopted the theory that when there was doubt about what course of moral action was to be followed, then the '*more* probable' opinion had to win the day. The Jesuits, on the other hand, believed that any opinion could be followed that was 'probable'. The Pope condemned the Jesuits' approach as too liberal. In the long term, however, the Jesuits' view, which favoured the right of human beings to make decisions for themselves, was the one that prevailed in the Church.

Prospero Lorenzo Lambertini was born on 31 March 1675, 18 months before Innocent XI was elected Pope. As Pope Benedict XIV, Lambertini was as easy-going as Odescalchi had been severe. He came from Bologna, the son of Marcello Lambertini and Lucrezia Bulgarini. His family was of some considerable standing in the city, but of no great wealth. Prospero did well at school, and went to Rome at the age of 13. There his abilities brought him to the attention of Innocent XII who provided enough money for him to continue his studies at Rome's university. After he had completed his degree in law and theology he began to practice in the papal courts. He quickly built up a reputation as a successful lawyer, and was attached to the Congregation of Rites. Among the many tasks of this Congregation was deciding upon the holiness of life of people who were being presented for canonization, and from 1702 Lambertini became the Promotor Fidei, or 'Devil's Advocate', whose job was, as it still is, to find objections to the sanctity of people being urged on the Church as potential candidates for canonization.

One of the cases with which he had to deal was that of a distant relative, Imelda Lambertini, who had died in 1322. She was so young when she entered her convent that she was not allowed, much to her distress, to receive Communion with the other nuns. On one occasion, so the legend had it, she was followed into the chapel and was discovered kneeling in prayer with the Sacrament hovering over her. The chaplain took the Host, and gave her Communion with it. Shortly after this occurrence she died, at the age of 13. Not surprisingly, Prospero Lambertini had his doubts. The Blessed Imelda was not beatified for another century.

Much consulted by successive popes, Lambertini was made a bishop in 1725 and a cardinal *in petto* (that is to say, he was appointed cardinal, but the Pope kept the fact secret) the following year. In 1727 his rank of cardinal was made public knowledge, and he was made Bishop of Ancona. Then, in 1731, he was appointed to the Archbishopric of Bologna, his native town.

As Archbishop, Lambertini's rule was benign and imaginative; he abolished public floggings, prohibited bullfights, founded a reformatory, and improved the standard of education in the seminary. He took firm action against superstition, insisting that all relics exposed for veneration be shown to be authentic. He required the local clergy to dress soberly: there were to be no brightly-coloured suits, or waistcoats embroidered with silver and gold thread; priests were not to dye their hair chestnut or blond.

He used to rise very early in the morning, though more out of an inability to sleep than from asceticism. Most mornings he would stroll out of his palace after breakfast and chat with passers-by as he wandered about the streets. In the evenings he would relax with friends or receive visitors, many of them from the world of scholarship or literature. The English writers Thomas Gray and Horace Walpole called upon Lambertini, and he made a great impression on them. In later years, Walpole wrote in praise of him, but

Benedict XIV was unimpressed. The Pope was, Benedict said, rather like the statues on the top of Saint Peter's–better seen from a distance.

While in Bologna, Lambertini published his great study, based upon his experiences in the Congregation of Rites, entitled *Of the Beatification of Servants of God, and the Canonization of the Blessed.* In this huge work he examined the history, the process, the mechanics and the economics of raising people to the status of saints, and he discussed the marks by which holiness of life might be assessed.

He was very happy at Bologna. Even after he became Pope he kept the diocese in his own care. He did not nominate anyone to succeed him until 1754, when he chose a close personal friend, who was also a native of the city. Indeed, he was very reluctant to accept the papacy; he told the assembled cardinals, that he had only done so because he did not want to oppose God's will, appear ungracious to those who had elected him, or to drag the con-

Above: In October 1744, during the War of the Austrian Succession, the Austrians retreated from southern Italy, passed Rome and, on 3 November, King Charles III of Naples was welcomed in Rome by Pope Benedict XIV as the liberator of the city. The King was received by the Pope in a coffee-house in the grounds of the Quirinal Palace, and the scene was depicted by Giovanni Paolo Pannini (1691-1765).

Above: *This dual portrait by Pannini shows Pope Benedict XIV with Cardinal Silvio Valenti Gonzaga, the man he chose for the office of Secretary of State on his election to the papacy. A contemporary described Cardinal Gonzaga as knowing everything without appearing to know anything, and the collaboration between the Pope and his Secretary of State was close and abiding.*

clave out any longer in the summer heat – two of the cardinals having already died in the course of it. The conclave had lasted from early March to 17 August 1740. Prospero Lambertini was unanimously chosen on the 255th ballot and took the name Benedict XIV.

His manner of life as Pope changed little from the life he had lived in Bologna. He still went about on foot. He did not live a Spartan existence, but nonetheless managed to cut back on papal expenditure on board and lodging. He also economized on defence expenditure for the Papal States. Though from time to time he was driven to protest against the havoc caused by foreign armies as they tramped across the states of the Church, he kept the states themselves out of war. Some have seen in this a natural indolence passing muster for a foreign policy, but this judgement seems unfair. He was active enough for the security and well-being of his subjects in other ways. To guard the coastline from Barbary pirates he bought two English frigates and built a galley, the *Benedettina*. To ensure adequate food supplies he constructed granaries in every town and village.

He has the unusual distinction of being the first man to draw up a list of the names of the streets and squares of modern Rome. It was, however, very incomplete, and in any case not of great help to visitors because he made no provision for road signs. He did a great deal for Rome. The Colosseum was saved from total destruction, and he commissioned Pannini to complete the Trevi Fountain begun by Salvi earlier that century. He rebuilt the church of Santa Croce in Gerusalemme, and linked this church by a broad avenue to the Lateran. Other churches were restored and embellished.

Much of the money to pay for these improvements he scrimped and saved out of household expenses, and from the running of the Papal States. Any money he had left over he spent on pictures, mosaics and statues for the

Vatican museums, and most particularly on manuscripts for the Vatican library. His own books he sent to Bologna, and built a library to house them.

He had an intense interest in all branches of learning, especially medicine. He set up no less than four learned societies in Rome, and endowed courses in medicine, astronomy and physics at the universities of Rome and Bologna. He was instrumental in promoting two women to professorships in Bologna, though one of them proved so shy that she never gave a lecture and retired into a convent.

With such a concern for scholarship it is not surprising that he was shocked at the behaviour of those who were responsible for producing the *Index of Forbidden Books*. They were, he found, banning works which he had read and enjoyed. New instructions were therefore issued which, while not abrogating the *Index* entirely, put strict limits on what the Congregation in charge of it could do without the pope's express permission. An author's right to defend himself against the censor was guaranteed, and Benedict reminded censors that they were not to confuse their own views with the official teaching of the Church.

Benedict himself held surprisingly liberal views for his day. He was ready to allow monks and nuns to return to the ranks of the laity by freeing them from their vows, and he insisted that priests hearing confessions should not be too severe with their penitents. Priests were to remember, he said, that smoking and snuff-taking were not inherently sinful. He was violently opposed to the castration of boy sopranos to preserve their voices, and condemned the practice. Those *castrati* already singing in church choirs could remain, but no new ones were to be engaged.

Towards the end of his life he developed a great interest in the Eastern Churches. He hoped for reunion, and he did not see this, as so many others did, as being achieved by the Eastern Churches adopting the Latin rite. This open attitude, however, did not extend to permitting what came to be called the Chinese rites. This was one of the many problems which troubled the Society of Jesus in the seventeenth and eighteenth centuries. From the earliest days of its missions to the Far East, the Society had adapted its manner of life to the situation in which it found itself. There were Jesuit Brahmins in India and Jesuit Mandarins in China, and in China particularly the Jesuits had tried to fit what was best in the local culture and religion into a Christian context.

This adaptation was not well received by the Church. Dominican and Franciscan missionaries saw the inclusion of ancestor worship and similar practices in the Christian liturgy as a prostitution of Catholicism. Their views prevailed, despite pleas made on behalf of the Jesuits by the Emperor of China himself. The Emperor eventually forbade any Christian service to be held within his dominions unless it conformed to the Jesuit version. But adaptation was forbidden, and by no pope more vigorously than by Benedict XIV.

It was a curiously untypical attitude from a man who, although quick-tempered, was genial and sympathetic to those exploited by authority, rather than to the exploiters. He shares with the modern Pope John XXIII the unusual distinction for a pope of having had his more humorous sayings collected for publication. He was not a man to be overawed by the prestige of his high office. Once when out walking he was accosted by a fanatical friar with the news that Antichrist had been born. 'How old is he?' the Pope asked. 'Just three years old', said the friar. 'Then I will leave the problem to my successor to deal with', replied the Pope.

He was probably the only pope to have been on good terms with the Grand Turk, the ruler of the Ottoman Empire, and one of the few who enjoyed reading Voltaire (although he was eventually obliged to allow Voltaire's writings to be put on the *Index*). This tolerant lover of learning, who forbade his clergy to ride to hounds, and ordered them to remain with

Below: *The Trevi Fountain, representing Neptune's palace, was built between 1732 and 1762. Popular tradition ascribes the plan to Bernini, but Nicolo Salvi (1697-1751) was chiefly responsible for its construction.*

their flocks in time of plague, died on 3 May 1758. Horace Walpole described him as 'a man whom neither wit nor power could spoil . . . the best of Roman pontiffs'.

The same could not be said of either of his two successors, both of whom were called Clement – the XIII and XIV of that name. Their reigns were bedevilled with the problem of the Society of Jesus, and Clement XIV was responsible for suppressing the Order which, for over 200 years, had been one of the most loyal defenders of the Holy See.

It was partly that very loyalty which led to the downfall of the Jesuits. They were unacceptable to governments bent on establishing national Churches – though without completely breaking with the Bishop of Rome – because they were a supra-national organization, closely linked to their Rome headquarters, with little local loyalty. They paid the penalty of this internationalism by being expelled from Spain, Portugal and Naples. The French were at first unwilling to take such a drastic step, but the abiding influence of the Jansenists, the Society's old adversaries, coupled with questionable financial dealings by some Jesuits and the growth of rationalism, conspired against the Society's survival.

The Franciscan Giovanni Ganganelli, chosen to be Pope Clement XIV on 19 May 1769 after a conclave that had dragged on since February, owed his election to the fact that the cardinals representing the Bourbon courts of France, Spain and Naples were convinced that he would suppress the Society, while other cardinals were equally sure that he would not. It was one of the tragedies of Ganganelli's life that he had given both groups grounds for their belief.

He was born near Rimini on 31 October 1705, and his family moved into the town itself after the death of his father, who had been a doctor. There he came under the influence of a relative who was a member of the Conventual Franciscans, and he joined the Order himself in 1723, taking the name Lorenzo in memory of his father. He studied in various places, finally taking a doctorate in Rome in 1731. He was then sent to teach philosophy and theology, and during this period of his life he was much helped by members of the Society of Jesus, and became very friendly with them.

The first step to his cardinal's hat was his appointment as First Consultor to the Inquisition by Benedict XIV. He was twice offered advancement within his own Order, but he declined to accept it and his patience was rewarded when Pope Clement XIII made him a cardinal in 1759. The Pope wanted to have someone in the Sacred College who would support him and the Society of Jesus—but after his elevation Ganganelli's attitude towards the Society began to change. The change was not immediately evident even to the extremely anxious observers within the Society itself. He continued to live a highly edifying life as a simple friar – humble, frugal, charitable and studious. But he slowly grew away from the influence of Clement XIII and closer to that of the Bourbon courts.

The Bourbons were putting pressure on the Pope to suppress the Society: Clement issued a bull extolling the Jesuits' virtues. Naples seized the papal town of Benevento and France occupied Avignon. The Pope remained adamant. His successor, however, capitulated.

Pombal, the First Minister of Portugal, was of the opinion that the most important matter with which the Catholic world had been occupied since the revolutionary appearance of Calvin and Luther was the suppression of the Society, and he told the Pope so. Clement XIV made concessions and temporized. He made Pombal's brother a cardinal. When the brother died, Clement conferred the red hat on the brother of Portugal's Foreign Minister. But Pombal was not to be fobbed off. In any case, the suppression of the Jesuits was only the first step in his campaign. His true intentions were revealed when he set up a Royal Board of Censorship. Its task was to forbid the circulation of any books which defended the rights of the Holy See or opposed the nationalization of the Portuguese Church.

A formal request to the Pope for the suppression of the Society was presented by the Bourbon courts just two month's after Clement's election. He tried to buy time. Members of the Society were removed from their teaching posts in Roman and other seminaries. Jesuits who had been expelled from Portugal and had settled in the Papal States were deprived of their meagre pensions, and bishops were instructed not to grant licences to teach or to preach to any Jesuit exiled from Parma, Naples or Spain. Books

Opposite: *Antonio Canova (1757-1822) took up permanent residence in Rome in 1781, and three years later was commissioned to produce a tomb for Pope Clement XIV. When he had completed this he was asked to execute a tomb for Pope Clement XIII, which is pictured here. The work lasted for over four years (1787-92), and it shows simply a man at prayer, rather than the highly baroque, allegorical monuments of popes, portraying them as men of power, which had been customary hitherto.*

that were being published in defence of the Society of Jesus were banned.

Much turned upon the attitude of Maria Theresa of Austria. Her son, the Emperor Joseph II, had arrived unexpectedly in time for the conclave, the first Emperor to visit Rome since Charles V. He let it be known that although his mother held the Society in great esteem, she would leave any decision about its future to the will of the Church, and would do nothing to oppose any move to suppress it. Nonetheless, it remained clear that Maria Theresa favoured the Jesuits, and this strengthened their hand. She was, however, eager that her daughter Marie Antoinette should marry the Dauphin, the future King Louis XVI of France; consequently, when the Bourbon King of Spain wrote to her in 1773, soliciting her support for the campaign against the Jesuits, she gave way.

On 16 August 1773 a papal emissary arrived at the doors of the Jesuit headquarters in Rome. He was accompanied by police and soldiers, and carried the papal Brief of Suppression. It was dated 21 July. Other prelates, similarly escorted, called simultaneously at all the other houses of the Society in Rome.

There was no doubt on anyone's part, least of all on the part of members of the Society, that the Pope had the right to suppress the Society should he so wish. But what made Clement's action all the more bitter was that he saw fit to give no reason for his action. The reasons, he said, were locked up in his breast. The theology, discipline and customs of the Society itself went uncondemned.

The Jesuit General and his assistants were imprisoned, and at first harshly treated, in Castel Sant'Angelo. The General, Father Lorenzo Ricci, eventually died there soon after the death of the Pope himself. On the instructions of Clement's successor, Pius VI, he was buried in the Society's main church in Rome, the Gesú.

Elsewhere Jesuits fared well or ill, depending on the whim of local civil or ecclesiastical rulers, but after the issue of his Brief of Suppression Clement XIV showed little interest in the fate of the Society. He turned his attention to the recovery of Avignon and Benevento from France and Naples. After lengthy negotiations they were returned to the papacy, but in humiliating circumstances. Clement tried to make the best of the occasion, and celebrate the event. The citizens of Rome received him coldly. He was out of favour, but not particularly because of his treatment of the Jesuits. They felt he was too extravagant, and were angered by the amount of money he was spending on the Museo Clementino (which he had founded and named after himself), though all he was trying to do was to rescue for Rome some of the antiquities which by this time were being removed from the city. Apart from his buying policy for the Museo Clementino, he did little to embellish the city. He did, however, considerably enrich the Vatican Library, and began a fine collection of coins and medals.

He died a year after the Society had been suppressed. He was in great pain for much of the last year of his life, but he kept up public engagements as best he could. On returning from one of them he collapsed outside the Quirinal palace; this was the residence to which the papacy moved in the eighteenth century because, although smaller than the Vatican, it was more comfortable and not so crowded.

After his death on 22 September 1774 Clement's body turned black and blue. There were rumours that he had been poisoned by some former Jesuits, and he had clearly feared that something of the sort might happen. Guards had been doubled, and he had travelled everywhere with a military escort. When he was staying at Castel Gandolfo food had been brought out from Rome each day in two heavily guarded vans. It may be true that he was poisoned. But even if so, it was most likely to have been an accidental self-poisoning – brought about as a result of taking large amounts of medicine for his many ailments.

LUD. DAVID
PARISIIS 1805

AN AGE OF REVOLUTIONS

T he suppression of the Society of Jesus was just the first step in an all-out attack on the Church. That was clear to both friends and foes of the Jesuits. The Pope elected on 15 February 1775 after a conclave of 134 days seemed very ill-suited to meet such a challenge. But Giovanni Angelo Braschi, who took the name Pius VI, had sanctity of a sort thrust upon him, as other people have greatness thrust upon them.

He was born on Christmas Day 1717 at Cesena. Cesena lay across the Apennine Mountains from Rome, in that part of the Papal States called the Romagna or, sometimes, the Legations, because the chief cities of the region, from Ferrara in the north to Rimini in the south, were administered by papal legates.

The Braschi family was noble and ancient, but not very wealthy. Giovanni studied in his home town, and in 1735 took a doctorate in law. He entered the papal civil service and without a notable display of either energy or genius rose rapidly through the ranks to the post of finance minister of the Papal States. He did not become a priest until he was over 40, and became a cardinal in 1771.

In the disputes over the Society, Cardinal Braschi succeeded in remaining neutral. That was one reason for electing him to the papacy: he had not irrevocably alienated either party. He was, however, committed to keeping the Society suppressed, and that was another reason for choosing him.

Pius VI was amiable and rather vain. A man of culture, with a special interest in classical antiquity, his purchases for the Vatican museum led to charges of extravagance being laid against him. He threw open the Vatican library to visiting scholars, and Rome once more began to attract men of learning. He ordered the erection of three Egyptian obelisks, brought to Rome by the Caesars – one outside the Quirinal, one opposite Santa Trinità dei Monti, and the third on Monte Citorio. Rome may have been full of ruins, but ruins were now romantic. Jacques Louis David visited the city, incorporated the ruins in his work and set a new classical style in painting. Goethe came to Rome, and so did Antonio Canova, to erect the magnificent memorial to Clement XIV.

Much as he delighted in embellishing his capital, Pius VI, like other princes of his age, was just as interested in improving the territory over which he ruled. He was particularly concerned with draining the Pontine marshes to the south of Rome, and visited the site each year, unless otherwise prevented, to see how the work was progressing. In the event, his efforts achieved little. Some arable land was reclaimed, and a shorter route opened up between Rome and Naples, but on balance the work may have made the area more rather than less unhealthy.

Concessions in the land which had been reclaimed, together with rents

Opposite: *David's portrait of Pope Pius VII (1800-23). Bullied and outwitted by Napoleon, who deprived him of the Papal States, Pius nevertheless survived to see the downfall of Napoleon and the restoration of the states in 1814 by the Congress of Vienna.*

from former Jesuit lands at Tivoli, enabled the Pope's nephew to buy the Duchy of Nemi. Duke Braschi finally became a prince of the Empire, and this revival of nepotism was one of the less attractive features of a pontificate that was full of contradictions.

The most extraordinary contradiction was the position of the Jesuits. The Society survived for a time both in Prussia and in Russia, and although Prussia eventually allowed Clement XIV's Brief of Suppression to take effect, Catherine of Russia held out. Catherine had acquired a large number of Catholic subjects by the partition of Poland, and she relished the paradox of the Pope trying to persuade a Russian Orthodox Queen to deprive her Catholic subjects of the Catholic clergy who ministered to them.

She was, moreover, especially appreciative of the scientific and educational work of the Jesuits in the town of Polotsk, and regularly rejected the rector's frequent request that his college be suppressed in accordance with Rome's instructions. Catherine took the opposite course. She actively encouraged learned Jesuits to settle in Polotsk, and finally persuaded the apostolic delegate to allow the Society to open a house for new recruits.

Like the attack on the Society, the challenge to the papacy came from Catholic, rather than from Protestant or Orthodox, rulers. The pious Maria Theresa died in 1780. Free of her influence, her son, the Emperor Joseph II of Austria, espoused Febronianism. This was the name given to the theories of the Catholic Assistant Bishop of Trier, who wrote under the name Febronius. He wanted to limit papal authority strictly to matters of faith, leaving all questions of Church discipline to the State. The State would then control the lives and the education of the clergy, and of members of religious orders. When the Emperor Joseph started to put these ideas into practice, Pius VI took a leisurely journey to Vienna to try to bargain with him. His visit was fruitless. The following year the Emperor made a return journey to Rome, and before he left the city at the beginning of 1784 had managed to wring even more concessions out of the Pope.

The Emperor's success encouraged his brother Leopold, Grand Duke of Tuscany. Leopold had his own brand of Febronianism, which was intermingled with strong doses of Jansenism. He appointed as Bishop of Pistoia a man who held similar views, Scipione de Ricci. Ricci introduced radical changes. Mass was said in Italian instead of Latin, relics were burned, pictures of the Sacred Heart of Jesus, a devotion then very much in vogue, were torn up.

In 1786 Scipione de Ricci held a synod which attracted well over 200 clergy, though many of them came from outside his own diocese. The synod's decrees endorsed the basic tenets of Jansenism, and embraced the four Gallican Articles of 1682. The changes proved too radical for the ordinary people of the diocese. In 1787 they rose in revolt, and Leopold did not fight to retain the discipline imposed by the synod. Other matters were occupying his attention. In 1790 he left Florence to succeed his brother Joseph as Emperor, and four years later Pope Pius VI plucked up enough courage to condemn the synod of Pistoia. Bishop Scipione de Ricci held out until 1805, but then he, too, submitted to Rome.

As some of the consequences of the attempt to 'nationalize' the Church became clear, there was less eagerness to adopt Febronianism. In 1786 representatives of the prince-bishops of the Empire, those prelates who, as electors of the Empire, were secular as well as ecclesiastical authorities, met at Ems. They met to discuss the Pope's attempt to establish a papal nunciature at Munich, an act which they regarded as interference in their sphere of influence. The oddly-named 'Punctuation of Ems' restricted Rome's right to intervene in German affairs. Now the Emperor Joseph began to see dangers ahead. He did not want power to be wrested from the Pope only for it to fall into the hands of the prince-bishops. Similarly the prince-bishops did not want the power to go to the Emperor. It was a stalemate. But that

Above: *Anxious to improve the Papal States, Pius VI undertook the enormous task of draining the Pontine marshes to the south of Rome. The project had little success, and the marshes were not properly drained until after Mussolini came to power in 1922. This anonymous painting shows the Pope paying his annual spring visit to see how the work was progressing.*

particular problem paled into insignificance when the French Revolution broke out.

The Estates General of France (an assembly born in 1302 out of the French king's conflict with Boniface VIII) that met at Versailles on 5 May 1789 was not at first an anti-Catholic, or even an anti-clerical, gathering. The lower ranks of the French clergy made up a surprisingly large proportion of the assembly. They were obsessed with the question of their status and the debate on the Constitution of the Clergy was intended to improve their position. But as the debate went on, the Constitution became increasingly radical, and it was decided that the French Church should be nationalized. Then it became evident that one result of nationalizing the Church would be that taxpayers would have to find the money to fund the clergy, and this would have imposed an immense burden. The only alternative was to reduce the number of those to be supported, and appropriate measures were adopted. All the religious houses for men, and all those for women which were not thought to be performing a useful function in society, were dissolved and their members dispersed. Even the number of diocesan clergy and bishops was to be cut back, and the pope was to lose authority over those who remained. This was the basis of the new Constitutional Church.

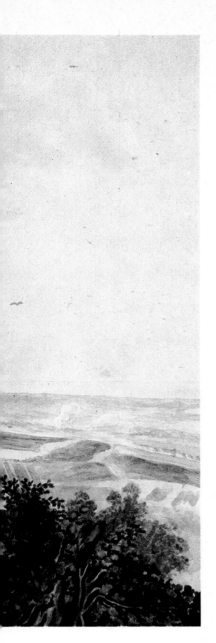

In March 1791 Pius VI condemned the Constitution of the Clergy, but only after the majority of French bishops had done so before him. Then Louis XVI, more loyal to Rome than some of his country's clergy, did likewise. It marked the French King's definitive break with the Revolution. In the event, only half-a-dozen bishops out of 150 accepted the Constitution, and only about half the lower clergy. Very many of the remainder, perhaps as many as 40,000, fled the country. Ten thousand came to England, half of them remaining in London where a few of the more active began new Catholic parishes which survive to the present day. A great many escaped to Rome, and there lent colour to the stories of the Revolution which were already circulating.

The Constitutional Church was in trouble almost as soon as it had been set up. As one recent commentator has remarked, the Constitutional clergy had accepted much in order to obey the government, only to find that the government was not really interested in them. But the disinterest shown by the government was not shared by Napoleon Bonaparte.

Napoleon's attitude, as he advanced down the length of Italy with his revolutionary army, was quite different from that of his masters in Paris. He believed that religion was a force to be harnessed, if possible, rather than destroyed. Harnessing religion, however, was not to prove easy. Napoleon incorporated the Legations (those northern Italian towns governed by papal legates) into the new Cisalpine Republic, based upon Milan. The Cardinal-Archbishops of the Legatine cities of Ferrara and Bologna fought the new regime every inch of the way.

The approach of 'Cardinal Citizen' Chiaramonti, Bishop of Imola, was different. In a sermon for Christmas 1797 he tried to show that there was nothing irreconcilable between the Revolution and Christianity. He argued that the newly imposed democracy would require from its citizens a higher degree of virtue than other forms of government had demanded in the past. 'Be good Catholics', he said, 'and you will be good democrats'. On his writing paper he had 'Equality' printed in one corner, and 'Liberty' in the other. But in the place of 'Fraternity' he had in the centre 'And Peace in Our Lord Jesus Christ'

The French army arrived outside Rome on 9 February 1798 to be greeted by the Cardinal Secretary of State, the Spanish ambassador, and Duke Braschi. General Berthier made camp outside the city, expecting his presence to give heart to revolutionaries inside the walls. No rising occurred. The city of Rome was occupied on 15 February, and when a rising did break out it was against the French invaders: it was brutally put down by firing squads in the Piazza del Popolo. But by that time Pope Pius VI had been declared deposed, and bundled off to spend his last days in France. He died in Valence on 29 August 1799. He had reigned for over 24 years. Apart from the quarter of a century traditionally ascribed to Saint Peter, it was the longest reign of any Bishop of Rome up to that time.

When he was forcibly removed from Rome, Pope Pius VI had left the Church in the charge of Cardinal Antonelli and six other cardinals. Antonelli had tried in vain to persuade him to create more members of the College of Cardinals, and to insist that the next conclave meet in Venice. Venice had the advantage of being in the Italian peninsula, but politically part of Austrian territory. The Pope refused, but he issued a bull which laid down that the next true conclave would be one which was held in the dominions of a Catholic ruler, and attended by the largest group of cardinals. By this means he hoped to guard against the possibility of a schismatic conclave, held under French auspices.

The conclave that came together on 30 November 1799 met, as Antonelli had suggested, in Venice, on the island of San Giorgio. It was attended by 34 electors, and was held under the protection of the Austrian Emperor. The Emperor was hoping for a compliant pope, one with whom he could form a strong alliance against the Revolution. The cardinals' choice, however, was not at all to his taste. They elected the 'Cardinal Citizen' Bishop of Imola, Gregorio Chiaramonti.

Like his predecessor, whose name he took on his election, Chiaramonti came from Cesena. He was born on 14 August 1742, and was baptized with the name Barnaba. He was educated by the Benedictines, and when he joined them in 1756 he changed his name to Gregorio. His family, like that of Pius VI, was ancient and aristocratic, and the two families were friendly. He grew up in a very pious environment. After her children had reached an age when they could look after themselves, Chiaramonti's mother became a Carmelite nun.

After Gregorio had studied and then taught in Padua, Rome and Parma, he came back to Rome to teach. Pius VI made him Abbot of Saint Paul's in the city, and then, in 1783, appointed him Bishop of Tivoli. It was not long, however, before he was moved to the more important see of Imola, with the rank of cardinal. That post taught him a good deal about the shortcomings of the constitution and administration of the Papal States, and during the French invasion he was prepared to co-operate with the army of occupation. He was also always ready to smooth out conflicts between the French and the local inhabitants.

News of his election was at first welcome to Napoleon, who now held the title of Frist Consul. He was also delighted to hear that Pius VII had turned down the Emperor's pressing invitation to go on from Venice to the safety of Vienna, and had chosen instead to return to Rome. He entered the city on 3 July 1800.

The main business which awaited him was the negotiations with France about the status of the Catholic Church in that country. The position was a delicate one. The first bishop of the Constitutional Church had been consecrated by Bishop Talleyrand, one of the few prelates to accept the Civil Constitution of the Clergy. Talleyrand had apostatized, married, and was now France's Foreign Minister. Napoleon seemed to be on the point of abandoning the Constitutional Church altogether. Any agreement with Rome which would undermine the Constitutional Church was clearly unacceptable to the clergy of that Church, and any agreement whatsoever between Napoleon and Pius VII was unacceptable to the Pretender to the French throne, Louis XVIII. A concordat between Rome and Paris, Louis reasoned, would only strengthen the usurper's authority in France.

Napoleon's bargaining position was a strong one. In return for a suitable concordat he would give back control of the Papal States to the Pope. But the man Pius chose to represent him was a tough negotiator. Cardinal Consalvi was not to be browbeaten. He won most of the concessions from the First Consul which Pius and the cardinals in Rome had wanted, including semi-official status for the Catholic Church in France.

The concordat was not at all to Napoleon's liking. He delayed publication until Easter 1802, and when it appeared there were 77 'Organic Articles' appended to it. These safeguarded the government's position. All documents entering France from Rome had to have official approval; no seminaries for training the clergy were to be established without Napoleon's agreement; all seminary professors had to subscribe to the Gallican Articles of 1682; the civil contract of marriage was to take precedence over the religious ceremony, and so on. Pius VII had been out-maneuvered by the First Consul, and not for the last time.

On the other hand, there were some definite gains for the papacy. Not only was the Pope's right to invest bishops recognized, but it was stated he also had the right to depose them, which was something new, and considerably strengthened his hand.

Napoleon's next move was to make himself Emperor. But, traditionally, emperors had been crowned by popes. Pius VII therefore received an invitation to go to Paris to perform the ceremony. The Roman cardinals

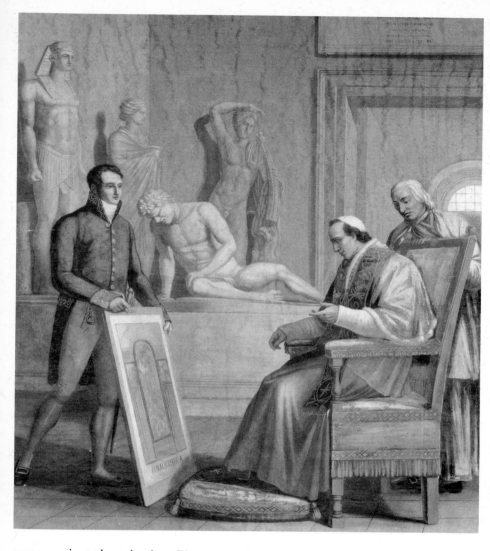

were against the trip, but Pius overruled them. Once in Paris, however, he discovered that Napoleon had not been through an ecclesiastical ceremony of marriage with Josephine, whom Pius was to crown Empress. Pius insisted that they have a sacramental wedding. This delighted Josephine, who was afraid, with good reason, that one day Napoleon would try to desert her. It considerably irritated the Emperor himself, however, and was to cause Pius problems in the future.

The Pope for the most part thoroughly enjoyed his trip to the French capital, the sightseeing and the applause of the crowds. As a reward for his services, Napoleon gave him a triple tiara. To the Pope's indignation, prominent among the gems which encrusted it was a large emerald which his predecessor had been forced to send to Paris, along with other jewels, antiques and works of art, as part of the price of the brief respites in the French army's inexorable march down Italy.

In addition to proclaiming himself Emperor, Napoleon now decided to become King of Italy. He was crowned in Milan, and his armies invaded Naples. All Italy was going to be his, he told Pope Pius, but he was prepared to respect the independence of the Holy See on certain conditions. The Pope was to banish from Rome citizens of all countries at war with France, and close papal ports to the ships of all enemy countries.

Pius' response was firm and dignified. 'We are the Vicar of a God of Peace,' he said, 'which means peace towards all, without distinction between Catholics and heretics . . . Catholics living in those countries [at war with France] are not small in number; there are millions in the Russian Empire

Above: *Napoleon persuaded Pius VII to come to Paris in 1804 to crown him Emperor, but he placed the Imperial wreath on his own head, reducing the Pope to a mere onlooker. Napoleon then crowned his wife Josephine Empress, as shown in this famous painting by David, which can be seen in the Louvre.*

. . . in the lands ruled by the King of England; they enjoy freedom in the practice of their religion, they are protected. We cannot foresee what would happen if the rulers of those states found themselves provoked by us.'

The inevitable happened. Two years after their invasion of Naples the French armies occupied Rome. In the following year, on 17 May 1809, Napoleon decreed that the Papal States were to be annexed to his Empire, and Rome itself was to become a 'free Imperial city'. The Pope was to be left in possession of all his palaces, and endowed with suitable revenue, but he was to lose all temporal power. On 10 June the French tricolour was hoisted over Castel Sant' Angelo.

Pius retaliated with the only power he had left. He excommunicated all who had been involved in stripping him of his temporal sovereignty. Then General Radet and a troop of soldiers broke into the Quirinal palace where Pius was sheltering, arrested the Pope and Cardinal Pacca, and hustled them into a coach. As it left Rome, Pope and Cardinal turned out their pockets and found they had only 20 sous between them. They found this funny.

Napoleon was not at all amused. He had given no instructions to arrest the Pope. Pius was an unwanted and embarrassing prisoner. He ordered that the Pope be taken to Savona near Genoa, had all papal archives moved to Paris, and declared Rome now to be the second city of his Empire. Duke Braschi, the late Pius VI's nephew, was made its mayor.

While a prisoner, the Pope refused to carry out any of the functions involved in running the Church. More particularly, he refused even to consider giving Bonaparte a divorce. The Emperor Napoleon wanted to marry Marie Louise, daughter of the Emperor Francis I of Austria, who as Francis II had also been the last Holy Roman Emperor.(He had resigned the latter title on 6 August 1806 after his defeat by Napoleon at the battle of Austerlitz in 1805. The Holy Roman Empire had existed for almost exactly a thousand years, but had become increasingly irrelevant.) For reasons of state, however, Francis did not oppose Napoleon's marriage to his daughter. He was not over-concerned about ecclesiastical niceties, but wanted some sort of Church approval for the wedding.

Napoleon coerced a Parisian court into agreeing that he had been forced into a marriage with Josephine, and in a way this was true. A contract entered into under duress was ruled invalid; Napoleon was free to marry again. Cardinals who refused to attend the wedding ceremony were stripped of their rank, and from then on were known as the 'black' cardinals, to distinguish them from the 'red' ones who attended. Within a year, Marie Louise had fulfilled her duty. She had provided Napoleon with an heir who was styled 'King of Rome'.

But even more of a problem to Napoleon than the divorce was Pius' refusal to invest any bishops. There were vacant dioceses right across Europe,

Right: The Concordat of 1801 between Napoleon and Pius VII deprived the Church of important political rights, but the papacy subsequently became a great spiritual influence. The signatures of Bonaparte, his Foreign Minister, Talleyrand, and the Pope appear on the document.

including that of Paris itself. The Emperor called a 'National Council' of bishops at Notre Dame in Paris, and managed to persuade the 95 present (half of them from Italy) to suggest to the Pope that bishops appointed by the Emperor would be invested with their office by their metropolitan arch-bishops if, after six months, the Pope had not done so himself. Pius agreed to this, provided that it did not apply to the Papal States. But for Napoleon it was all or nothing. He had the captive Pope hurried from Savona to the Palace of Fontainebleu, where the Emperor would be in a better position to browbeat him.

At first, the move proved successful. Pius agreed to discuss certain proposals which the Emperor then presented to the world as the outline of a new concordat. But one of the terms of this 'agreement' was that the cardinals whom Napoleon had imprisoned should be released from custody. They made their way to the Pope's side, and persuaded him to cancel what little agreement had so far been reached.

By this time the Emperor was in military difficulties, and everyone knew it. Even when he offered the Pope full restoration of temporal sovereignty, Pius refused to be drawn. At last, Napoleon gave instructions for his return to Rome. For the Pope the journey back was a triumphal progress. He arrived in the city on 24 May 1814, and one of his first major acts, on 7 August, was to restore the Society of Jesus.

The Pope's popularity was immense. He had earned the admiration of Europe, first of all as an opponent of Napoleon, and then by his bearing as his prisoner; and the respect with which he was regarded contributed greatly to the decision made at the great Peace Congress of Vienna to restore the Papal States to him. He was even given back the Romagna region across the Apennines. It may have made little political sense, but it was the only part of the Papal States that was financially profitable. If the popes were to live in the style which, up to then, had been thought appropriate they would need the Romagna to provide the income.

Pius' advisers, and especially Cardinal Consalvi, were not unaware of the problem. Under the French the laity had played a large part in the government of the Romagna, and they would be unwilling to give that up now that the region had been restored to the papacy. Although Consalvi kept effective political power in the hands of ecclesiastics, he made a modest attempt to maintain lay involvement.

But there were those among the cardinals who wanted to put the clock back to before the Revolution. They wanted to remove from all administrative positions anyone who had in any way collaborated with the French; they wanted to dismiss all liberal-minded university professors; they wanted to send the Jews back to the ghettoes from which the French had freed them. They had some small success, but as long as Consalvi was Pius VII's Secretary of State, the power of the reactionary cardinals was limited.

Then, in July 1823, Pius fell while alone in his study and broke a thigh-bone. Louis XVIII of France, who had been put on the throne after the defeat of Napoleon, sent him a special adjustable bed; Francis I of Austria sent him two dozen bottles of his best Tokay – but the Pope never recovered. He died on 20 August, and Consalvi immediately fell from power.

The heterogeneous nature of the Papal States, the clash between progressive and reactionary forces within them, and the anachronism of a modern state being governed by ecclesiastics made the collapse of the Papal States inevitable. It came during the pontificate of Pope Pius IX.

Giovanni Maria Mastai-Ferretti was himself a native of the Papal States. He had been born at Singaglia, just north of Ancona, on 13 May 1792. His parents, Jerome Mastai-Ferretti and the Countess Catherine Solazzi had something of a reputation for their liberal and reformist outlook. Their son began his studies at Volterra, but they were interrupted by an attack of epilepsy. After his recovery, Giovanni went to the Roman College, and was ordained priest in 1819. After ordination he spent some time working in a

Left: *Pope Pius IX (1846-78) – Pio Nono – summoned the First Vatican Council to meet in December 1869. The following year it defined the controversial doctrine that, when propounding a doctrine concerning faith or morals to be believed by the whole Church, the pope is infallible – in other words, cannot make a mistake.*

Roman orphanage, and then was invited to accompany the apostolic delegate to Chile and Peru for two years. On his return in 1825 he decided not to continue his career in the papal diplomatic service, and took charge of the Roman hospice of San Michele.

He was appointed Archbishop of Spoleto in 1827, and five years later was moved to the more important post of Bishop of Imola, a position once held by Pius VII. This post was usually held by a cardinal, but Ferretti did not receive his red hat until 1840. Though the Pope (Gregory XVI) and his Secretary of State were aware that they needed someone like Ferretti, with popular appeal and liberal sentiments, to handle this difficult assignment, they were themselves in no way enamoured of his views.

In fact, they had misunderstood him. He was no intellectual, and not very much of a liberal. He did not approve of the tight police regime which the Pope was trying to impose on the Papal States to maintain order, but he had no great commitment to reform. He produced an outline for economic and administrative changes at Imola, but his plan did not deal with the much more contentious issue of political reform. Ferretti was undoubtedly popular, but his popularity sprang from his simplicity and his piety, from his sense of humour and his generosity, from his numerous acts of charity and his unfeigned concern for the spiritual good of his diocese.

Cardinal Ferretti was one of the three whose task it was, in the conclave of 1846, to read out the names of the candidates and the votes cast for them. At the third ballot, on 16 June, he found himself reading out his own name 18 times. He faltered and could not go on. He paused to recover, and then went on to read out his own name 36 times, at which point he had obtained the necessary two-thirds majority. A month later he had allowed hundreds of exiles to return to the Papal States, and granted an amnesty to over a thousand political prisoners. These acts were greeted with enormous enthusiasm: the papal carriage was pulled by the crowd through the streets of Rome beneath a shower of flowers.

These reforms were rapidly followed by others. The press was granted freedom from censorship. A lay municipal government was set up in Rome. There was a largely lay council of ministers established for the whole of the Papal States, and other measures were taken to remove clerics from office and replace them with laymen.

But then he began to be overtaken by events. The Austrians marched into the papal city of Ferrara to forestall a revolution there, or so they claimed. Pius strengthened his army on the border, but then made the mistake of placing it under the command of a general who was Piedmontese, and the Piedmontese were at war with the Austrians. The papal army joined in. The Pope insisted that the Austrians withdraw from Ferrara, and in so doing unwittingly became the champion of a united Italy – or so he was hailed by those who wished to see the unification of the peninsula. In reality, Pius had little sympathy with the idea, and said so. In a statement of 29 April 1848 he listed all the reforms he had introduced, but it was not right, he said, for a pope to go to war, and he had no wish to unite all Italy under his presidency.

Left: *In 1848, Pius IX fled from the democratic revolution in Rome to take refuge at Gaeta in the Kingdom of Naples. He left Rome disguised as a simple priest, as J. P. Sanese shows in this drawing.*

This declaration marked his break with the liberals in Italy.

However, like other rulers in that year of revolutions, he had been forced to grant a democratic constitution. This brought little but chaos to Rome, and culminated in the assassination of the Prime Minister he had appointed. So Pius IX, or Pio Nono as he was known to the Italians, fled from his capital. He left the city on 24 November, disguised as an ordinary priest. He took refuge in Gaeta, just inside the Kingdom of Naples, and was given hospitality in the royal palace there.

The ruling junta in Rome now called for a constitutional assembly, to be elected by universal suffrage. In Rome only half those eligible voted, in the Pope's birthplace less than one in a hundred. Some of the votes cast were recorded for Pio Nono himself, others for the Jesuit General, and even some for Saint Peter, but the result of this boycott of the election by those sympathetic to the Pope was that the assembly, when it met, was a very anti-clerical body. It voted to end the temporal power of the papacy, and to establish a Roman Republic. From the papal refuge in Gaeta, Cardinal Antonelli, Pius' Secretary of State, made an appeal to the Catholic powers to restore the authority of the Pope.

The French acted first. By the end of July 1849 the administration of Rome was back in the hands of a triumvirate of cardinals, under French protection. Pio Nono returned on 12 April 1850 with an escort of French

Above: *On their arrival at Gaeta, Pio Nono and his companions had to stay in a cramped hotel, where only the Pope had a room to himself. The King of Naples arrived the following day with members of his court in three ships, and the Pope was offered accommodation in the royal palace at Gaeta, which he accepted. He also received an offer of asylum from Queen Victoria.*

199

troops. He took up residence in the Vatican, which once again became the place where the pope usually lived, and so it has remained.

For a decade there was relative calm in the Papal States, and major reforms were introduced. But in the north the Kingdom of Piedmont kept alive the ideal of a united Italy. The only obstacle to Piedmont's advance was the presence in Rome of a French garrison. But then, in September 1860, the cession of Nice and Savoy to France by Piedmont brought about Napoleon III's compliance in the occupation by Piedmont of all the Papal States, except for an area around Rome.

The French garrison remained in the city – which the Piedmontese had declared was to be the capital of a united Italy – until the defeat of France in the Franco-Prussian War of 1870. Napoleon III fell from power and the troops were withdrawn. On 19 September that year Pius IX paid a visit to the Lateran basilica. He ascended the Scala Santa on his knees, and from the top blessed his tiny army. He ordered them, however, to offer only a token resistance to the Piedmontese attack. When the attack began the following day the Pope waited anxiously for his generals to surrender. When they did not do so he gave orders for a white flag to be run up on the cupola of Saint Peter's. The Papal States had fallen for ever.

In fact, the new government offered Pio Nono very generous terms. He was to be treated as a sovereign, and allowed to send and receive diplomatic representatives. But the terms implied a complete separation of the spiritual and temporal authority of the Pope, and Pius would have none of it. The new Kingdom of Italy, he said in an unrestrained attack on it in 1877, was incompatible with the independence of the Holy See.

But as his temporal authority declined, his spiritual authority grew. From Gaeta he had sent a letter to all Catholic bishops, asking their opinion about the teaching that the Virgin Mary, alone of all mankind, had been conceived in her mother's womb without the least stain of original sin upon her soul. This belief in the 'Immaculate Conception' had a long history in the Catholic Church, and there had been a Mass to celebrate it in the missal ever since the fifteenth century. But hitherto Catholics had been free to believe or not to believe in the Immaculate Conception. After favourable replies from the bishops of the Church, Pius IX decided to declare it a dogma of faith, something that must be believed by all Catholics. This he did, on his own authority, on 8 December 1854.

An even more controversial exercise of papal authority occurred just a decade later when Pius IX issued the *Syllabus of Errors*. This contained 80 propositions, the most notorious among them being the last. People were quite mistaken, the document said, if they believed that 'the Roman Pontiff can and ought to reconcile and harmonize himself with progress, liberalism, and recent civilization'. In Italy it was well enough understood that 'progress, liberalism and recent civilization' were being condemned because of the way in which the Piedmontese had interpreted them: the closure of convents and monasteries, the imposition of secular education, general anti-clericalism. But such niceties were lost on the world at large. Pio Nono's popularity had been high outside Italy because of all the suffering he had undergone in 1848 – even Queen Victoria had written him a letter of sympathy – but now it took a plunge, at least outside the Catholic Church.

Within the Church, attitudes were mixed. Pius IX's prestige had grown in the course of the longest reign so far in papal history, and people were increasingly looking to Rome for guidance. There was a growth in 'ultramontanism' (literally, government from 'beyond the mountains') because men saw in a centralized authority a counterbalance to the spread of revolutionary principles. The papacy built upon this newfound interest in its doings, and its influence reached out to all parts of the Church, in small matters as well as in great. Priests around the world began to wear the Roman-style soutane with its short cape, as well as the 'Roman' collar. The

Roman title of 'Monsignor' was freely bestowed, and the number of non-Italian cardinals significantly increased under Pius IX's pontificate. *Ad limina* visits of bishops to the Pope were insisted upon.

The culminating point was the Vatican Council, which opened on 8 December 1869. There were some 700 bishops present from all around the globe, and though the largest single group was still Italian, it was a sign of the times that 120 of the bishops were English speaking.

The Council fathers dealt swiftly with the first major document put before them. It was a statement of the Church's position on revelation and the relationship between faith and reason. The second major document was more problematical. It dealt with the doctrine of the Church itself.

The great issue of the day, much debated before the Council, was the infallibility of the pope. Curiously, this question of whether the pope could make a mistake when teaching Catholic doctrine, did not occur in the text and Pius IX (who firmly believed in papal infallibility) did not want to thrust his own views on the Council. 'I do not know whether I shall come out of this Council fallible or infallible', he said, making an Italian pun, 'but I shall certainly come out of it bankrupt.'

But just as Pio Nono did not want to pressurize the Council in favour of infallibility, so he was annoyed by government pressure from England and elsewhere to influence the fathers in the Vatican to vote against infallibility. Eventually he let himself be persuaded by the majority, led by Archbishop Manning of Westminster, and approved the preparation of a special document. It described what was meant by papal primacy over the whole Church, and laid down the meaning and the limits of papal infallibility. This was solemnly approved on 18 July 1870, just before the Council was brought to a sudden end by the outbreak of hostilities between France and Prussia which led to the final withdrawal of French troops from Rome.

Because the Council came to such an abrupt halt there was no time to situate papal infallibility within the wider context of the infallibility of the Church as a whole. Perhaps that would never have happened in any case. Many of the fathers at the Council wanted the definition of infallibility to bolster the pope's spiritual authority as a compensation for his loss of temporal power, so were quite content with what they had achieved.

But unfortunately some of the interpretations of the doctrine of infallibility went too far in stressing the pope's personal responsibility. The German bishops made this point in a collective statement in 1875, and Pius IX wrote a letter agreeing with them. Such subtleties, however, were lost on the great majority of Catholics, and on almost all non-Catholics. They were left with the impression that the pope, and only the pope, spoke for the Church. The bishops were merely his representatives round the world. If the bishops met in council, an English Jesuit theologian wrote in the nineteenth century, they only did so to give the pope moral support.

The image of the Church in people's minds was that of a pyramid. The Pope was at the top. His authority spread out to the bishops, and from the bishops to the priests. The laity formed the base of the pyramid. It was a vision of the Church that owed more to the Middle Ages than to the Renaissance. There was indeed a new interest in the philosophy and theology of the Middle Ages in the second half of the nineteenth century, and Pius IX's successor was to foster it. Even so, it must be doubtful if the high degree of centralization achieved by the Roman Church would have been possible had it not been for the personal prestige enjoyed by the Bishop of Rome, Pope Pius IX.

The citizens of Rome, itself, however, did not share the rest of the Catholic world's regard for their Bishop, who had kept them out of the united Kingdom of Italy for so long. He died on 7 February 1878, but his tomb in San Lorenzo Fuore le Mure was not ready until three years later. When his body was finally moved there—late at night for fear of the hostility of the crowds—the incensed mob threw bricks and stones at his coffin.

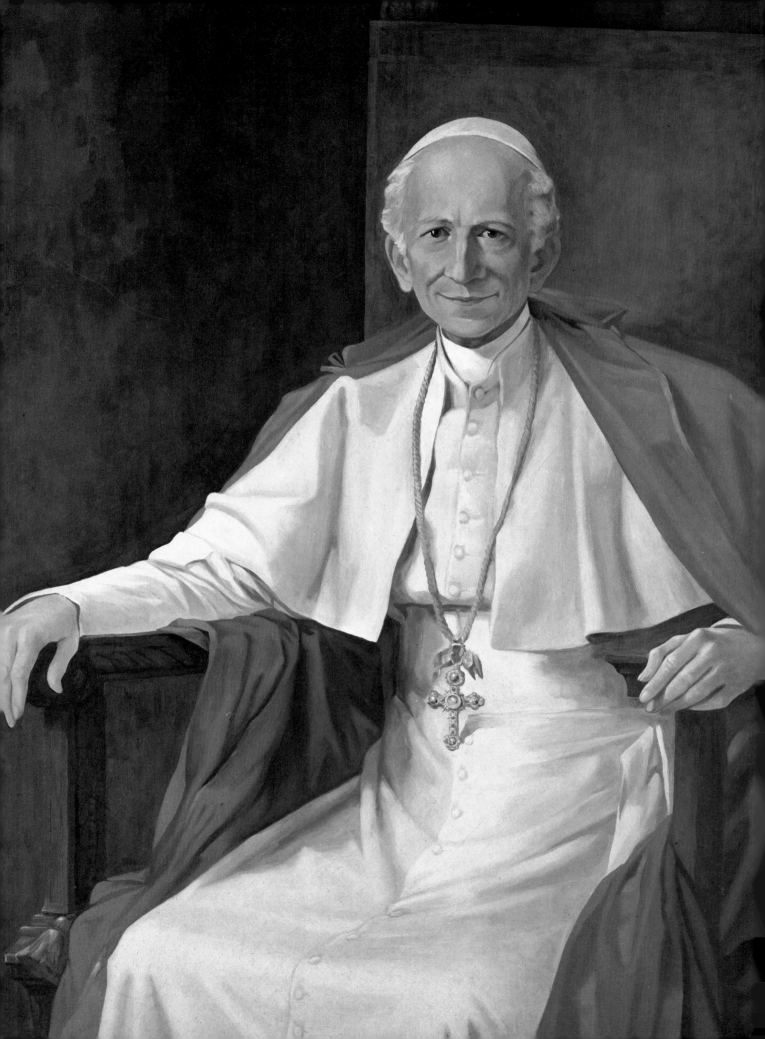

THE WORLD'S CONSCIENCE

The man chosen to succeed Pio Nono – and who took the name Leo XIII – was something of a surprise. Cardinal Giocchino Vincenzo Pecci had spent little time in Rome, and to many of the electors was an unknown quantity. The cardinals who chose him on 20 February 1878 after only three ballots had been impressed with the efficient way he had organized the conclave, and the moderates among them wanted someone who was not too closely identified with the policy of Pius IX. They were hoping for a less rigid approach to what had become known as 'the Roman Question': the isolation of the papacy (the pope as the 'prisoner in the Vatican') from the rest of Italy since the formal annexation of Rome by the Piedmontese.

A few months before his death Pius IX had appointed Cardinal Pecci the Camerlengo of the Roman Church. This office carried with it, in addition to responsibility for directing the conclave, the task of administering Church property while the papal throne was vacant. Though it was his skill in fulfilling this office that brought him to the attention of the other electors, his experience of the Church had been wide, both as a diplomat and as a pastoral bishop.

He was born in Carpineto in central Italy on 2 March 1810, the sixth of the seven sons of Colonel Ludovico Pecci and Anna Prosperi Buzi. From 1818 to 1824 he attended the Jesuit school at Viterbo, and then went on to the Roman College. In 1832 he enrolled in the Academia dei Nobili Ecclesiastici, and studied law at the University of Rome. Five years later he was ordained, and immediately appointed a 'domestic prelate' to the Pope, a largely honorary rank which carried with it the title of 'Monsignor'. This was done, in part at least, as a reward for the outstanding courage he had shown during an outbreak of cholera.

His career began with an appointment to Benevento as apostolic delegate. He stayed there until 1841 when he was transferred to Perugia to fill an equivalent post. He was energetic in the pursuit both of bandits and liberals, and revealed himself to be a highly capable administrator, building roads and making other improvements to the economic well-being of the region, including setting up a savings bank for farmers.

After only two years in Perugia Monsignor Pecci was consecrated Archbishop and sent as papal nuncio to Brussels. It was a difficult post. His predecessor had crossed swords with the local hierarchy and had been recalled to Rome. Pecci was much more conciliatory, and was therefore accused by the papal Secretary of State of being insufficiently vigorous in the defence of the rights of the Holy See. In pursuance of the Holy See's policy, he prevented the Catholics of Belgium and the moderate liberals in the country from coming to an understanding. This interference in the

Opposite: *Pope Leo XIII (1878-1903) wrote the encyclical 'Rerum Novarum', the first formal statement of Catholic social teaching, and the first endorsement by any ruler, civil or ecclesiastical, of the aspirations of the working class.*

internal affairs of Belgium annoyed the King, who demanded Pecci's recall. So in 1846 he found himself once more back in Perugia, this time in charge of the spiritual, rather than the temporal, welfare of the region. It was to be an immensely formative period in his life.

Archbishop Pecci's Jesuit brother, Joseph, himself later to become a cardinal, was on the staff of the diocesan seminary, and was an enthusiastic student of the writings of the great thirteenth-century theologian, Saint Thomas Aquinas. With his brother's help, Archbishop Pecci established an Academy of Saint Thomas in 1859.

He maintained this interest after he had become Pope. The year after his election he published an encyclical urging all Catholics to look to the teachings of Saint Thomas for guidance in philosophy. He stressed in particular the detailed study of Thomas's writings. This might seem obvious, but at the time it was a great step forward. The Pope was recommending that the original writings should be used, rather than bad textbook versions of what Thomas was reputed to have said. But before the original text could be studied it had to be established. In 1880 the Dominicans were given the task of producing a definitive edition of Aquinas's works. The Leonine Edition, named after Pope Leo XIII, is still slowly appearing in enormous folio volumes.

Pope Leo is often criticized for commending to the Church the study of medieval philosophy and theology, rather than encouraging the development of a more modern synthesis. But he took this step from the best of intentions. He wanted to do two things: to improve the education of the clergy, and to provide the Church with a coherent philosophical and theological system. The possibility of the coexistence of faith and reason was very much under attack in the nineteenth century. Leo wanted to show that it was not only possible but had already been achieved.

The writings of Saint Thomas also provided Pope Leo with a view of the world which divided it into two 'perfect societies', that of the Church and that of the State. As Archbishop of Perugia he had not been a whole-hearted supporter of the illiberal phase of Pius IX's pontificate. He realized, as Pio Nono had not, that civil authorities had a legitimate autonomy within their own sphere, and that the era of Christian princes who listened to the instructions of the popes of Rome had passed – if it had ever existed. But this was a relatively new idea not acceptable to many of the aristocracy, or even of the middle classes of France, Germany or Italy.

For the Church to have any influence in the future, reasoned Leo, it would have to appeal directly to the working class which was being increasingly attracted by socialism. He wrote an encyclical letter against socialism in 1878, but his real appeal to the working class came later when, in 1891, he issued the first of the papal social encyclicals, *Rerum Novarum*.

Groups of Catholics had been discussing social questions long before Leo put pen to paper, and some individual bishops had been particularly active. Cardinal Manning of Westminster, for example, had become famous for his support of the strike of London dockers in 1889. There were competing social philosophies in the Church, and this fact itself put pressure on the Pope. In Italy in particular, those who were most active in writing or speaking about social morality were criticizing the emerging industrial society from a point of view that went back beyond the French Revolution. They wanted to restore the *ancien régime*, and return to an agricultural economy.

So *Rerum Novarum* was a relatively cautious document, and certainly no 'workers' charter', as it is sometimes claimed to be. Leo attacked the excesses of capitalism, but provided no analysis of the state of affairs capitalism had produced. There was a good deal of abstract argument in the encyclical, but very little reference to actual situations. There was no direct endorsement of workers' trades unions. What Leo recommended was a system of trade associations, ones which embraced both workers and employers in the same organization. It had overtones of the medieval guild structure.

On the other hand, Leo defended workers' rights as a matter of strict justice. And however restrained it may now seem, the approval he gave to workers' movements was of immense psychological importance. It was the first time in history such a thing had been done by any authority of the standing of the Holy See.

Pope Leo might not have been altogether happy with such liberal institutions as a free press and parliamentary democracy, but for the most part he was prepared to urge Catholics to accept them. Though his first encyclical denounced the excesses of liberalism, he believed that Catholics ought to participate in governmental structures of whatever complexion, for the common good, and for the good of the Church.

But this readiness to espouse a modest liberalism did not extend to Italy. After his election he refused to give the customary blessing 'to the City and the World', a gesture that was ill-received by the Romans. He tried for a time to bring about a reconciliation between the Holy See and King Victor Emmanuel of Italy. When this failed he made it clear that his predecessor's prohibition on Catholics taking part in Italian politics was still in force. This was a disastrous decision. It forged an alliance between the Catholic Church in Italy and the right-wing parties which were also unwilling to be reconciled to the new regime. Leo was in favour of an Italian Catholic political party, as long as it did not take part in politics—an odd viewpoint.

After direct negotiations with the Kingdom of Italy came to nothing, Leo tried to internationalize the Roman Question. He pinned his hopes on Germany. The German Chancellor, Otto von Bismarck, had passed a great deal of anti-Catholic legislation in the 1870s, and Leo worked patiently to have it removed from the statute book. His quiet diplomacy was successful, and relations between Germany and the Holy See improved.

Leo also had to cope with an anti-clerical government in France. He realized that at the root of the attitude of the government in Paris towards the Church was the unwillingness of Catholics in France to be reconciled to the new Republican regime. Many of the clergy and more active laity were staunchly monarchist. The Pope refused to connive at Catholic conspiracies against the regime, and asked the Archbishop of Algiers to rally Catholics to the support of the government. Though not too happy about the idea, the Archbishop did so in a speech made in 1890 which became known as the 'toast of Algiers'. It earned him a lot of vituperation. Rather tardily, Leo came to the Archbishop's defence. He wrote an encyclical letter calling upon French Catholics to forget their differences with the Republican regime. They were exhorted to accept the prevailing political institutions on the dubious principle that 'civil power is of God, and always of God'.

This message was not very palatable to the great majority of the French bishops. They depended for much of their financial support on people whose sympathies lay with the monarchist cause. So the outcome of the call to rally to the side of the government was a further split in the ranks of French Catholics. But the government in Paris was grateful for Leo's efforts, and the situation of the Church in France was somewhat eased.

Leo was undoubtedly a skilful diplomat, but his efforts to make the Holy See a force on the world scene came to little. The Roman Question kept getting in the way. He was anxious, for example, to be invited to the Peace Conference held at The Hague in 1899, but the current Italian government vetoed the proposal.

The Pope had to employ his talents as a diplomat in fields other than politics. He was hampered by the French and the Portuguese when he tried to reorganize the Church's missions in China and India, though he managed eventually to set up a proper hierarchy of bishops in India. He used the opportunity offered by a Congress on the Eucharist held in Jerusalem to show the Churches of the East that the Holy See was well-disposed both to the Churches themselves, and to their proud traditions. He wanted to make it clear that if the Churches of the East were reunited with Rome, there would be no attempt made to Latinize their liturgies, or impose Western structures. These things had happened in the past, with disastrous results. Ill-will had built up towards Rome, and the Churches of the East had split into warring factions.

The same enlightened attitude, however, did not extend towards relations with Anglicanism. Unofficial talks between the two Churches began after a chance encounter on the island of Madeira between the English Lord Halifax and the French priest, Fernand Portal. Cardinal Vaughan, the Archbishop of Westminster, was not at all enthusiastic about reunion with the Anglicans, but Leo XIII certainly was, at least at first. He wanted to write a personal letter to the Archbishop of Canterbury. Cardinal Vaughan dissuaded him from doing so, and the Pope had to content himself with a very general exhortation 'To the English', calling for prayers for unity.

It was not very long before the question arose whether Catholics could regard the Anglican clergy as being true priests. A commission was set up in Rome to consider the matter, and Vaughan managed to pack it with people who shared his views. The outcome was inevitable. In a bull entitled *Apostolicae Curae*, which was issued in 1896, Pope Leo XIII declared that Holy Orders as bestowed in the Church of England were 'absolutely null and utterly void' as far as Catholics were concerned. There were no anti-Catholic demonstrations in England, but the snub was bitterly resented.

Discussions about reunion had begun as private conversations. Cardinal Vaughan had engineered that they be put on an official footing, and that they should take place, not in England or France, but in Rome. Decisions affecting local Churches, and the lives of Catholics even in minor details, were increasingly being made in Rome. It was a movement towards centralization which local bishops encouraged, especially after the definition of papal infallibility. Leo XIII helped it along. The authority of papal nuncios, the Pope's representatives in different countries, was increased, so that they could control local hierarchies. Papal legates were sent specially to preside over very important meetings in the name of the Bishop of Rome. Religious orders were encouraged to move their headquarters to Rome, or at least to open houses of study in the city. The larger the number of priests who received their training in Rome, the greater would be the influence of the Holy See throughout the Church, or so successive popes believed.

Naturally, Leo believed that the influence of the papacy would be benign. When Italian anti-clericals started to blame the popes for all the ills of Italy he responded in 1883 by opening the enormously rich Vatican archives to historians so that they could set the record straight. The documents should speak for themselves, decided the Pope. Ludwig von Pastor began to use the archives to write his history of the papacy. The third volume in the series covered the life and times of the notorious Pope Alexander VI. There were people in the Roman Curia who wanted to put the book on the *Index*, but Leo refused to do so. The Church, he said, had nothing to fear from the truth. It was a great act of faith, but he stood by it, even in the case of Alexander VI.

Before Leo opened the Vatican archives, use of them had been so surrounded by restrictions that research was next to impossible. Historians could not trust their luck when they were allowed such easy access. After Leo's death, on 20 July 1903, Pastor sought and received from the new Pope confirmation that historical research could go on as it had under Leo.

In this gesture, Pius X showed himself to be open-minded. In his personal life he was, as he has since been declared, a saint. But neither this openness of mind to historical research, nor his personal holiness, made him in any way sympathetic towards people whose studies led them to question views accepted within the Catholic Church. He was no intellectual. It was a catastrophe for the Church that, immediately after his election, he had to

Left: *The pontificate of Pope Saint Pius X (1903-1914) was one of the most controversial in modern times. No intellectual himself, immediately upon his election he was faced with the monumental problem of reconciling the received truths of the Faith with the demands of contemporary scholarship.*

face the problem of reconciling faith with modern scholarship.

Giuseppe Melchiore Sarto was born on 2 June 1835 in the northern Italian village of Riese, where his father was a minor official. He went to the seminary in Padua in 1850, and was ordained eight years later. He worked for a while as an assistant priest, and then as a parish priest at Salzano. In 1875 the Bishop of Treviso asked him to return to the seminary as spiritual director to the students, and at the same time to act as chancellor of the diocese. In 1884 he was appointed Bishop of Mantua, and in 1893, three days after having been made a Cardinal, Patriarch of Venice. During the

conclave which followed Leo XIII's death, a Catholic power – Austria – exercised its traditional right of veto against one of the favourite candidates. It was the last time such a thing was to happen. After he had been elected on 4 August 1903, Pope Pius X abolished this privilege for ever.

At first sight, Cardinal Sarto was an excellent choice to succeed Pope Leo. He had behind him a great deal more pastoral experience than the majority of his predecessors of recent centuries. He had a somewhat florid complexion, was rather stout, and of medium height. His voice was warm and gentle, his manner friendly. He was simple and straightforward, and extremely pious. But he reacted to the problem of Modernism with a severity, and a lack of comprehension, that were to damage the Church for a generation.

Not that he was wholly to blame for his failure to understand. The 'heresy' of Modernism was enormously difficult to tie down. There were almost as many forms of it as there were Modernists. It arose out of the wholly praiseworthy attempt to apply the lessons learned from the theory of evolution and the techniques of modern historical scholarship to the study of the Bible and the history of doctrine. Modernists found it impossible to accept that God had revealed absolute truths to the Church once and for all, and that the Church had transmitted these truths down the ages in an unchanging, and unchangeable, form.

Much of what the Modernists wrote made very good sense, for the 'heresy' attracted in varying degrees some of the brightest intellects of the late

nineteenth and early twentieth centuries. But there were also some things written and said which were clearly incompatible with Christianity. They were more likely to occur, however, after the individuals who made them had been excommunicated, or their books put on the *Index*.

The Church's reaction was extreme. The Biblical Commission, which Pope Leo XIII had founded to foster biblical scholarship, effectively put an end to such scholarship with a series of reactionary decrees. A decree of 1906, for example, required Catholic scholars to believe that Moses had written the first five books of the Bible, and a decree in 1911 insisted that Saint Matthew's Gospel was the first of the four Gospels to be written. There were many other decisions, most of them highly debatable if not downright wrong. But Catholics were obliged to accept them. Pope Pius X, in a letter he wrote in 1907, commanded members of the Church to give their assent not only to all that the Biblical Commission had already laid down, but even to anything it would decide in the future. In Pius' view, papal infallibility extended to the subordinate agencies of the Church.

In Rome's eyes, the errors of the Modernists were not limited to biblical matters. A long list was condemned by the Pope in his encyclical called *Pascendi*, published in September 1907. Naturally, there were protests. One man complained that, as it was described in *Pascendi*, Modernism did not exist. He was excommunicated. Students for the priesthood were forbidden to read secular newspapers and magazines lest they be infected by the spirit of the age. Lecturers had to submit textbooks and lecture notes for approval. All candidates for the priesthood had to take the anti-Modernist oath, and to repeat it every time they took a step up the ecclesiastical ladder. Bishops were required to establish councils to fight Modernism, seek out individual Modernists and confiscate their writings. Every three years they were to report on their success. 'Never in the history of Christian tradition and spirituality,' wrote one Modernist, 'had a greater outrage been perpetrated upon that regard for truth which is the elementary obligation of every human being.'

The worst aspect of the witch-hunt against Modernists was the setting up of a secret 'thought police'. The organization was called the *Sodalitium Pianum*, or Sodality of Saint Pius V, but because it operated undercover it was referred to more frequently by its code-name 'Sapinière'. Monsignor Humberto Benigni supplied Pius X with daily reports, and Pius X supplied 'Sapiniere' with money. The mere accusation of Modernism, against which there was no defence, was enough to put an end to ecclesiastical careers, or to debar someone from teaching.

As the Holy See understood it, Modernism in theology had a counterpart in social and political life. To guard against this, Pius X thought it important that Catholic organizations involved in secular matters should be kept under the control of the clergy. The danger of socialism in Italy, and a fear that the papacy might be totally isolated, pushed the Holy See closer to the 'liberal' Italian government, and Pius IX's prohibition against Catholics involving themselves in Italian political life was allowed to fall into abeyance; it was finally abolished in 1919. But the Pope did not want to see a specifically Catholic political party, even a conservative one, because that might threaten clerical control of the laity.

When the anti-clerical government in Paris annulled the concordat which Napoleon had made with Pius VII, the threat to the clerical control of the Church in France became acute. The French government decided to set up lay associations to administer Church property. The French bishops came to the conclusion that, in the circumstances, the proposal was the best that could be hoped for. Pius X, however, utterly rejected the idea. He managed to make it appear that, in so doing, he was speaking on behalf of the bishops of France, which was quite untrue.

The attitude of the Holy See towards the government in Paris encouraged those who believed that a union of Church and State was indispensable to the well-being of Catholicism. These *integristes*, as they were called, found their spiritual home in *Action Française*, an extreme right-wing group which believed that all the ills of France stemmed from the abandonment of Catholic religious practice and the destruction of the monarchy. Its leader was an atheist, Charles Maurras, several of whose books were condemned by the Church in 1914. Pope Pius refused to allow the condemnation to be made public. He praised Maurras as a 'valiant defender of the Holy See and the Church'. *Action Française* was eventually condemned by Pope Pius XI in 1926, though it survived to flourish in Vichy France during World War II. Pius X, however, tried to appoint as bishops in France priests who were well-disposed towards it. 'It is acting in defence of authority, and in defence of order', he said, and that, for Pope Pius, was high praise indeed.

Order was the Pope's ruling passion. He identified it with clerical control. He was not greatly interested in political affairs: his chief concern was the spiritual wellbeing of the Church. Career diplomats in the Vatican's service were replaced by pastoral bishops, or by men who had served as heads of their religious orders. Their task was not so much to negotiate with governments as to report on the state of a country's dioceses, and to ensure that the instruction given in seminaries was untainted by Modernism. Diocesan bishops were required to send in regular and detailed reports in addition to those provided by the diplomatic representatives, and *ad limina* visits had to be made at fixed times.

The comprehensive surveillance he exercised over the Church was, Pius believed, the duty owed by an infallible pope to worldwide Catholicism. Love of the pope, he once informed a group of priests, was an important means of achieving holiness, and love put into practice was expressed in obedience to the pope's instructions. He would have been failing in his job

Below: The Lateran Treaty, which put an end to the conflict between the Holy See and the Kingdom of Italy, was signed in February 1929. The pope was no longer 'a prisoner of the Vatican'. This painting, completed by an Italian artist for the London Graphic that same month shows the papal court in full regalia. Pope Pius XI is being carried along on the portable throne, the Sedia Gestatoria, and on either side of him are the fans of ostrich feathers. Much of this magnificence was abolished by Pope Paul VI – the Noble and the Palatine Guards were dissolved, for example – but the Sedia Gestatoria was retained, so that the crowds could see the pope during solemn processions.

Right: *Pope Pius XII (1939-58) at prayer. Very many Catholics came to regard him as a saint, and the process which might eventually result in his canonization was begun by Pope Paul VI at the same time as he initiated the process for the canonization of Pope John XXIII, Pius' successor.*

had he not given the instructions, and made sure they were obeyed.

It would be wrong to think of him as a harsh man. He was personally very devout, and encouraged devotion to the Eucharist. All Catholics, he urged, should receive it more frequently, and he lowered the age when children might first receive it. For innovations such as these, and for restoring to the Church's liturgy the hauntingly beautiful Gregorian chant, he is now remembered by Catholics, and honoured as a saint. He died on 20 August 1914 heartbroken, it was said, by the outbreak of World War I. He was canonized just 40 years later by a pope who shared his vision of the Church, and who had been elected to office just before Europe became engulfed in World War II.

Pius XII was born in Rome on 2 March 1876, and christened Eugenio Maria Giuseppe. His family, the Pacellis, were from Tuscany, and they had been supplying the Holy See with lawyers since the early years of the nineteenth century. It was no surprise, therefore, when Eugenio Pacelli himself decided to study law, after completing his studies in philosophy and theology at the Gregorian University and the Lateran in Rome. He was awarded a doctorate in canon law in 1902. By that time he was already a priest and working in the Secretariat of State. In 1904 he joined

Above: *Each Easter Day the Pope comes out on to a balcony in front of Saint Peter's and gives a blessing 'Urbi et Orbi' – to the City (of Rome) and the World. This picture of 200,000 people crowding into Saint Peter's Square between the Bernini's columnades was taken in 1948.*

the team set up by Pius X to codify the law of the Church, a task which was only completed in 1917.

For a while he taught ecclesiastical diplomacy, and in 1917 he was required to put his teaching into practice. He was consecrated an archbishop, and sent to Bavaria as papal nuncio. He served at Munich for three years, and was then promoted to Berlin. There he stayed, becoming a fluent German speaker and Germanophile, until in 1930 he was appointed Pope Pius XI's Secretary of State.

He took office just as one long-standing problem had been solved. In 1929 the Lateran Treaty – which a lawyer brother of Cardinal Pacelli had helped to draw up – settled the dispute between the Kingdom of Italy and the Holy See. The Pope was left as sovereign of the Vatican City State, with extra-territorial rights over some other buildings in Rome, and over Castel Gandolfo. The terms, which included what then seemed a huge financial settlement by Italy upon the Holy See, were generous. They were achieved at the price of silencing the church's opposition to Mussolini's rise to power, and killing any hope of reviving the Catholic Popular Party – of which the future Pope Paul VI's father had been a founder-member.

Treaties and concordats were very much in vogue, and Pacelli's term of office as Secretary of State saw the signing of a whole string of them. As a lawyer and diplomat he believed that concordats were the best way of

Left: *Cardinal Eugenio Pacelli, the future Pope Pius XII, entered the Vatican's diplomatic service in 1917 when he was sent to Germany as nuncio (or ambassador) to Munich and then on to Berlin in the same role in 1920. Ten years later he became Cardinal Secretary of State, the Pope's foreign minister. His time in Germany made him a fluent German speaker, and very much a Germanophile – though he was never taken in by Hitler.*

preserving the Church's freedom of action. He remained convinced of this despite his experiences with Hitler.

It was the German leader himself who first suggested a concordat with Rome. Pacelli had few illusions about Hitler, but since both the laity and the bishops in Germany seemed ready to trust him, the Secretary of State went ahead. On paper the concordat of 1933 was a triumph. It granted all that the Vatican asked. The only problem was that Hitler ignored it, and the remaining years of the decade saw a constant stream of notes of protest from the Vatican to Berlin. They did no good. Pius XI's encyclical *Mit brennender Sorge* was a bitter condemnation of the Nazi Party. It had been drafted by Pacelli, and the Pope ordered it to be read in all German churches on Palm Sunday 1937. When Hitler visited Rome during the following year the Pope ostentatiously left the city.

Cardinal Pacelli had been groomed for the papacy. He had a wide

knowledge of foreign affairs, and during his time as Secretary of State he had visited both North and South America, Eastern Europe and France. The dying Pope Pius XI had ensured that all foreign cardinals would be in Rome for the conclave, and had made it plain that Pacelli was his candidate. He was chosen by 48 votes out of 65 on 2 March 1939, after the shortest conclave since that which elected Urban VIII in 1623.

Pope Pius XII had to turn his attention immediately to the conflict in Europe. He tried to keep the peace, and when that failed relayed messages from the German resistance to the Allies. He met with King Victor Emmanuel III of Italy and wrote letters to Mussolini in a vain attempt to prevent Italy from siding with Germany. Finally he tried to have Rome declared an 'open city', free of troops and not, therefore, a military target. That initiative, too, was doomed to failure. As a British official remarked in 1944, the Pope had done as much as anyone in his position could do.

Nonetheless, his behaviour during the war years has become a matter of bitter controversy. In particular, he has been accused of being insufficiently active on behalf of the Jews. Both the Pope personally and the Church gave considerable help to Jewish (and other) refugees, and Pius twice unequivocally condemned the extermination of the Jews. It must be remembered that complaints about the Pope's 'silence' came only long after the war. In its immediate aftermath people remembered his assistance to the victims of persecution, his pleas for peace, and his championing of human rights.

He hated the war, and it brought him agonies of indecision. He believed, rightly or wrongly, that in certain instances it would have done more harm than good to have spoken out. He also felt himself obliged to remain neutral, and to use the instruments of diplomacy to which he was accustomed. It rapidly became clear that traditional diplomacy was irrelevant, but he was unsure what he should put in its place.

Part of the problem was his conviction that Communism presented at least as great a danger as did Fascism. His worst fears were to be fulfilled after the war when the Churches of Eastern Europe which had been in communion with the Bishop of Rome were one by one eliminated by the Communist regimes. Church leaders were made the victims of show trials, and found guilty. In his Christmas message in 1951, Pope Pius XII spoke of 'the Church of silence'.

One result of the persecution in Eastern Europe was the arrival in the West of many Eastern-rite Christians. Pius at times showed himself strangely insensitive to the special problems of these refugees, and appointed Latin-rite bishops to attend to their spiritual needs. Ham-fisted efforts by Rome to codify Eastern canon law also caused alarm among the Eastern Churches, who saw their autonomy being eroded. Nor was the Pope particularly sensitive to the Churches of the Reformed tradition. After vague stirrings during the Pontificate of Leo XIII, popes had issued stern warnings against ecumenism. Under Pius XII it advanced scarcely at all.

But for all that, there was much of the reformer about Pope Pius. Though his encyclical of August 1950, *Humani Generis*, issued stern warnings about certain theological developments, it was followed by little of the witch-hunt which the attack on Modernism had engendered. Some distinguished professors of theology in France were removed from their posts, but their scholarly exile was not permanent. On the other hand, *Divino Afflante Spiritu*, published in 1943, gave renewed vigour to Catholic biblical studies.

The first encyclical ever to be entirely devoted to the Church's liturgy was published in 1947: it laid great stress upon the community nature of worship. There were numerous minor reforms which, taken as a whole, made a powerful impact on Catholics. They made the Church's worship more readily accessible to the worshippers and, of more moment in the long term, they demonstrated, in a period of relative stability, that the Vatican did not consider the liturgy to be unchangeable.

Opposite: *Archbishop Cesare Orsenigo, who succeeded Eugenio Pacelli as Papal Nuncio in Berlin, is shown here greeting Hitler and Ribbentrop. Orsenigo remained at his post until his death in March 1946, but was regarded as politically compromised by the post-war regime in Germany, and his personal situation became very difficult during the last few months of his life.*

Above: *In this picture, taken at Castel Gandolfo in September 1957, Pius XII can be seen with the British Minister to the Holy See (then Sir Marcus Cheke) on the Pope's left. He has just presented the lady on the Pope's right, the Regent Paramount Chief of Basutoland which in 1957 was still a British colony.*

Pius XII was a man of wide culture and sharp intelligence. He was prepared to write and to speak on almost any topic. He devoted over 200 documents to the way of life of monks and nuns, and he tried to remedy defects in the organization of religious orders. It was in this context that he used the word *aggiornamento* (bringing up to date), which became so much associated with his successor as Bishop of Rome.

Averaged out over his pontificate, the number of his speeches was almost one a day. They ranged widely. Medical ethics was a particularly common topic, and though he never wrote an encyclical on social questions, he often spoke of them, and was the first pope to use the expression 'social teaching of the Church'. By training and inclination he was a legalist. His addresses framed a rigid behaviour code. Catholic consciences were constantly being instructed, little was left to their own decision.

It was natural, therefore, that Pope Pius should have planned to reform the Roman Curia (which he made considerably more international) in such a way that cardinals would become papal legates, ensuring that the will of the sovereign pontiff be implemented by local bishops, and carried out by the laity. The plan was never put into practice, but it was the logical extension of Pius X's vision of the role of the papacy. It was the structural expression of the doctrine of papal infallibility as it had been understood immediately after Vatican I.

In the opinion of Romolo Murri, an Italian priest closely associated with the foundation of Christian Democracy, the great advantage of the definition of papal infallibility was that it freed Catholics from having to engage in theological disputes. They could spend more time on social and political issues. But now the Pope was taking charge of those matters as well. It was a case of 'creeping infallibility'. Pius XII was the last Pope to date to invoke explicitly the doctrine of papal infallibility. He did so in November 1950 when he solemnly proclaimed the dogma of the Bodily Assumption of the Virgin Mary into heaven.

He died eight years later, on 9 October 1958. His voice had been often heard on the radio. His ascetic, emaciated figure was becoming known through the medium of television. He was an object of devotion to millions of Catholics throughout the world who were thrilled with rumours of his vision of Christ at his bedside.

Increasing ill health in his later years intensified his natural predilection for solitude, and this in turn enhanced the air of mystery which surrounded him. The impact of his pontificate was such that many came to see the role of the papacy in the Church and in the world in the same exalted and highly dramatic way that Pius himself saw it. For many, Pius XII for a long time remained, and for some still remains, the absolute model of what a pope ought to be.

Above: *By the time of his death in 1958 the remote, emaciated and ascetical Pope Pius XII had come to be almost worshipped by millions of Catholics, as this photograph so vividly illustrates. It was taken just four years before he died when 6,000 young women from 34 countries were received in audience in Saint Peter's by Pope Pius. These women had come to Rome on a pilgrimage for the 'Marian Year', a year dedicated to special devotion to the Blessed Virgin.*

FINDING A NEW ROLE

Powerful though the memory of Pius XII may have been, it did not so bemuse the cardinal-electors of the conclave of 1958 that they chose someone just like him. On 28 October they selected Angelo Giuseppe Roncalli, Cardinal-Patriarch of Venice, who took the name John XXIII with the characteristic comment that the reigns of most of his predecessors of that name had been brief. So in place of the tall, gaunt aristocrat, the Church was to be ruled by a small, plump peasant. When he was being photographed (which was often) Pius XII was accustomed to gaze away from the camera, his eyes raised mystically heavenward. Pope John beamed straight into the lens, and the world breathed a sigh of relief.

He was 77 years of age at his election, and many thought he must have been a compromise candidate, or a transitional Pope. But in some circles he had been hot favourite. There were, in any case, few possibilities. Pius XII had not appointed any cardinals for five years, and there were only 51 electors, nearly a quarter of whom were 80 or more years old. In the event, it took 11 ballots to choose Roncalli. It was a struggle for him to fit into the white robes which were waiting. The Vatican prepares three sets of such robes for the new pope: one small, one medium and one large. Officials, however, had been unprepared for someone of Roncalli's girth. 'Everyone wants me to be pope except the tailors', he said, and moved off to give his blessing in the constricting clothing, muttering darkly about the shackles of the papacy.

The Roncalli family farmed rented land – which the Pope's father was eventually able to buy from the local Count – at Sotto il Monte, near Bergamo. Giovanni and Giulia Marianna were poor. 'There are three ways a man can be ruined,' Pope John once explained, 'women, gambling and farming, and my father chose the most boring.' The family was large. Angelo was the eldest son, and the third of 13 children. The house was crowded with aunts, uncles and cousins, as well as with the children.

Angelo was born on 25 November 1881. At the age of 12 he entered the diocesan seminary, and there won a scholarship which took him to Rome, where he studied for a doctorate in theology. He was ordained a priest in 1904, and began graduate work in canon law, but this was interupted by a summons to serve as secretary to Count Giacomo Radini-Tedeschi, the newly appointed Bishop of Bergamo.

The Count's liberal views were well known in Rome, and not at all to the taste of Pope Pius X, but he was too important a person to be ignored. He was therefore sent to a diocese where he would have little opportunity to devote himself to the social problems which so interested him. Instead, Bishop Radini-Tedeschi threw himself wholeheartedly into the other pastoral concerns of his diocese. Roncalli was to learn a great deal from him

Opposite: *Angelo Giuseppe Roncalli was born in 1881 and became Pope John XXIII in 1958. Though elected as an interim Pope, his desire for 'aggiornamento' (up-dating) in the Church, his personal holiness and the friendliness of his character together with his wit, made an enormous impact upon his fellow Catholics, and upon the world at large. In 1962 he opened the Second Vatican Council, but lived only long enough to see the Council complete its first session. He died, much loved and deeply mourned, in 1963.*

Above: *Pope John XXIII (1958-63) photographed* (top) *as a young priest at his ordination, in 1904, and* (bottom) *during the First World War, in which he served first as a sergeant in the medical corps and then as a lieutenant in the chaplains' corps.*

about the pastoral apostolate, and became his fervent admirer. After Radini-Tedeschi's death he wrote a biography of the Bishop, and sent a copy of it to another admirer, Pope Benedict XV.

The Bishop of Bergamo died just before the outbreak of World War I. Roncalli, who had broken off his studies a decade before to serve in the Italian army, now returned to the ranks, first of all as a sergeant in the medical corps, and then as a lieutenant in the corps of chaplains.

After the war Benedict XV remembered the young biographer of Bishop Radini-Tedeschi. Roncalli was summoned to Rome, and made national organizer for the Association for the Propagation of the Faith. His function was to raise money for the Church's missionary activity, and this appointment gave him opportunities for travel. It also brought him into contact with people of influence, some at least of whom shared the concern for social issues which he had learned from the Bishop of Bergamo. But the early years of the pontificate of Pope Pius XI were not hopeful ones in Rome for those who were liberals, or opposed to the rise of Italian Fascism. Roncalli may have been something of an embarrassment. Whatever the reason, in 1925 he was suddenly named Apostolic Visitor to Bulgaria, and exiled to Sofia with the rank of Archbishop. In 1934 he was promoted to the status of Apostolic Delegate to Turkey and Greece.

These were thankless tasks. Both posts required a good deal of patience, tact and good humour – all qualities which Roncalli possessed in abundance. But in all three countries he was at first faced with hostile governments. In Turkey and Bulgaria he had some success in establishing friendly diplomatic relations. Dealing with Athens, however, was much more difficult. One of the chief problems was a suspicion about the intentions of the Holy See harboured by the Greek Orthodox Church – a suspicion which had been confirmed by the efforts made by Rome to foster the growth of Latin-rite Catholicism in traditionally Orthodox areas. It was a feeling shared by many of the non-Latin-rite Christians who were in communion with Rome. In addition to his diplomatic activities on behalf of the Holy See, Archbishop Roncalli had pastoral responsibility for all Christians in communion with Rome, whether belonging to the Latin rite, or divided among the various Eastern Churches. His experience taught him a good deal about the complexities of Eastern Catholicism, as well as the sensibilities of the Orthodox Churches.

Then, in 1944, came a new appointment which was even more of a surprise than the earlier ones. From the diplomatic backwater of Istanbul he was suddenly ordered to take up the prestigious post of papal nuncio in Paris. The government which had just been set up in a newly-liberated France demanded that the Vatican recall its former nuncio who had been accredited to the collaborationist Vichy regime. Perhaps someone in the French Foreign Ministry remembered Roncalli, for the French had exercised a form of protectorate over Latin-rite Christians in the lands where Roncalli had served before World War II. Certainly Pope Pius XII had come to respect the Archbishop's skill.

And all his skill was to be needed. It was not an easy time to be an ecclesiastical diplomat in Paris. The new government was demanding the resignation of 33 bishops whom they accused of collaborating with the Germans. Roncalli examined each case carefully, and eventually whittled the number down to three. He then won the approval of the government by seeking, and obtaining, elevation to the rank of cardinal for three more prelates who had been sympathetic to the Free French, and whom General de Gaulle wished to honour.

Roncalli also had to cope with some very difficult problems internal to the Church. It was his duty, for example, to see that the encyclical *Humani Generis* was implemented in France, and that the suspect theologians (most of whom were French) were removed from their teaching posts. It was not a task that he relished. Nor was he particularly happy when he was asked to report upon

the 'worker-priests'. These were priests who had taken jobs in factories so that they could better understand, and more closely identify with, workers for whom the Christian faith had lost its meaning and influence. Pius XII believed that the experiment had done little to win such people back to Christ, and had done a great deal to radicalize the clergy. He wanted the whole experiment closed down. Archbishop Roncalli's advice was to do nothing, but it was not taken. Later on, as Pope, he allowed a modified form of the worker-priest movement to begin again.

There have been differing views about his success as nuncio in Paris, but there can be little doubt about his personal popularity both with his colleagues, including the Soviet ambassador, and with the statesmen with whom he came into contact. His easy manner was a relief from much of the stuffiness traditionally associated with diplomacy. On one occasion he found himself seated next to a lady wearing a very low-cut dress. Afterwards he was asked if he were not angry, or at least embarrassed. Not at all, he replied, because while he was sitting there everyone else was looking in the direction of the papal nuncio to see how he was taking it, rather than at the lady in question.

At the end of 1952 Pius XII belatedly decided to make him a cardinal. The President of the French Republic, who was an atheist, insisted on exercising the ancient privilege of the French kings, and bestowing on the

Above: *This photograph of Pope John XXIII was taken in May 1963 as he worked in his study in Saint John's tower in the Vatican – a remote room to which the Pope used to retire for peace and quiet. A month after this picture was taken he died of an illness which had begun the previous November.*

nuncio his red biretta, the sign of his rank in the Church. The gesture was a remarkable one. It may have had some influence on Pope Pius' next surprise for Cardinal Roncalli. He was to be moved to the Patriarchal See of Venice. After more than a quarter of a century of exile from his native country, Angelo Giuseppe Roncalli was coming home.

Though the Italy he found in 1953 was very different from the one he had left in 1925, he soon learned to adapt, and was once again a great popular success. He even managed to get along with the Communist mayor of the city. He wrote regular short letters to the clergy and to the people of his diocese, and won their affection. He visited all the parishes under his charge, and started 30 new ones. He showed concern about the decaying fabric of one of the world's most beautiful cities, and successfully opposed an attempt to bring the gambling casino into the centre of Venice from the Lido. Yet in the midst of all his time-consuming activities and duties, he still found time to complete his five-volume edition of Saint Charles Borromeo's account of his visitation to Bergamo.

He was also trapped by Vatican politics. The Pope required him to oppose the move towards the left which was being made by the Christian Democratic Party in Venice. He obediently did so, but as gently as he possibly could. When the Italian Socialist Party held a congress in the city he sent it an address of welcome, a gesture that was not at all well received by the right wing of the Church.

So the man whose smile was splashed across the newspapers in October 1958 came from a very complex background. He had written a biography, and edited a manuscript. He had served the Church in some of the most difficult trouble spots for a Vatican diplomat, and had done so with a deceptive ease. On the surface he appeared easy-going, and perhaps a little simple, yet he spoke French, Bulgarian, Russian, Turkish and modern Greek, as well as his native Italian and the Church's Latin. He was fond of Italian literature, and appreciative of art. He was something of a connoisseur of music, and had arranged for Igor Stravinsky's 'Sacred Canticle' to be given its first performance in the cathedral at Venice.

John XXIII's first actions as Pope did not help to make it clear just what sort of a person had been elected. He increased the number of members of the sacred college of cardinals, a badly needed reform, but he also increased the percentage of Italian cardinals from 30 to 40, which was taken to be a conservative move. He wrote two stirring social encyclicals, *Mater et Magistra* and *Pacem in Terris*, but in between them he published another, bringing back Latin as the language of instruction in seminaries.

It may all have been part of the Pope's diplomatic technique, giving a little in one direction so that more important gains might be made in another. Or it may have been that he had lived for so long away from Rome that he was not always aware when he was being used in the power struggle between different parties in the Church. But though at times he may have seemed to favour the forces of reaction in the Church, there was no doubt at all where his own aspirations lay. 'So long as I am able,' he said, 'I prefer to be one who dispenses warmth rather than cold.'

He gave immediate evidence of what he meant when, to the consternation of those responsible for his security, he set about visiting churches and hospitals in Rome, as any bishop in any other diocese would have done. His most famous visit, the day after Christmas 1958, was to the Regina Coeli prison in Rome. 'You can't come to me, so I have come to you', he explained to the astonished inmates. They were completely won over by his confession that he knew something about prisons – a cousin of his had once been gaoled for poaching.

This remark was too much for the editorial staff on the Vatican's newspaper, *L'Osservatore Romano*. They left it out of the account of the visit, and consistently modified his speeches to make them fit into the sort of image they considered appropriate. It was not this form of censorship which eventually

Above: *A very young-looking Edward Kennedy was received in audience by Pope John XXIII on 21 May 1961. Kennedy had been sent to Italy by his brother John, then President of the United States, as a goodwill ambassador for the celebration to mark the centenary of the unification of Italy.*

spurred Pope John to take action, however, but the odd sight of a reporter taking dictation from him on his knees. (In Pope Pius XII's time, Vatican officials were reputed to have received telephone calls from the Pope on their knees.) John told the man to stand up, and ordered the paper's editor to cut down on the flowery phrases with which *Osservatore* customarily introduced the words of the Pope, or described his activities.

The Vatican daily was not at all happy when, in a gathering of cardinals on 25 January 1959, John announced that there was to be a Council of the whole Church. The paper forebore to mention the fact, except as a brief news item, until it became clear that John really meant to do what he had said. 'We are not here on earth to guard a museum,' he once remarked of the Church, 'but to cultivate a garden.'

Before the Council could begin there were to be long battles with curial officials who were afraid of the forces which might be unleashed by it. Pope John was once asked how many people worked in the Vatican. 'About

Left: *A photograph of Pope John XXIII taken in October 1962 as his train stood in the railway station at Spoleto. He was on his way to the shrine of the Blessed Virgin at Loretto and to that of Saint Francis at Assisi to pray for the success of the Second Vatican Council, which opened later that same month. It was an historic journey, for it was the first time in over a century that a pope had left the confines of Rome.*

half', he replied (the expected answer would have been some 2250), and a good many of the active ones were putting difficulties in the way of his cherished project.

Despite the opposition, however, it began on 11 October 1962. In his opening address, Pope John emphasized that the purpose of the Second Vatican Council was to renew the religious life of Christians. It was to bring up to date the teaching, discipline and organization of the Church, with the ultimate goal of the reunion of all Christians.

The gathering in Saint Peter's reflected a very different world from that of Vatican I. Though Western Europe still accounted for the largest single grouping out of the 2500 or so bishops meeting in the basilica, more than 20 per cent came from Latin America, and another 20 per cent was evenly divided between Asian and Black African representatives.

From the countries of the Eastern bloc, only Yugoslavia was fully represented from the first. But Pope John's intervention in the Berlin crisis of 1961, and his disinterested and impassioned plea for peace, so impressed Mr

Opposite: *The Second Vatican Council began under Pope John XXIII in October 1962, but by the second session John was dead, and the ceremony of its opening was performed by his successor, Pope Paul VI. The picture shows Pope Paul standing in front of the papal altar in Saint Peter's Basilica, where the plenary meetings of the members of the Council were held.*

Above: *Giovanni Battista Montini in his formal dress as a cardinal, a rank in the Church to which he was appointed in December 1958 by Pope John XXIII. Four and a half years later, in June 1963, Montini was to succeed Pope John, and reign as Bishop of Rome for 15 years.*

Khruschev, the Russian leader, that not only were more bishops from Iron Curtain countries allowed to attend, but Khruschev's son-in-law was despatched to Rome and had a private audience with the Pope. It was all a far cry from the bitter anti-Communism of Pius XII.

Having failed to prevent the Council meeting, highly-placed and conservative-minded members of the Vatican's civil service tried at the outset to control the gathering. They were thwarted by men who had not flown halfway round the world to be told what to do, or whom to elect to the various committees which were to draft the Council's documents. Pope John supported the bishops against his curial officials.

He had made it quite clear that he did not want the Council to issue definitions or condemnations. 'There are thirty centimetres of condemnations in this document', he complained to one of his aides about a preparatory draft of one text. 'Nowadays the Church prefers to use the arm of mercy rather than that of severity', he told the assembled bishops in his opening address, and no definitions or condemnations were issued. Instead, the Council contented itself with producing a series of statements of varying lengths and differing quality on a range of topics, two of the most important being on subjects which Vatican I had been forced to abandon: papal infallibility and divine revelation.

Because the Council of 1870 had not had time to discuss the Church as a whole, the doctrine of papal infallibility had been left high and dry, without having been placed in the context in which it was to be understood. Vatican II pointed out that infallibility was something the pope enjoyed as head of the whole college of bishops. The concept of 'collegiality', or the corporate responsibility of the whole body of the bishops for the well-being of the Church, became part of the Church's official teaching.

As the Council was beginning professors from the Lateran, a Roman college Pope John had raised to the status of a university, were attacking Jesuit scholars from the Biblical Institute. The charge was that they had employed modern techniques in interpreting the Bible, and two eminent lecturers at the Biblical Institute were temporarily removed from their posts. The document on divine revelation, however, freed such scholars from fear of further attacks. It situated the Scriptures back within the Church, where they belonged, rather than leaving them, as Vatican I had seemed to do, as isolated books containing a series of God's statements to mankind.

Apart from these two 'Dogmatic Constitutions', there were 14 other Constitutions, Decrees or Declarations. Among the documents of the second rank, the fairly brief statement on religious freedom and the much lengthier one on the role of the Church in the modern world were outstanding, but all had something worthwhile to say. Most of them have had a considerable influence on the life of the Catholic Church ever since.

But before any of the documents had been finally agreed, Pope John was dead. For a year he lived with a painful cancer, though this did not prevent him from making, less than a month before his death, the first visit of a pope to a president of Italy. He went to the official presidential residence in the once-papal Quirinal palace to congratulate winners of prizes given by the Balzan Foundation. He had himself the day before been given the Foundation's Peace Prize. It was a fitting climax to the life of a man who had begun his papal career complaining that the lion of Saint Mark, which stood for the See of Venice on his papal coat of arms, looked far too fierce. He had instructed Monsignor Bruno Heim, the expert in ecclesiastical heraldry and later Apostolic Delegate to Great Britain, to draw a lion which seemed more friendly.

Pope John XXIII died on 3 June 1963. There were demonstrations of sympathy in Moscow. Jewish, Moslem, Buddhist as well as Christian leaders expressed their sorrow. The flag of the United Nations was flown at half-mast. These were not empty gestures. John's warmth, friendliness, compassion and humour had communicated itself to people far outside the

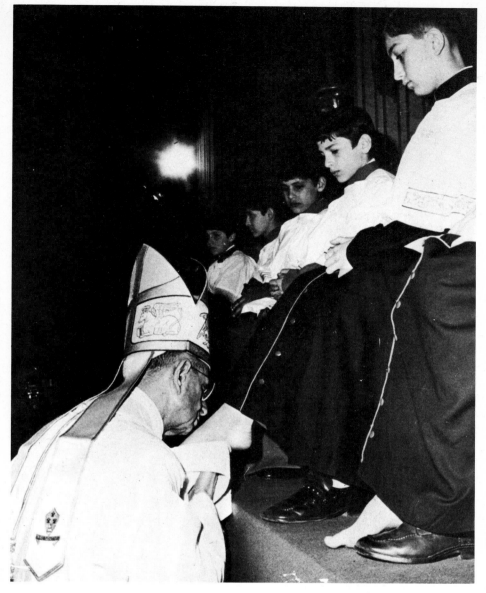

boundaries of the Catholic Church. It was the world as a whole that mourned the loss of a spiritual leader.

The Roman Church expressed its gratitude for John's life when the process for his canonization was begun by his successor, Pope Paul VI, in November 1965. But it was typical of Giovanni Battista Montini that he introduced at the same time the cause of the much less attractive figure of Pius XII. Pope Paul was caught between two worlds.

As Cardinal-Archbishop of Milan he had been very active in the opening stages of the Council. Shortly after Pope John's death he pledged himself to carry on the work which his old friend had begun. But all Montini's experience of Church government had been acquired under Pius XII, either as a member of Pacelli's department when the future Pope was Secretary of State, or practically running the Secretariat himself in the closing years of Pius' pontificate. The tension between the two vastly dissimilar styles of Pius and John was to plague Paul throughout his pontificate.

Like Pope John, Montini came from northern Italy. He was born on 26 September 1897 in the small town of Concesio, near Brescia. His father Giorgio was a well-to-do lawyer who preferred to think of himself as a journalist and politician committed to social and political reform. Giovanni's

younger brother qualified as a doctor, and fought in the Italian Resistance. His elder brother entered politics, and became a senator.

Giovanni's childhood was conventional but solemn. He suffered from ill health, and was turned down for the army. At the age of 19 his health suddenly improved, but he was still rejected for military service. In the meantime, however, he had entered the diocesan seminary, and in May 1920 he was ordained priest. In November the same year he went to Rome for further studies. Three years later he was sent to the papal nunciature in Warsaw but, once again, his health let him down and this brought him back to Italy. In October 1924 he began his more than 30 years of service in the Secretariat of State.

His spare time he devoted to the anti-Fascist Federation of Catholic University Students. He regarded anything to do with Mussolini with distaste, and when the Italian leader visited the Vatican in 1932 he made it clear that relations between Italy and the Holy See would improve if Montini were forbidden to have further contact with student groups. Montini's promotion to be assistant to Cardinal Pacelli in 1937 was a sign of the Vatican's growing disillusionment with Fascism.

His last years in the Secretariat of State were difficult ones. Pius XII had become something of a recluse, and Montini was one of the few who had relatively easy access to him. 'Why go to the Mountain [*Monte*] when one can get what one wants from the foothills [*Montini*]' ran the Roman joke of the day. But Montini was unhappy with the situation, at odds with Pius over the policies he was supposed to put into operation, and out of sympathy with the conservative Monsignor Tardini who worked beside him. In 1955 he was relieved to be appointed to the Archbishopric of Milan.

This great northern industrial city was under Communist control. He struggled to revive a decaying Church, and it was a measure of his success that the first anniversary of his arrival was marked by a bomb being thrown through the window of his residence. He did not simply build churches. He constructed schools, community centres and despensaries in the poor areas of the towns, and organized an enormous mission throughout his diocese. For this purpose he brought in great numbers of clergy equipped with little motorbikes – they were called the 'flying friars' – while he sped around the countryside in the fastest car he could find. He later carried this passion for speed to Rome with him, and would sit in the back of the papal limousine with a stop watch, encouraging his chauffeur to drive faster and faster.

Through his work for the poor he became known as 'the priest of the left', a title he detested. The champion of all who were oppressed, he believed that this did not commit him to any particular political ideology.

His work in Milan was much admired, his work in the Curia had made him well known. Although Pius XII had not made him a cardinal he was thought by some to be a candidate in the election of 1958. Pope John created him a cardinal in the December after that conclave, and in 1963 it took the electors only 42 hours to make him Pope Paul on 21 June.

For the first few months of his pontificate, Paul tried to follow not only the policies, but even the style of his predecessor. But he shared something of Pius' exalted vision of the office to which he had been called, and finally he found it easier to model himself upon Pius rather than upon John.

This inevitably brought conflict. In the spirit of collegiality he encouraged local groups of bishops to meet in episcopal conferences to deal with problems peculiar to their geographical area. He also established a series of regular meetings in Rome for bishops' representatives to discuss more general questions. He created more cardinals, and made the Curia international.

But some questions he reserved to himself, and refused to submit to collegial decision. One was the celibacy of the clergy, and on that he published an encyclical in 1967 reaffirming the traditional teaching. The other was artificial contraception. The encyclical *Humanae Vitae* condemning artificial methods of birth control appeared on 25 July 1968, and immediately

Opposite: *Paul VI appears at one of the windows of the papal summer residence of Castel Gandolfo in July 1968. The banner draped below depicts his coat of arms: the fleur-de-lis representing his affection for things French, and a conventional representation of a mountain, a play on the family name of Montini.*

aroused a storm of protest. It was well known that a committee set up to advise the Pope had suggested that some forms of contraception should be approved. The Vatican carefully orchestrated protestations of loyalty from all over the world, but it was abundantly evident that the encyclical did not enjoy the wholehearted support of all the bishops. They had not expected the Pope to act quite so unilaterally. The decision was ignored by many Catholics, and treated warily by vast numbers of the clergy. Those who defied the Pope's teaching did not think it necessary to leave the Church: they rejected papal claims to decide for Catholics which way they ought to behave.

I t was a turning point in Paul's pontificate. He wrote no more encyclicals, and later confessed to a Vatican diplomat 'Now I understand Saint Peter – he came to Rome twice, the second time to be crucified.' The controversy dragged on throughout his reign, and overshadowed it.

Yet Paul did a great deal else for which he deserves to be remembered. He carried out a number of reforms, some of them of great importance. After four centuries of controversial existence, for example, the *Index of Forbidden Books* was abolished. A retiring age for bishops was introduced, and no cardinal over the age of 80 was to vote in papal elections. He did away with some of the more flamboyant aspects of the papal court and of clerical attire.

Pope John had created a stir when he had travelled by train as far from Rome as Assisi, starting from the Vatican railway station built by Pius IX but never used. No Pope since Pio Nono had gone such a distance from the Vatican. But now Pope Paul went to the Holy Land, where he met the Patriarch of Constantinople, and he visited him again in Istanbul. The Patriarch returned the visit, and much better relations began between the Roman and the Orthodox Churches.

Paul went to the World Council of Churches in Geneva, and to India, Colombia, Uganda and Australia. He landed at Manila in November 1970, and was attacked by a thirty-year-old Brazilian, dressed as a priest and wielding a knife. His life was saved by the huge figure of a British missionary bishop, and the story was given out that he had been unharmed, although it appears now that he did receive a slight injury.

The world's press, and some of the Catholic papers, did not take kindly to his visit to the shrine of the Virgin at Fatima. The devotion was suspect, and Portugal's politics were disliked. But huge crowds greeted him there as they did everywhere. He admitted to a journalist that it was the support of the common people, who flocked to Rome in their millions for the Holy Year of 1975, that gave him the confidence to go on despite mounting criticism of the latter part of his pontificate. This criticism had come from the intellectuals in the Church. The ordinary Catholic understood that beneath the shy, rather cold manner Paul was a man deeply moved by the physical as well as the spiritual distress of so much of mankind. 'Wherever there is suffering', he had said in his first sermon in Milan, 'or where there is injustice or legitimate aspiration for social improvement, there will be the frank and solid defence of a pastor and father.'

That commitment had been made just to one city. In *Populorum Progressio*, on the duty of aiding the developing nations, published in 1967, Paul committed the Church to work for justice throughout the whole world. The newspaper of the American business world, *The Wall Street Journal*, attacked the encyclical, but it was rapturously received by millions. Where Pius XII had spoken to the consciences of Catholics, Paul VI addressed himself to the conscience of all mankind.

It was natural, then, that he should journey to New York to make a speech to the United Nations. It was also natural that such diverse personalities as Mrs Golda Meir or General Idi Amin should wish to visit him in Rome. He even received Communist leaders. President Tito came, and so did

Left: *Pope Paul VI being carried on the Sedia Gestatoria, the portable throne, during a Palm Sunday procession. Palms are attached to the top of the crucifix which serves as a pastoral staff, or 'crozier'. Recent popes have wished to discontinue the use of the sedia gestatoria, but so many people have come to see the processions that to do so would have been to deny them the sight of the Pope himself.*

President Podgorny of the U.S.S.R. Vatican officials were encouraged to make use of the contacts established, and to travel to Eastern bloc states. There they worked quietly, and to some extent successfully, to create normal – or as normal as possible – relations between the Communist regimes and the Catholic Church.

Pope Paul VI died on 7 August 1978. His great achievement was to put the Catholic Church, and the papacy itself, in the centre of the world stage. His pontificate, following upon that of Pope John, had defined the papacy's new role. Yet Paul himself, 'timid by temperament and courageous only out of virtue' as an admirer said of him, was ill-suited to play the part.

On 26 August, the cardinals believed that they had found the right man to succeed Pope Paul; 'God's candidate', the English Cardinal Hume described him. On the very first full day of the conclave they elected Albino Luciani, the Patriarch of Venice with the unruly quiff of hair and jaunty skull-cap. In honour of his two distinguished immediate predecessors he chose the name John Paul I.

POPE JOHN PAUL II

The pontificate of John Paul I began with high hopes. He was eminently approachable. He smiled broadly. He said 'I' when he meant 'I', instead of using the first person plural 'we' when referring to himself, as popes had done for centuries. He refused to be crowned or enthroned – these ceremonies being symbolic of earthly power. He chose instead to be invested with the 'pallium', the white woollen stole symbolizing bishops' unity with each other through their unity with the Bishop of Rome.

And then he died. It was 29 September, and Albino Luciani had ruled the See of Saint Peter for just 33 days. The world mourned the shortest pontificate since 1605, when Pope Leo XI had ruled for only 27 days.

The 111 electors hurried back to Rome. The task they were faced with in October was quite different from the one they had undertaken in August. They were now to replace a man very unlike Pope Paul VI. John Paul I had been a cheerful man of wide literary culture – he had written a series of letters to figures from fiction, from Mr Pickwick to Pinocchio, for a devotional magazine. He had been a seminary professor, then a bishop for 20 years, and then Patriarch of Venice, and had possessed a deep but simple piety.

On 14 October the conclave began. At a quarter to seven in the evening two days later, less than half an hour after the traditional white smoke signifying the election of a new pope had poured from a chimney above the Sistine Chapel, the senior Cardinal-Deacon came out on to the balcony of Saint Peter's. 'I bring you news of great joy,' he said in the hallowed Latin phrase, 'we have a pope, the most eminent and most reverend Lord, Karol, Cardinal of the Holy Roman Church, Wojtyla. He has chosen the name John Paul II.'

A thousand miles away the Polish Minister for Religion was holding a press conference in Warsaw. He expressed the hope that whoever became pope would continue the policy of *rapprochement* between the Holy See and Eastern Europe. 'And if they elect a Polish pope, I'll treat you all to champagne,' he said jokingly to the assembled journalists. Half an hour later he was pouring the champagne.

No doubt the Minister had believed his offer to be a safe one. The last non-Italian pope had died 455 years before. But the cardinals knew that there was no one left among the Italians to match the personality of Luciani, and that, in any case, the Italians were so sharply divided between progressives and conservatives that there was little hope of one of them being chosen. Among the non-Italians there were some eminently good candidates, but it was difficult to find one with all the qualities necessary to win him the two-thirds plus one majority.

Cardinal Wojtyla, however, had studied in Rome. He returned there for the Vatican Council, and came back often on curial business, or to attend

Opposite: *Pope John Paul II was elected to office on 16 October 1978. He is the first non-Italian to be Bishop of Rome for 455 years, and the first Polish pope ever. On his stole are embroidered the patron saints of the Church of Rome: Saints Peter and Paul on one side, and the Virgin Mary, to whom he has a great devotion, on the other.*

meetings of the synod of bishops. He spoke Italian almost flawlessly. But he was equally at home in French, German or Russian, and was soon to demonstrate that he could hold his own in Spanish and English as well.

He was born in Wadowice, some 50 kilometres south-west of Cracow, on 18 May 1920. His father, also called Karol, was a junior officer in the army; his mother, Emilia, had been a school teacher. He had a brother, Edward, who was 15 years older than himself. Edward became a doctor and died tragically of scarlet fever caught from a patient. Emilia died giving birth to a stillborn daughter. Only the two Karols, father and son, were left.

The younger Karol went to school in Wadowice and then, after his father had moved to that most beautiful of European cities, he attended the six-hundred-year-old Jagiellonian University in Cracow. He prepared himself for a degree in philosophy, also studying Polish language and literature. In his spare time he had started to read for a diploma in drama; he had decided to capitalize on his undoubted talent by becoming an actor. But his whole world collapsed when German troops invaded Poland on 1 September 1939. In November the University was forced to close down. To avoid transportation to forced labour camps in Germany, Karol Wojtyla took a job, first in a quarry and then in a chemical factory. John Paul I was the first pope whose father was a worker (and a socialist) rather than a peasant, businessman or aristocrat; John Paul II is the first who has actually been a worker. But he also remained an actor: he ran a clandestine theatre club to raise the sagging morale of his wartime friends.

During convalescence after an accident he reflected upon his life and decided to give up thoughts of an acting career and become a priest. It was not a surprising choice to those who knew him well. At school he had been outstanding both as a scholar and an athlete but, without a trace of priggishness, he had also been remarkable for his piety. He had learned it from fiercely devout parents. And so, while working by day in the chemical factory, and at night helping the student resistance movement against the Nazis, he studied in the illegal theological department of the Jagiellonian. By 1944 he was a marked man; the Gestapo hunted for him. He disappeared.

A romance has been concocted for this period of his life. He fell in love, it is said, and was secretly married. But his wife died and so he became a priest. The truth may be less romantic, but it is more dramatic. The Archbishop of Cracow, realizing that Wojtyla's life was in danger, hid him in his episcopal palace along with four other seminarians.

When the war was over he was ordained. He became a priest on 1 November 1946, and was then sent to Rome for further studies. The topic of his doctorate, which he finished only after he had returned home, was the problem of faith in the writings of the sixteenth-century Spanish mystical writer, Saint John of the Cross.

He returned to Poland in 1948, after a visit to France to study the Young Christian Workers' Movement. Back home he found that the Nazi tyranny had been replaced by a Communist one. The government was showing itself increasingly hostile to the Church, to which 90 per cent of the population of the country belonged. By the end of that year 400 priests had been detained. Four years later, the number had risen to a thousand. By 1955, 2000 bishops, priests and laymen were in prison. Cardinal Wyszinski, the leader of the Polish Church, was immured in a monastery. Seminaries were closed, and their students locked away in labour camps.

The Church had to struggle on and stay alive for the future. Karol Wojtyla did parish work, and made a considerable reputation as a preacher. He was then sent to study philosophy, and to prepare himself for a teaching certificate. As a student of philosophy he was particularly attracted to the personalist Max Scheler. He wrote a thesis, his second, on the possibility of building a Christian ethic on Scheler's teaching.

By 1953 he was lecturing in the underground seminaries which the Church was running in defiance of the State. The following year he was teaching philosophy in that strange anomaly, the Catholic University of Lublin, the only non-state-run university in the whole of the Eastern bloc.

In 1958 he took his holidays canoeing on the Masurian Lakes, a typical way for him to spend his free time. Messengers arrived to tell him he had been appointed Assistant Bishop in Cracow. He left his canoe to make a formal acceptance, and then returned to it.

As a bishop he lived in a small, two-roomed apartment, and went about on a bicycle. He tried to stay in the same flat even when, in January 1964, he became Archbishop of Cracow. But when he was out one day, friends came and took his belongings to the episcopal palace in the centre of the city, and so he had no choice but to follow them. He turned up on the doorstep with a pair of skis over his shoulder.

Stories of his informality abound. People of all kinds had ready access to his office, even after he had become Cardinal-Archbishop in 1967. It was a case of first come, first seen. Part of his palace he turned into a rest home for the chronically sick, and established a special ministry for the sick and disabled which he put in the sympathetic charge of a priest who was himself chronically ill. He continued to take some part of his holidays with student groups, and his guitar went with him, to accompany his fine baritone voice as he sang Polish folk-songs around a camp fire.

Wojtyla's style was friendly and familiar, a far cry from his predecessors in the See of Cracow, all of whom had been aristocrats. His own protector, the Cardinal Saphieha, who had sheltered him from the Nazis, had been a prince in his own right. But Cardinal Wojtyla himself was happiest when he was dropping in unannounced for meals or visits with his friends and

Below: *After the Second World War the young priest Karol Wojtyla was sent to Rome for higher studies. In this photograph, taken in 1947, he is pictured in a group of Polish and Belgian clergy, flanked by two members of the Vatican's Swiss Guard. Wojtyla is fifth from the right in the back row.*

their families, or when he was out skiing on his beloved Tatra Mountains.

As an Assistant Bishop he had taken an active part in the Second Vatican Council. Now he set to with a will, and with an enthusiasm not always shared by others among the Polish bishops, to put the decrees of the Council into operation. He attended every one of the synods Pope Paul summoned to Rome, and this gave him an idea. He set up a permanent synod of clergy and laity who met in small groups throughout his diocese to discuss and carry out the provisions of Vatican II. He brought three Polish seminaries together to make them into one Pontifical University, recognized outside Poland but not by the authorities in the country, and thereby improved – or so he hoped – the standard of education of the clergy. He organized monthly seminars in his own palace for the most diverse groups, including actors – for whom he still felt a strong affinity. He made a point of attending the seminars himself. One week-long seminar was convened on the history of Cracow, and he founded a review to publish learned articles about the city.

He travelled abroad, to North America, the Far East, and in Europe. He went to international conferences of philosophers to read papers he had written. He went to the synods of bishops, and benefitted greatly from the contacts they brought him and the worldwide network of friends he made. In 1976, in a gesture which may have been a hint given by Pope Paul as to the man he wanted to succeed him, Cardinal Wojtyla was invited to Italy to

Below: *After the increasingly care-worn appearance of Pope Paul, one of the characteristics of Pope John Paul II which endeared him to the world was his ready smile, and evident humanity.*

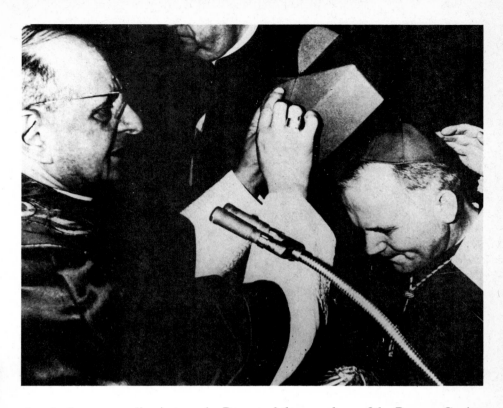

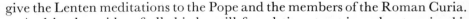

give the Lenten meditations to the Pope and the members of the Roman Curia.

And in the midst of all this he still found time to swim, play tennis, ski, and go canoeing. He composed poetry, which was often published under a pseudonym. He wrote a major work of philosophy which was on the point of being published when he was elected to the papacy.

He took a philosophical journal into the conclave with him in October 1978. It was a Marxist one. Several of the cardinals were observed taking in the *Sign of Contradiction*, the collection of his Lenten addresses to Pope Paul. That the press did not think of him as a serious candidate shows that the journalists had not done their homework.

After the Cardinal-Deacon had announced him, he strode out on to the balcony, and the bemused crowd set up a weak cheer. He broke with tradition: he addressed the people in Saint Peter's Square in Italian. He called himself 'a man from a far country'. 'If I cannot explain myself too well in your – I mean our – language, you will correct me if I make a mistake.' The slip may have been accidental, or a deliberate 'theatrical' touch. Either way, the crowd loved him for it.

The Polish President and his Minister for Religion were present at the installation Mass. At the Pope's insistence, it began at 10.00 a.m. so as not to interfere with a football match on television in the afternoon. He was sensitive to such things: once he himself had had to leave a meeting in Italy early to see the home team play Brazil.

The Mass was the first one ever shown on Polish television. Like his predecessor, he chose to be invested with the pallium rather than crowned with the papal tiara. At his first formal meeting with the Church's cardinals he stressed his commitment to collegiality and ecumenism, and emphasized the need for new structures to make collegiality work.

His first appointments to posts of special responsibility within the Vatican's civil service indicated a new approach to the papal office. Under Pope Paul, whose own training had been in diplomacy, the Secretary of State had been a pastorally-experienced cardinal. Pope John Paul has had a great deal of pastoral experience, and has chosen a professional diplomat, Cardinal Casaroli, who will ensure that diplomatic objectives serve the pastoral ends of the Church, and who is skilled in dealing with Communist regimes.

Traditionalists in the Roman Curia shivered when John Paul put a Spaniard in charge of Italian affairs. But Italian affairs have preoccupied Italian popes ever since the Papal States first began. Now, with a non-Italian pope, Italy has become part of the Holy See's foreign policy and not part of its domestic concerns. The Pope still speaks to Italy, but only with the voice of moral authority. He does not wish to interfere, as the Vatican has done so often, in the workings of the State. Many an Italian politician will breathe a sigh of relief. So will many a non-Italian, who believed that the papacy's preoccupation with Italy obstructed its worldwide role.

And Pope John Paul II is nothing if not a worldwide Pope. His first journey outside Italy was at the beginning of 1979 when he went to Mexico, via the Dominican Republic, to attend the opening session of the Conference of Bishops from Latin America. It was a major gathering, for which the Churches of Latin America had been preparing for several years. But twice it had to be postponed – by the deaths of Pope Paul and Pope John Paul I. The theme of John Paul's address was one which has since become familiar: the dedication of the Church to its spiritual goals.

Many commentators saw in the Pope's words a condemnation of 'liberation theology', the theology which has sprung out of the struggles of the oppressed peoples of Latin America for the achievement of human dignity. The Pope was horrified when he saw what the press had made of his address. At Oaxaca he spoke much more directly to the thousands of South American Indians who had made their way to see him. He unequivocally committed himself, and the Church, to the cause of the poor and underprivileged.

After Mexico he visited Poland: for him this was the most difficult and emotionally demanding of any of his journeys. Paul VI had wanted to make a similar visit, but the Polish authorities had been cool. John Paul II wanted to return to Cracow to celebrate the ninth centenary of the martyrdom of Saint Stanislaw, the Patron Saint of Poland. His feast day was 8 May. The government did not think it advisable to combine the feast day with a papal visit: too much nationalist fervour might be generated. Instead, the Pope was allowed to return to his homeland in June, when the celebrations were at an end. The bureaucratic caution had been misplaced. The delay simply meant that the Poles took two holidays instead of one.

The Pope spent nine days in Poland. He spoke often in public, regularly departing from his prepared text to say words of encouragement to a people who are just as oppressed, if in a more subtle fashion, as those he had met in Oaxaca. Sometimes the remarks were too subtle for the hundreds of Western journalists who poured into the country to cover the visit. At the Presidential palace, for example, there was a curious exchange between the Pope and Prime Minister Gierek. Mr Gierek was unusually nervous. He spoke of the 'thirty-five years of socialism' which the regime was busy celebrating to counteract the 1000 years of Christianity and the 900 years since the death of Saint Stanislaw that the Church had been celebrating.

John Paul's reply ignored the 35 years of socialism. Instead, he congratulated the Prime Minister on rebuilding the royal palace in Warsaw. But every Pole knows very well that the royal palace has been rebuilt with the money of Polish exiles. They also know that the regime itself was unhappy at the idea of restoring a royal symbol of Poland's former glories.

The little verbal duel over, the Pope strode vigorously away from the microphone. He had to be hurried back because he had forgotten to present the President with the mosaic he had brought.

The crowds were enormous wherever he went. At his birthplace of Wadowice he said Mass for 30,000 people – twice the town's population – in the church square. Afterwards he and his cardinals lunched in the simple parish house with the priest who had taught him catechism as a boy.

In Warsaw 220,000 packed into Victory Square. The huge dais and the massive cross erected by the authorities rather dwarfed him and separated

him from the people, but it made a splendid picture for the congregation at Mass to carry away with them. 'For he's a jolly good fellow' – Polish version – was sung for the Pope, and then 'We want God'. The people were always ready to sing. Over 40,000 of them gathered in front of the Cathedral at Gniezo while the Pope led them in the singing of hymns and Polish folk-songs for 90 minutes beyond his scheduled time.

As a young man, hurrying from the chemical factory to his secret theology classes during the war, he would have seen German soldiers from the notorious camp at Auschwitz-Birkenau sipping beer in the cafes under the splendid colonnade that divides the city's main square. Four million people died in the camps, and at Birkenau a shoe may still scuff up a fragment of bone. The Pope went to Auschwitz without the crowds, and with a minimum of attendants. He prayed, laid flowers, and lit a candle in the starvation cell where the Franciscan priest, Maximilian Kolbe, died.

His last Mass in Poland was said on the outskirts of Cracow, before a congregation of more than a million people. With the memories of Auschwitz still fresh in his mind, he tried to rekindle in men's hearts 'faith in man, and faith in hope and love'.

Above: *Wherever John Paul II has travelled – Mexico, Poland, Ireland, the United States – he has been able to establish an instant rapport. Here he has been photographed in Poland, against a sea of people disappearing into the distance.*

He returned by air from Cracow to Rome. Somewhat incongruously, he reviewed troops before he left the airport, embraced the President of Poland, and climbed the steps of the plane in tears. He had come to Poland, he said, to cure his homesickness. It seemed only to have made it worse. But those he left behind were heartened by the visit. Poles are never very sure where religion ends and nationalism begins. Their pride in a Polish Pope gave them confidence to continue their struggle to profess their faith.

There could scarcely be a greater contrast than that between Poland and Ireland, where the Pope went next, in August 1979, on his way to New York. Again the massive crowds, now bigger than ever, with a million and a half people attending mass in Dublin's Phoenix Park. But this time the Pope was able to give Communion to the President of the Republic, and to all the members of his government.

This was a 'pastoral' visit, not an official diplomatic one. The government had left the organization to the Church, and the Church had done wonders and everyone had a splendid view of the Pope as he toured in his 'Popemobile', a yellow Ford truck converted into a form of travelling inspection platform.

If the Republic of Ireland has no problems of major conflict between Church and State, it has an abiding problem of violence. At Drogheda, the nearest point Pope John Paul came to the border which divides the Republic from Northern Ireland, he made an impassioned plea for peace between the warring parties. Many of the crowd who applauded him had come down from the North in hundreds of buses and thousands of private cars. They knew the suffering at first hand. 'Violence destroys what it claims to defend', repeated the Pope, 'the dignity, the life, the freedom of human beings.'

In Galway, on the other hand, the atmosphere was one of carnival. There he spoke to young people in a crowd of 300,000. 'I love you', the Pope told them. 'We love you, too', they roared back, and punctuated the 12 minutes of applause with snatches of 'He's got the whole world in his hands.' John Paul had to wipe away tears, while the teenagers, many of whom had spent the previous night in their sleeping-bags in the park, threw flowers.

The reason for the Pope's visit to Ireland was the centenary of an alleged apparition in which the Virgin Mary, Saint Joseph and Saint John the Evangelist were seen gathered round an altar with a lamb upon it – the symbol of Christ. This took place, it was claimed, near the gable-end of a church at Knock. John Paul II has a great devotion to the Virgin, as the very unheraldic letter M on his coat of arms signifies. He has been systematically visiting the shrines of Italy. In Mexico he went to the shrine of Guadalupe, in Poland to that at Czestochowa. So now he went to Knock, Ireland's national shrine. In 1976 a large modern church had been built to hold congregations of up to 10,000. For the Pope's visit the congregation that came to Mass in the small town was half a million.

The United States is not a Catholic country, and in that respect differs from the other countries the Pope has visited. Even in Mexico, where a self-consciously secular government referred to John Paul as 'Senor Wojtyla', the population for the most part shared John Paul's beliefs. But in America he was moving among a people who were not all of his faith. Yet once again, he won the hearts of those who flocked to hear him, and many of them were not Catholics. A million people gathered in Philadelphia, for example, and less than a third of that city's population are Catholics.

Again, the crowds were for the most part enormous. No political leader, no presidential candidate, no film or rock-music star has been accorded such a welcome. In New York City there were 60,000 people tightly packed into the stands of the Yankee Stadium and another 15,000 on the turf. There were 20,000 teenagers in Madison Square Garden. A crowd of 200,000 braved the cold, wind and rain to hear Mass in Washington D.C.'s Mall.

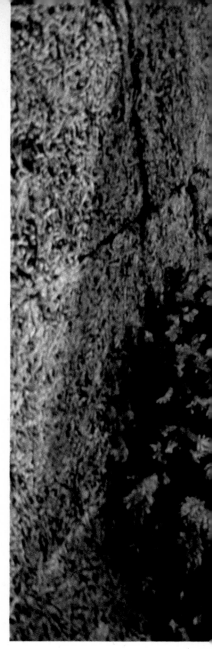

The main purpose of the visit to America was to address the United Nations' General Assembly. The hall was packed. Even accompanying cardinals had to wear identity tags to gain admittance. The delegates listened quietly and courteously, and then gave him one of the longest ovations in the history of the Assembly. *The New York Times* held its edition back an hour to print the text of the speech, a fervent plea for the upholding of human rights, and the dignity of man.

The trip to the United States also had its quiet moments. At Des Moines in Iowa the Pope became, once more, for one Sunday morning, a parish priest in a country church. It also had its moments of conflict: when John Paul met a gathering of nuns in the Immaculate Conception Cathedral in Washington, there was a call for women to be allowed to share in all the ministries of the Church, a thinly-veiled reference to the ordination of women priests, against which the Pope has taken a firm stand. And it was not always a triumphal progress. In New York and Boston the crowds were quieter and smaller than they had been elsewhere.

But for the most part the crowds in the States were huge – as they had been elsewhere – a token of the Pope's immense popular impact. He has retained his actor's flair for projecting himself through the medium of television. He is the first pope to have thoroughly understood the power of the media.

Above: *In June 1979, Pope John Paul II revisited the site of Auschwitz concentration camp, 'this Golgotha of the modern world' as he called it in a sermon. Here he is praying before the wall against which prisoners were executed by firing-squads. Auschwitz is not very far from Cracow, where John Paul spent the war years.*

It is not just flair, however, which wins hearts – not just the majestic, vigorous presence of a strong man with a lively mind. He also has a message which brings hope to millions, one which is deeply rooted both in his Catholic faith and his philosophical study.

It is to be found in his first encyclical, *Redemptor Hominis*, which he began writing in the November after his election and published the following March. The first words of the encyclical (after which it is named in the manner of papal documents) mean 'Redeemer of mankind'. It is in the redemption brought by Christ, says the Pope, that 'man finds again the greatness, dignity and value that belong to his humanity'. The emphasis is shifted from the 'other-worldly' spirituality which had become common in the Church. The Pope focuses on man's striving to fulfil the potentiality of his own nature, which he can only achieve in Christ.

The encyclical is the abstract working-out of his conviction; the speeches he has made as he has travelled around the world have given it more concrete shape. In Mexico it was the unjust distribution of wealth which was attacked as destructive of human dignity, in Poland it was the totalitarian denial of intellectual and spiritual freedom, in Ireland the threat of violence, at the United Nations the general denial of human rights.

But part of his Christian humanism is an insistence upon some of the traditional moral demands of the Catholic Church: a firm 'no' to contraception, abortion and divorce. Such is the magnetism of his personality that he is listened to, and admired, by many who would not share his convictions on these issues. Yet John Paul sees them as part of the same message.

He has been described as 'conservative in substance and modern in style'. It is not a bad motto for a Bishop of Rome whose task it is to see that the faith of the Church is preserved and yet reinterpreted to each successive generation. The encyclical presents this reinterpretation to today's believers. The Pope's travels, his use of the media, even the fact that he wears a wristwatch (which he frequently consults but regularly ignores), are all signs of the 'modern style'. There is even a record of his folk-singing heading for 'golden disc' status, if not higher.

There are some within the Catholic Church who find this new-style papacy disturbing. It seems to be running counter to the developments which were breaking down the monolithic, pyramidal structure of the Church to give more independence to local conferences of bishops. Under John Paul the papacy will have to find new ways of linking the Churches around the world with the Church of Rome at the centre.

This is no new task. While preserving their essential function as the source of unity among all the Churches of the Catholic Communion, the bishops of Rome have taken on a variety of different guises. They have been Lombard dukes, medieval monarchs, Renaissance princes, enlightened despots – or their religious equivalents. In a world in desperate need of spiritual ideals there is no reason at all why the Bishop of Rome should not become a spiritual leader for all mankind, not solely for his companions in the Catholic faith. John Paul II is able to call men back to the values they sometimes acknowledge, but for the most part prefer to forget.

Politicians often have a tenuous hold on power. This obliges them to be more sensitive than churchmen to the forces at work in the world. There are indications that they have already awakened to the potentialities of the new role which Pope John Paul is making for himself. The Foreign Minister of Russia has visited the Vatican, and conversed alone, in Russian, for two hours with the Pope. President Jablonski of Poland was anxious to invite him to his residence; so was President Carter in the United States. Not all who are so eager to receive, or to be received, by the Pope share his convictions. Few are ready to openly reject them. They would not wish to appear to be on the side of oppression against liberty, or of death over life. There is another challenge which John Paul presents to the traditionalists

within his own Communion. He is a Slav, not an Italian. During his visit to Poland he made it clear that he hoped to be able to appeal, through the Polish people, to all the Slavs of Eastern Europe and beyond. He has, moreover, already travelled almost as much as Pope Paul, and has made visits to the scattered Churches of the Roman Communion an integral part of his pontificate.

From his background and from his travels, he is aware of the immense cultural variety which is to be found within the Catholic Church. It is a cultural variety which has long been rejected but which has to be built into the life of the Church, if the Church is to become as universal as its 'Catholic' title claims. The process will not be easy, for Christianity is still too often seen solely in terms derived from Western Europe.

So Pope John Paul II sets the Church not one but many challenges: to accommodate his worldwide role; to rethink the relationship of the local Churches with the Church at Rome; to integrate a Christianity which is authentically representative of the many different peoples who are linked within the one Communion.

Those, then, are the challenges he sets. But he has also something immensely valuable to offer: a confidence in man's common humanity, as it has been redeemed in Christ.

Below: *Before his election to the papacy, Karol Wojtyla had been trained as a philosopher. His many speeches and letters as Pope John Paul II have shown that he has a clear-cut position on the dignity of man, and of man's need for God.*

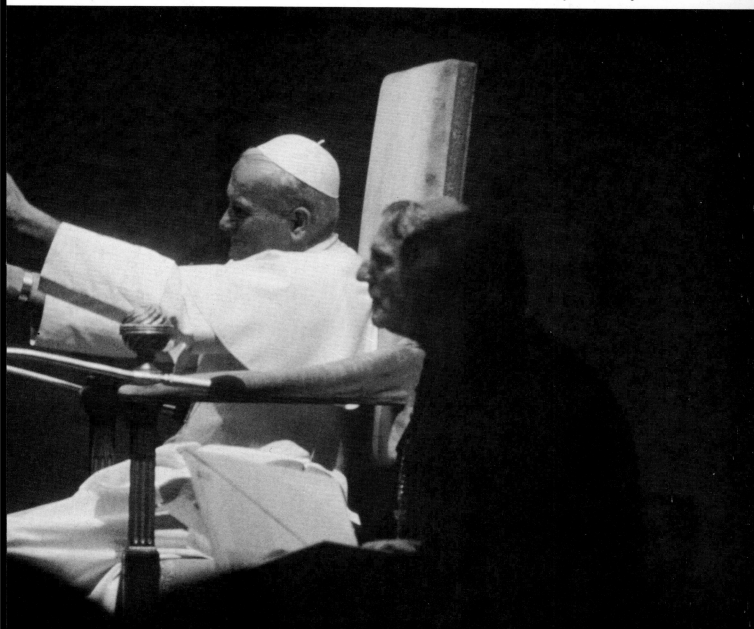

FURTHER READING

The story of the popes is part of the history of the Catholic Church, and the easiest way to learn more about the men who succeeded to the See of Saint Peter is to read general histories of the Church. There are many of these available, but perhaps the best is *Histoire de l'Eglise*, generally referred to as 'Fliche-Martin' from the names of its first editors, Augustin Fliche and Victor Martin. This was published in Paris by Bloud et Gay over a 30-year period (1934-64) in 21 volumes, and covers the history of the Church up to the death of Pius IX. Only a very small proportion of it, alas, has been translated into English. Two shorter works are being translated at present: *The Christian Centuries* (Darton, Longman & Todd, London, 1964-)will eventually comprise five volumes, and *A Handbook of Church History* (Burns & Oates, London, 1965-) will eventually have seven.

General Church histories are an essential guide to the very early period in the rise of the papacy because so little is known about it that more detailed information is not available from other sources. Also, one of the very interesting aspects of its story which can be traced through general histories is the way the papacy gradually emerged as a separate historical subject, as distinct from the broader history of the Church. Fortunately, there are many good, readily available histories of the early Church. That of Bishop J.W.C. Wand, *The History of the Early Church* (Methuen, London, 1937), is still one of the best accounts. It should be read alongside one of the more modern treatments, either that of Professor Henry Chadwick or the one by Professor William Frend; both books are called *The Early Church* and published in London, Professor Chadwick's by Penguin Books in 1967 and Professor Frend's by Hodder & Stoughton in 1973. In addition to these, a good deal of incidental information about the papacy, together with much other interesting material, can be found in *The Roman Catacombs and their Martyrs* by Ludwig Hertling and Engelbert Kirschbaum (Darton, Longman & Todd, London, 1960).

A reader who is prepared to undertake serious study of the papacy, or of individual popes, cannot do better than look at the monumental works of Horace K. Mann and Ludwig von Pastor. Mann's *The Lives of the Popes* begins with the reign of Pope Gregory the Great and ends in 1304. This, too, appeared over a period of 30 years (Routledge & Kegan Paul, London, 1902-32), and consists of 18 volumes. This may seem a great many, but they are fairly easy to read. Pastor's 40 volumes of *The History of the Popes* (Routledge & Kegan Paul, London, 1891-1953) is much more ponderous, but is indispensable. It begins with the establishment of the papacy in Avignon, and ends with the death of Pius VI in 1799.

If these multi-volume works seem far too much to tackle, even over several years, there is a selection of shorter studies available, particularly covering the Middle Ages. Professor Walter Ullmann has written a great deal about the period, especially on the legal questions of the time. He has presented what he has to say in an easily digestible form in his *Short History of the Papacy in the Middle Ages* (Methuen, London, 1972). Partly in reaction to what he sees as excessive concern with the papal ideology, Jeffrey Richards has recently published *The Popes and the Papacy in the Early Middle Ages* (Routledge & Kegan Paul, London, 1979). The main focus of *The Lands of Saint Peter* by Peter Partner (Eyre Methuen, London, 1972) is the Papal States during the Middle Ages.

The Avignon period has been examined by a number of historians, but the *doyen* of them all is Guillaume Mollat, and his *The Popes at Avignon* (Nelson, London, 1963) is the classic study. John Holland Smith continues the story in *The Great Schism* (Hamish Hamilton, London, 1970). The flavour of that curious blend of violence, scandalous living and high culture which characterizes the Renaissance can be caught in Michael Mallet's *The Borgias* (Bodley Head, London, 1969), which ranges far wider than the pontificate of Alexander VI, and some of it is to be found, too, in a rather dated but still useful study of *The Medici Popes* by Herbert Vaughan (Methuen, London, 1908).

General histories of the modern papacy are harder to find in English. E.E.Y. Hales has made a special study of the period, and his *Revolution and the Papacy* (Eyre & Spottiswoode, London, 1960) can be recommended. J. Derek Holmes continues where Mr Hales left off, in his *The Triumph of the Holy See* (Burns & Oates, London, 1978). Recent events, of course, still await a historian, but a journalist who knows a great deal about the contemporary papacy is Peter Hebblethwaite. His *The Year of the Three Popes* (Collins, London, 1978) is worth looking at. Andrew Greeley's *The Making of the Popes* (Futura, London, 1979) gives the reader an insight into the sort of considerations that go into choosing a pope in our own generation.

The city of Rome itself is a major actor in the story. There are two monumental studies, Hartmann Grisar's *A History of Rome and the Popes in the Middle Ages* in three volumes (Routledge & Kegan Paul, London, 1911-12), and Ferdinand Gregorovius's *A History of the City of Rome in the Middle Ages* (Bell & Sons, London, 1900-09) in eight volumes. Professor Richard Krautheimer has promised a book on Rome, which will be well worth reading, but meanwhile we have to be satisfied with the relevant portions of his *Early Christian and Byzantine Architecture*, which appeared in the Pelican History of Art series (London, 1965). Peter Llewellyn's *Rome in the Dark Ages* (Faber & Faber, London, 1971) has a good deal to say about the papacy as well as about the city, and is a good balance to Professor Ullmann's legalistic approach. Robert Brentano's *Rome before Avignon* (Longmans, London, 1974), and Peter Partner's *Renaissance Rome* (University of California Press, Berkeley, 1976) are both excellent studies, particularly the latter. Maurice Andrieux's *Daily Life in Papal Rome in the Eighteenth Century* (Allen & Unwin, London, 1968) is an interesting book.

There are, of course, innumerable lives of individual popes available. Two classics worth reading despite their age are T. Jalland's *The Life and Times of Saint Leo the Great* (SPCK, London, 1941), and F. Homes Dudden's even older *Gregory the Great* (Longmans, London, 1905). Both works are in two volumes. T.S.R. Boase's *Boniface VIII* (Constable, London, 1933) is a thorough study of a puzzling character, but is in need of updating. Joseph Gill's *Eugenius IV* (Burns & Oates, London, 1962) brings clarity to a troubled period, as *Pio Nono* by E.E.Y. Hales does for the last days of the Papal States (Eyre & Spottiswoode, London, 1954). Biographies of modern popes abound, but too many tend to be uncritical eulogies. One that is not is Roy MacGregor-Hastie's *Paul VI* (Frederick Muller, London, 1966). Paul Johnson's *John XXIII* (Hutchinson, London, 1975) can be recommended; and Mary Craig's life of John Paul II, *A Man from a Far Country* (Hodder & Stoughton, London, 1979) is a good read.

CHRONOLOGY OF THE POPES

The official sequence of the Bishops of Rome is published in the Annuario Pontificio, *the Vatican's yearbook. The list which follows has been taken from the* Annuario, *although some of the dates have been altered in the light of recent research, and additional information given. Where the year of a pope's birth is known – or can be conjectured – it has been included, with his place of birth or nationality. It must be remembered, however, that nationality cannot be understood in terms of modern political boundaries. Thus, for many centuries a 'Greek' might have been born in what is now the Republic of Italy.*

Popes who abdicated, resigned, or were otherwise deposed are indicated by an asterisk (*), and those who met violent deaths – other than martyrdom – by a dagger (†). Pope John XXI is a special case for two reasons: first, although he died a violent death, it was the result of an accident – part of the new wing he had added to the papal palace at Viterbo fell on him while he was sleeping; secondly, there never was a Pope John XX.

The names of those regarded by the Holy See as anti-popes are given in italics. All dates before 175 are conjectural.

	Pope	Origin	Date of Election	Date of Death or Abdication
1	Peter	Galilean	48	69
2	Linus	Italian	69	78
3	Cletus	Roman	78	90
4	Clement I	Roman	90	99
5	Evaristus	Greek	99	105
6	Alexander I	Roman	105	115
7	Sixtus I	Roman	115	125
8	Telesphorus	Greek	125	136
9	Hyginus	Greek	136	140
10	Pius I	Italian	140	155
11	Anicetus	Syrian	155	166
12	Soter	Italian	166	175
13	Eleutherus	Greek	175	189
14	Victor I	African	189	199
15	Zephyrinus	Roman	199	217
16	Callistus I	Roman	217	222
	Hippolytus		*217*	*235**
17	Urban I	Roman	222	230
18	Pontianus	Roman	21 July 230	28 September 235*
19	Anterus	Greek	21 November 235	3 January 236
20	Fabian	Roman	10 January 236	20 January 250
21	Cornelius	Roman	March 251	June 253
	Novatian		*251*	*258*
22	Lucius I	Roman	25 June 253	5 March 254
23	Stephen I	Roman	12 May 254	2 August 257
24	Sixtus II	Greek	30 August 257	6 August 258
25	Dionysius	Greek	22 July 259	26 December 268
26	Felix I	Roman	5 January 269	30 December 274
27	Eutychianus	Italian	4 January 275	7 December 283
28	Caius	Dalmatian	17 December 283	22 April 296
29	Marcellinus	Roman	30 June 296	25 October 304
30	Marcellus I	Roman	27 May 308	16 January 309
31	Eusebius	Greek	18 April 309	17 September 309
32	Miltiades	African	2 July 311	11 January 314
33	Sylvester I	Roman	31 January 314	31 December 335
34	Mark	Roman	18 January 336	7 October 336

	Pope	Origin	Year of Birth	Date of Election	Date of Death or Abdication
35	Julius I	Roman		6 February 337	12 April 352
36	Liberius	Roman		17 May 352	22 September 366
	Felix II			*355*	*365**
37	Damasus I	Roman	c. 304	1 October 366	11 December 384
	Ursinus			*366*	*367**
38	Siricius	Roman		15 December 384	26 November 399
39	Anastasius I	Roman		27 November 399	19 December 401
40	Innocent I	Italian		22 December 401	12 March 417
41	Zosimus	Greek		18 March 417	26 December 418
42	Boniface I	Roman		29 December 418	4 September 422
	Eulalius			*418*	*419**
43	Celestine I	Italian		10 September 422	27 July 432
44	Sixtus III	Roman		31 July 432	19 August 440
45	Leo I	Italian		29 September 440	10 November 461
46	Hilarius	Sardinian		19 November 461	29 February 468
47	Simplicius	Italian		3 April 468	10 April 483
48	Felix II	Roman		13 March 483	1 March 492
49	Gelasius I	African		1 March 492	21 November 496
50	Anastasius II	Roman		24 November 496	19 November 498
51	Symmachus	Sardinian		22 November 498	19 July 514
	Laurentius			*498*	*505**
52	Hormisdas	Italian		20 July 514	6 August 523
53	John I	Italian		13 August 523	18 May 526
54	Felix III	Italian		12 July 526	22 September 530
55	Boniface II	Goth		22 September 530	17 October 532
	Dioscorus			*530*	*530*
56	John II	Roman		2 January 533	8 May 535
57	Agapitus I	Roman		13 May 535	22 April 536
58	Silverius	Italian		8 June 536	11 March 537*
59	Vigilius	Roman		29 March 537	7 June 555
60	Pelagius I	Roman		16 April 556	4 March 561
61	John III	Roman		17 July 561	13 July 574
62	Benedict I	Roman		3 June 575	30 July 579
63	Pelagius II	Goth		26 November 579	7 February 590
64	Gregory I	Roman	c. 540	3 September 590	13 March 604
65	Sabinianus	Italian		13 September 604	22 February 606
66	Boniface III	Roman		19 February 607	12 November 607
67	Boniface IV	Italian		25 August 608	8 May 615
68	Adeodatus I	Roman		19 October 615	8 November 618
69	Boniface V	Neapolitan		23 December 619	25 October 625
70	Honorius I	Italian		27 October 625	12 October 638
71	Severinus	Roman		28 May 640	2 September 640
72	John IV	Dalmatian		24 December 640	12 October 642
73	Theodore I	Greek		24 November 642	14 May 649
74	Martin I	Italian		21 July 649	18 June 653*
75	Eugenius I	Roman		10 August 654	2 June 657
76	Vitalian	Italian		30 July 657	27 January 672
77	Adeodatus II	Roman		11 April 672	17 June 676
78	Donus	Roman		2 November 676	11 April 678
79	Agatho	Sicilian		27 June 678	10 January 681
80	Leo II	Sicilian		17 August 682	3 July 683
81	Benedict II	Roman		26 June 684	8 May 685
82	John V	Antiochene		23 July 685	2 August 686
83	Conon	Sicilian?		21 October 686	21 September 687
	Theodore			*687*	*687**

	Pope	Origin	Year of Birth	Date of Election	Date of Death or Abdication
	Paschal			*687*	*687**
84	Sergius I	Syrian		15 December 687	8 September 701
85	John VI	Greek		30 October 701	11 January 705
86	John VII	Greek		1 March 705	18 October 707
87	Sisinnius	Syrian		15 January 708	4 February 708
88	Constantine I	Syrian		25 March 708	9 April 715
89	Gregory II	Roman		19 May 715	11 February 731
90	Gregory III	Syrian		18 March 731	10 December 741
91	Zachary	Greek		10 December 741	22 March 752
92	Stephen II	Roman		23 March 752	25 March 752
93	Stephen III	Roman		26 March 752	26 April 757
94	Paul I	Roman		29 May 757	28 June 767
	Constantine II			*767*	*769†*
	Philip			*768*	*768**
95	Stephen IV	Sicilian		7 August 768	3 February 772
96	Hadrian I	Roman		9 February 772	26 December 795
97	Leo III	Roman		26 December 795	12 June 816
98	Stephen V	Roman		22 June 816	14 January 817
99	Paschal I	Roman		25 January 817	11 February 824
100	Eugenius II	Roman		21 February 824	27 August 827
101	Valentine	Roman		August 827	September 827
102	Gregory IV	Roman		October 827	25 January 844
103	Sergius II	Roman		January 844	27 January 847
	John			*844*	*844**
104	Leo IV	Roman		10 April 847	17 July 855
105	Benedict III	Roman		29 September 855	17 April 858
	Anastasius			*855*	*855**
106	Nicholas I	Roman	c. 800	24 April 858	13 November 867
107	Hadrian II	Roman	c. 797	14 December 867	14 December 872
108	John VIII	Roman		14 December 872	16 December 882†
109	Marinus I	Italian		16 December 882	15 May 884
110	Hadrian III	Roman		17 May 884	17 September 885
111	Stephen VI	Roman		September 885	September 891
112	Formosus	Italian		6 October 891	4 April 896
113	Boniface VI	Roman		April 896	April 896
114	Stephen VII	Roman		May 896	August 897†
115	Romanus	Italian		August 897	November 897
116	Theodore II	Roman		December 897	December 897
117	John IX	Italian		January 898	January 900
118	Benedict IV	Roman		January 900	June 903
119	Leo V	Italian		July 903	September 903†
	Christopher			*903*	*904†*
120	Sergius III	Roman		29 January 904	14 April 911
121	Anastasius III	Roman		April 911	June 913
122	Lando	Italian		July 913	February 914
123	John X	Italian		March 914	May 928†
124	Leo VI	Roman		May 928	December 928†
125	Stephen VIII	Roman		December 928	February 931†
126	John XI	Roman	c. 915	March 931	December 935*
127	Leo VII	Roman		3 January 936	13 July 939
128	Stephen IX	Roman		14 July 939	October 942
129	Marinus II	Roman		30 October 942	10 May 946
130	Agapitus II	Roman		10 May 946	December 955
131	John XII	Roman	937	16 December 955	4 December 963*
132	Leo VIII	Roman		6 December 963	May? 964*

	Pope	Origin	Year of Birth	Date of Election	Date of Death or Abdication
133	Benedict V	Roman		22 May 964	23 June 964*
	Leo VIII (again)	Roman		23 June 964	1 March 965
134	John XIII	Roman		1 October 965	5 September 972
135	Benedict VI	Roman		19 January 973	June 974†
	Boniface VII			*974*	*974**
136	Benedict VII	Roman		October 974	10 July 983
137	John XIV	Italian		10 December 983	20 August 984†
	Boniface VII (again)			*984*	*985*†
138	John XV	Roman		August 985	March 996
139	Gregory V	German	c. 975	3 May 996	18 February 999
	John XVI			*997*	*998**
140	Sylvester II	French	c. 945	2 April 999	12 May 1003
141	John XVII	Roman		June 1003	6 November 1003
142	John XVIII	Roman		January 1004	July 1009
143	Sergius IV	Roman		31 July 1009	12 May 1012
144	Benedict VIII	Roman		18 May 1012	9 April 1024
	Gregor			*1012*	*1012**
145	John XIX	Roman		April 1024	1032
146	Benedict IX	Roman	c. 1017	1032	1044*
147	Sylvester III	Roman		20 January 1045	10 March 1045*
	Benedict IX (again)	Roman	c. 1017	10 March 1045	1 May 1045*
148	Gregory VI	Roman		5 May 1045	20 December 1046*
149	Clement II	German		25 December 1046	9 October 1047
	Benedict IX (again)	Roman	c. 1017	8 November 1047	17 July 1048*
150	Damasus II	German		17 July 1048	9 August 1048
151	Leo IX	German	1002	12 February 1049	19 April 1054
152	Victor II	German		16 April 1055	29 July 1057
153	Stephen X	French		3 August 1057	29 March 1058
	Benedict X			*1058*	*1059**
154	Nicholas II	French		24 January 1059	27 July 1061
155	Alexander II	Italian		30 September 1061	21 April 1073
	Honorius II			*1061*	*1072**
156	Gregory VII	Italian	c. 1020	22 April 1073	25 May 1085
	Clement III			*1080*	*1100**
157	Victor III	Italian		24 May 1086	16 September 1087
158	Urban II	French	c. 1042	12 March 1088	29 July 1099
159	Paschal II	Italian		14 August 1099	21 January 1118
	Theodoric			*1100*	*1100**
	Albert			*1102*	*1102**
	Sylvester IV			*1105*	*1111*
160	Gelasius II	Italian		24 January 1118	29 January 1119
	Gregory VIII			*1118*	*1121**
161	Callistus II	French		2 February 1119	13 December 1124
162	Honorius II	Italian		15 December 1124	13 February 1130
	Celestine			*1124*	*1124**
163	Innocent II	Roman		14 February 1130	24 September 1143
	Anacletus II			*1130*	*1138*
	Victor IV			*1138*	*1138**
164	Celestine II	Italian		26 September 1143	8 March 1144
165	Lucius II	Italian		12 March 1144	15 February 1145†
166	Eugenius III	Italian		15 February 1145	8 July 1153
167	Anastasius IV	Roman	1073	12 July 1153	3 December 1154
168	Hadrian IV	English	c. 1115	5 December 1154	1 September 1159
169	Alexander III	Italian	c. 1110	7 September 1159	30 August 1181
	Victor IV			*1159*	*1164*

	Pope	Origin	Year of Birth	Date of Election	Date of Death or Abdication
	Paschal III			*1164*	*1168*
	Callistus III			*1168*	*1178**
	Innocent III			*1179*	*1180**
170	Lucius III	Italian		1 September 1181	25 November 1185
171	Urban III	Italian		25 November 1185	20 October 1187
172	Gregory VIII	Italian		21 October 1187	17 December 1187
173	Clement III	Roman		19 December 1187	March 1191
174	Celestine III	Roman	1106	30 March 1191	8 January 1198
175	Innocent III	Italian	1161	8 January 1198	16 July 1216
176	Honorius III	Roman	c. 1150	18 July 1216	18 March 1227
177	Gregory IX	Italian	1147	19 March 1227	22 August 1241
178	Celestine IV	Italian		25 October 1241	10 November 1241
179	Innocent IV	Genoese	c. 1207	25 June 1243	7 December 1254
180	Alexander IV	Italian		12 December 1254	25 May 1261
181	Urban IV	French		29 August 1261	2 October 1264
182	Clement LV	French		5 February 1265	29 November 1268
183	Gregory X	Italian	1210	1 September 1271	10 January 1276
184	Innocent V	Savoyard	1225	21 January 1276	22 June 1276
185	Hadrian V	Genoese		11 July 1276	18 August 1276
186	John XXI	Portuguese		8 September 1276	20 May 1277†
187	Nicholas III	Roman	1217	25 November 1277	22 August 1280
188	Martin IV	French		22 February 1281	28 March 1285
189	Honorius IV	Roman	c. 1210	2 April 1285	3 April 1287
190	Nicholas IV	Italian	1227	15 February 1288	4 April 1292
191	Celestine V	Italian	c. 1215	5 July 1294	13 December 1294*
192	Boniface VIII	Italian	c. 1234	24 December 1294	11 October 1303
193	Benedict XI	Italian	1240	22 October 1303	7 July 1304
194	Clement V	French	1264	5 June 1305	14 April 1314
195	John XXII	French	1244	13 August 1316	4 December 1334
	Nicholas V			*1328*	*1330**
196	Benedict XII	French	1285	20 December 1334	25 April 1342
197	Clement VI	French	1291	7 May 1342	6 December 1352
198	Innocent VI	French	1282	18 December 1352	12 September 1362
199	Urban V	French	1310	16 October 1362	19 December 1370
200	Gregory XI	French	1329	30 December 1370	27 March 1378

POPES OF THE ROMAN OBEDIENCE:

	Pope	Origin	Year of Birth	Date of Election	Date of Death or Abdication
201	Urban VI	Neapolitan	c. 1318	9 April 1378	15 October 1389
202	Boniface IX	Neapolitan	1356	2 November 1389	1 October 1404
203	Innocent VII	Neapolitan	c. 1336	17 October 1404	6 November 1406
204	Gregory XII	Venetian	1336	30 November 1406	4 June 1415*

POPES OF THE AVIGNON OBEDIENCE:

	Pope	Origin	Year of Birth	Date of Election	Date of Death or Abdication
	Clement VII			*1378*	*1394*
	Benedict XIII			*1394*	*1417**
	Clement VIII			*1423*	*1429**

POPES OF THE PISAN OBEDIENCE:

	Pope	Origin	Year of Birth	Date of Election	Date of Death or Abdication
	Alexander V			*1409*	*1410*
	John XXIII			*1410*	*1415**
205	Martin V	Roman	1368	11 November 1417	20 February 1431
206	Eugenius IV	Venetian	1383	3 March 1431	23 February 1447
	Felix V			*1439*	*1449**
207	Nicholas V	Italian	1397	6 March 1447	24 March 1455
208	Callistus III	Spanish	1375	8 April 1455	6 August 1458

	Pope	Origin	Year of Birth	Date of Election	Date of Death or Abdication
209	Pius II	Venetian	1405	19 August 1458	15 August 1464
210	Paul II	Venetian	1417	30 August 1464	26 July 1471
211	Sixtus IV	Italian	1414	9 August 1471	12 August 1484
212	Innocent VIII	Genoese	1432	29 August 1484	25 July 1492
213	Alexander VI	Spanish	1431	11 August 1492	18 August 1503
214	Pius III	Italian	1439	22 September 1503	18 October 1503
215	Julius II	Italian	1443	31 October 1503	21 February 1513
216	Leo X	Florentine	1475	9 March 1513	30 November 1521
217	Hadrian VI	Flemish	1459	9 January 1522	14 September 1523
218	Clement VII	Florentine	1478	18 November 1523	25 September 1534
219	Paul III	Roman	1468	13 October 1534	10 November 1549
220	Julius III	Roman	1487	7 February 1550	23 March 1555
221	Marcellus II	Italian	1501	9 April 1555	30 April 1555
222	Paul IV	Neapolitan	1476	23 May 1555	18 August 1559
223	Pius IV	Italian	1499	25 December 1559	9 December 1565
224	Pius V	Italian	1504	7 January 1566	1 May 1572
225	Gregory XIII	Italian	1502	13 May 1572	10 April 1585
226	Sixtus V	Italian	1521	24 April 1585	27 August 1590
227	Urban VII	Roman	1521	15 September 1590	27 September 1590
228	Gregory XIV	Italian	1535	5 December 1590	15 October 1591
229	Innocent IX	Italian	1519	29 October 1591	30 December 1591
230	Clement VIII	Italian	1536	30 January 1592	3 March 1605
231	Leo XI	Florentine	1535	1 April 1605	27 April 1605
232	Paul V	Roman	1550	16 May 1605	28 January 1621
233	Gregory XV	Italian	1554	9 February 1621	8 July 1623
234	Urban VIII	Florentine	1568	6 August 1623	29 July 1644
235	Innocent X	Roman	1574	15 September 1644	7 January 1655
236	Alexander VII	Italian	1599	7 April 1655	22 May 1667
237	Clement IX	Italian	1600	20 June 1667	9 December 1669
238	Clement X	Roman	1590	29 April 1670	22 July 1676
239	Innocent XI	Italian	1611	21 September 1676	12 August 1689
240	Alexander VIII	Venetian	1610	6 October 1689	1 February 1691
241	Innocent XII	Italian	1615	13 July 1691	27 September 1700
242	Clement XI	Italian	1649	23 November 1700	19 March 1721
243	Innocent XIII	Roman	1655	8 May 1721	7 March 1724
244	Benedict XIII	Roman	1649	29 May 1724	21 February 1730
245	Clement XII	Florentine	1652	12 July 1730	6 February 1740
246	Benedict XIV	Italian	1675	17 August 1740	3 May 1758
247	Clement XIII	Venetian	1698	6 July 1758	2 February 1769
248	Clement XIV	Italian	1705	19 May 1769	22 September 1774
249	Pius VI	Italian	1717	15 February 1775	29 August 1799
250	Pius VII	Italian	1742	14 March 1800	20 August 1823
251	Leo XII	Italian	1760	28 September 1823	10 February 1829
252	Pius VIII	Italian	1761	31 March 1829	30 November 1830
253	Gregory XVI	Italian	1765	2 March 1831	1 June 1846
254	Pius IX	Italian	1792	16 June 1846	7 February 1878
255	Leo XIII	Italian	1810	20 February 1878	20 July 1903
256	Pius X	Italian	1835	4 August 1903	20 August 1914
257	Benedict XV	Genoese	1854	3 September 1914	22 January 1922
258	Pius XI	Italian	1857	6 February 1922	10 February 1939
259	Pius XII	Roman	1876	2 March 1939	9 October 1958
260	John XXIII	Italian	1881	28 October 1958	3 June 1963
261	Paul VI	Italian	1897	21 June 1963	6 August 1978
262	John Paul I	Italian	1912	26 August 1978	29 September 1978
263	John Paul II	Polish	1920	16 October 1978	

INDEX